Hot Rod Hardware

Timothy Remus

Published by:
Wolfgang Publications Inc.
1310 Sunny Slope Ln
Stillwater, MN 55082

First published in 2000 by Wolfgang Publications Inc., 1310 Sunny Slope Ln, Stillwater MN 55082

ISBN number: 1-929133-01-4

Printed and bound in the USA

Hot Rod Hardware

Acknowledgements

Though the topic, Hot Rod Hardware, might put some people to sleep, it's of enormous importance to the gearheads in the crowd. The subject of nuts, bolts, fasteners and high pressure plumbing is also of great importance to various members of industry. And it was to industry that I turned for help early on in this project.

Frank Akstens, Senior Staff Engineer at the Industrial Fasteners Institute, is a man who knows a great deal about fasteners. Frank is accustomed to discussing the merits of quality fasteners with purchasing agents at Ford Motor Company or Caterpillar. Yet he was more than willing to discuss the topic with me, pointing out as he did where purchasing agents (and individual hot rodders) make mistakes by buying on the cheap. Or by not taking the time to understand the difference between Bolt A and the similar Bolt B.

Tony Peterson from Atlantic Fasteners is another industry expert who took time to send me some of their technical information, with permission to use some of it in the book. ARP is a firm well known to anyone who races and a growing number of somewhat less intense automotive enthusiasts. If anyone knows what goes into the manufacture of a quality fastener it's the employees at ARP, and I'm lucky that one of those employees, Tom Smith, consented to an interview.

We need decorative bolts too, and for information on that topic I turned to Walter Mullally. With Walter's help I was able to gain a better understanding of the issues surrounding the use of chrome and stainless fasteners.

The plumbing information and many of the images used in the book came to me compliments of Alvin Rocha from Earl's and Fred Grossmann from Aeroquip. Last-minute images of torque wrenches come with a little help from local Snap-on man Gerald Schlagel. Also local and of great help were fabricators Jim Petrykowski and Neal Letourneau.

From within the automotive aftermarket I have to thank a variety of experts on everything from U-joints to hood hinges. The list includes Alan Zordan from Borgeson, Dan Fink from D.F. Metalworks, Don from Don's Hot Rods and Rocky from Rocky Hinge Company.

Rounding out the list of people I'm indebted to is John Dianna from Buckaroo Communications who kindly allowed me to use the hood-hinge sequence in Chapter Eight. For layout I must thank my old friend Mike Urseth and our newest employee, Joe Plumbo. As always I have to close by thanking my lovely and talented wife, Mary Lanz. When Hollywood buys the movie rights to *Hot Rod Hardware* she'll see that the late nights were all worthwhile.

Introduction

While there are other fastener books on the market most of those take a very nuts and bolts approach to the subject, i.e., they approach the topic from a very technical and competition-oriented perspective. As the name would suggest, this book is written in mostly non-technical terms for "hot rodders" - automotive enthusiasts who own and build street cars.

All of this is not to say that hot rods don't need good fasteners and quality plumbing. They do and those needs are met by a continually expanding line of products from the automotive aftermarket. Whether it's Grade 8 bolts or decorative bolts with a bow-tie embossed on the head, the fasteners you want are available today. The same is true of plumbing the car with extremely high quality hose and attractive anodized fittings, the parts you want are available now from a wide range of suppliers.

The potential problems however, are three-fold: First, from among all the hardware that's available, how do you decide which is best for your particular needs? Second, what are the trade-offs in using the more exotic hardware? Third, where can these components and fasteners be located?

We've tried to answer these questions with an eye toward the needs of the hot rod and street rod builder. Interviews with owners and engineers from within the automotive aftermarket bring their expertise to the subject and help illustrate issues you might not even have thought about yet. Illustrations and tables show the differences in various similar products and show how best to use them. We've even included some chassis and body hardware designed specifically for the street rod market.

Whether it's a '32 Ford or '61 Impala, it's your special vehicle and it deserves the very best, from the fasteners that hold the big block together to the AN hose that runs from the fuel pump to the Holley carburetor.

Chapter One

Why Hardware Matters

Who Cares?

The subject of hardware might seem too esoteric, too far-fetched, to really matter. After all, why should anyone worry about using the right bolts, or the right hardware. For that matter, what is the right hardware? If the door latch is held in place with plain old hex headed bolts instead of button-head Allens, what difference does it make? And does anyone really care?

There are at least three reasons why *you* should care and why hardware is important. The

This is one street rodder who fully understands the importance of hardware. From the chrome bolts to the high-end plumbing, everything here is top shelf. Note the chrome alternator and the upper radiator hose.

first is a structural reason. Strong, high quality bolts and capscrews are just that, strong. A Grade 8 steel bolt is a much stronger bolt than a grade 3 or 5 bolt that you get out of the bin at the local hardware store (for now we're calling them all bolts, capscrews are discussed in Chapter Two). You don't want the bolts that mount the caliper bracket to the spindle to shear when a panic stop transfers nearly the entire weight of the car, multiplied by velocity, to and through the front caliper mounting bolts.

Though the customs may not be as hardware intensive as an old hot rod with missing hood, there's still the need for quality fasteners and trick door latches.

You need more than shear strength for most of the bolts that hold your car together (look for a discussion on tension and shear loading farther along in the book). You need a bolt good enough that it won't stretch unduly when loaded. A bolt that stretches more than just a few percent won't stay tight. Bolts that aren't really tight will unscrew themselves.

The second reason for using high quality bolts is aesthetic. The difference between a nice car and a really nice car often comes down to the hardware. They say the devil's in the details. That includes the nuts, bolts and brackets you use to tie it all together. The difference between

It doesn't have to be exotic to exhibit high quality. There's nothing wrong with simple plumbing arrangements like a molded radiator hose as long as it's a brand-name hose correctly installed.

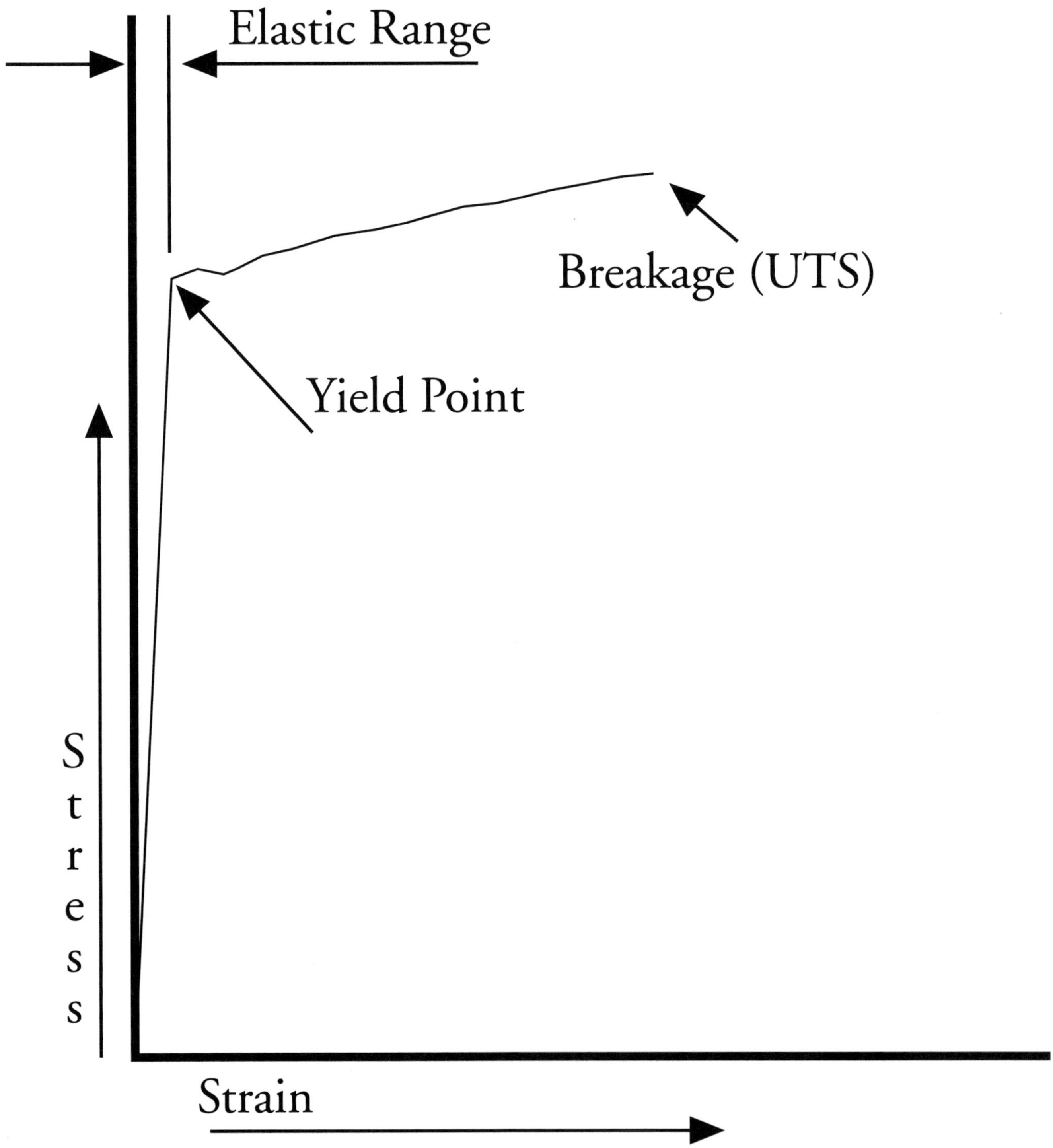

Good bolts act like a spring. At lower levels of stress (the load/the area of the bolt) the bolt will snap back to it's original dimension after the load is removed. At the yield point, however, the bolt is stretched past the point where it snaps back. If the stress is increased further the bolt reaches the breaking point (ultimate tensile strength).

the Deuce that wins and the runner up might come down to the quality of the hardware.

Next time you see a show winning car or truck, don't just look it over from a distance of ten feet. Get closer and closer in your inspection. After you've admired the long straight body panels and perfect pearl paint, look at the engine, and at the chassis.

Note the hardware that holds the whole thing together. The gas line clamps aren't P clamps, simple straps of steel with rubber liners, as might be seen on an OEM application. No, the hoses are held in place and kept from harm's way with some very graceful and balanced clamps cut from billet aluminum. Each of these clamps is like a miniature piece of sculpture, a polished aluminum creation nice enough to sit on a shelf by itself. Some of the hardware seen on hot rods could go to the Museum Of Modern Art and are pretty enough to be respected in their own right. The fact that these are functional clamps simply adds to their allure.

The high class hardware doesn't stop at the clamps and brackets. Valve covers may be held in place with the chrome Allen bolts and the hoses are probably high tech braided hoses from Earl's or Aeroquip, each with it's own anodized and colorful aluminum end.

The third reason for using high end hardware is a certain attitude about the whole project. The idea that everything about this project should be first class and as good as it can be. If you break it down, that new car is really nothing more than a collection of hardware. The only excep-

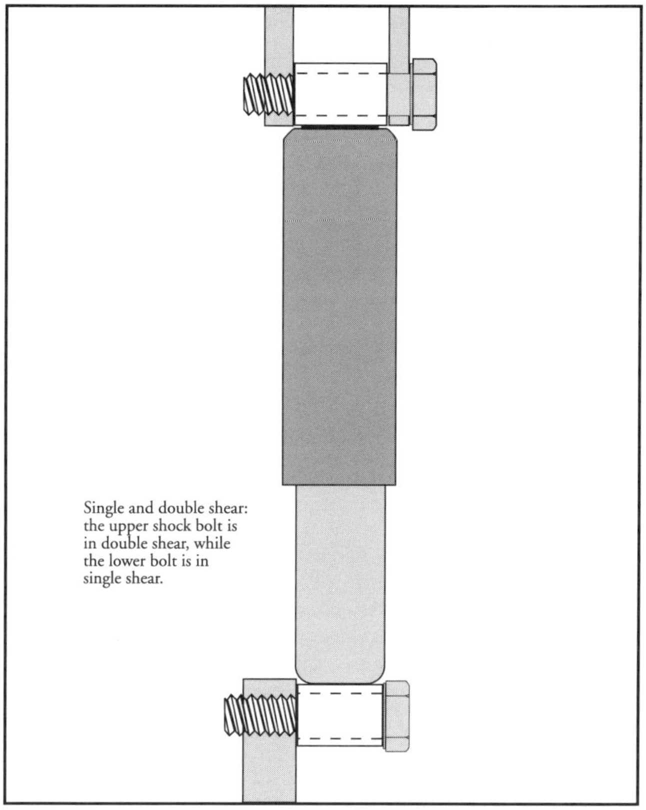

Bolts are much stronger in double (upper mount) than in single shear. Fully threaded bolts must not be used in shear applications as the shear load is placed on the threaded portion instead of the unthreaded shank.

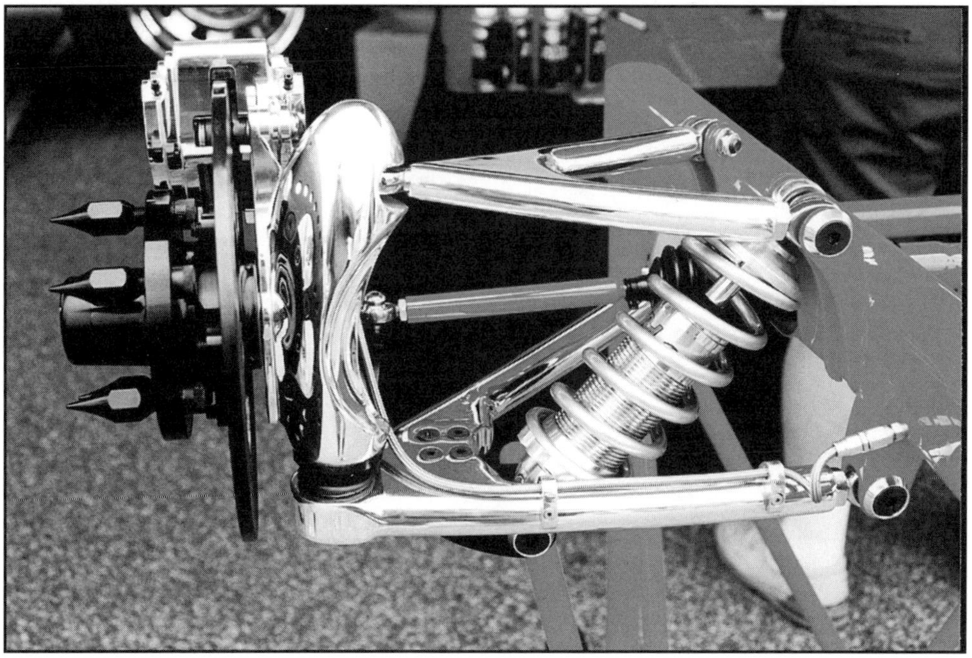

The latest from a man who definitely understands the importance of hardware – Boyd Coddington. Note the lug nuts, the Allen head fasteners used for the lower shock mount and the A-arm pivots and the brake line routing.

Old timey hot rods don't need the latest in trick billet brackets and AN plumbing, and thus might be a little easier to build. And though it might look really bitchin' the holes in the axle do more weakening than lightening.

tion might be the body panels. Everything else, from the bolts and nuts that hold it together, to the door latches, to the engine itself, can be considered hardware. If you've sweat blood assembling that big block with just the right camshaft, and pistons that fit the bores just right, why screw it together with mis-matched bolts and nuts.

You need a Zen-like dedication to building a vehicle as first-class as it can be. That means more than nice paint and expensive accessories. It means quality from one end to the other. From the headlight buckets to the spreader bar in back – and the bolts that hold all those pieces in place.

When it comes to hardware we always think nuts and bolts. Yet most of the parts on the car are "hardware" especially things like brake and suspension components.

Types of Loads

The loads that bolts are subjected to can be broken down into two types: tension or shear. A tension load is perhaps the more familiar of the two. The bolt that holds a body panel in place or the bolt that holds the cylinder head down against the block, both of those bolts are loaded in tension.

The bolt that holds the upper shock mount in place is loaded in shear. In other words, the forces are acting perpendicular to the axis of the bolt. And though you might tighten this bolt to 40 or 50 foot pounds, the true load is the one trying to shear the bolt into two or three pieces.

Most of the bolts we use are loaded in tension, clamping something together with little or no side load. Though logic would seem to imply the opposite, bolts are only about 60 percent as strong in shear (single shear) as they are in tension. Consider too that shear can be further subdivided into single and double. A double shear joint is much, much stronger than a single shear joint (see the illustration for clarification here).

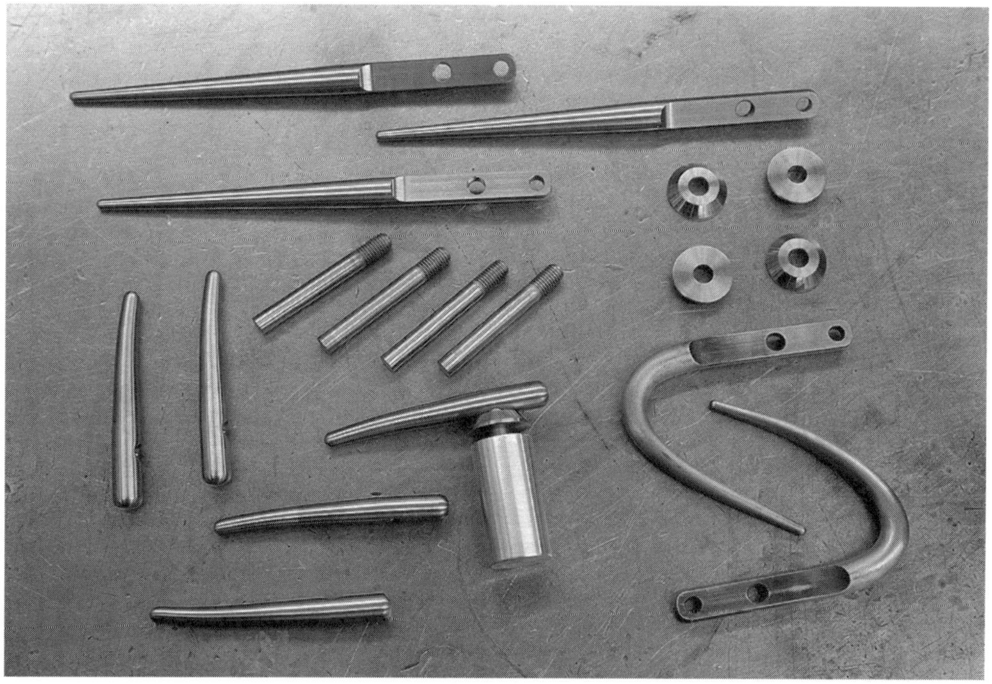

Some of the best hardware is the home-made variety, like these latch components from a Steve Moal roadster.

Measure the load

The *load*, measured in pounds, is the force that is placed on a bolt or the force the bolt is subjected to as it does it's job of resisting an external force.

If you look in a bolt catalog or technical book, each grade or type of bolt is followed by a psi figure. A good steel bolt might be rated at 150,000 psi. The per square inch figure is achieved by dividing the load in pounds by the cross sectional area of the bolt. This is known as the *stress* within the bolt. Stress doesn't describe the strength of a particular bolt but rather the strength of the material

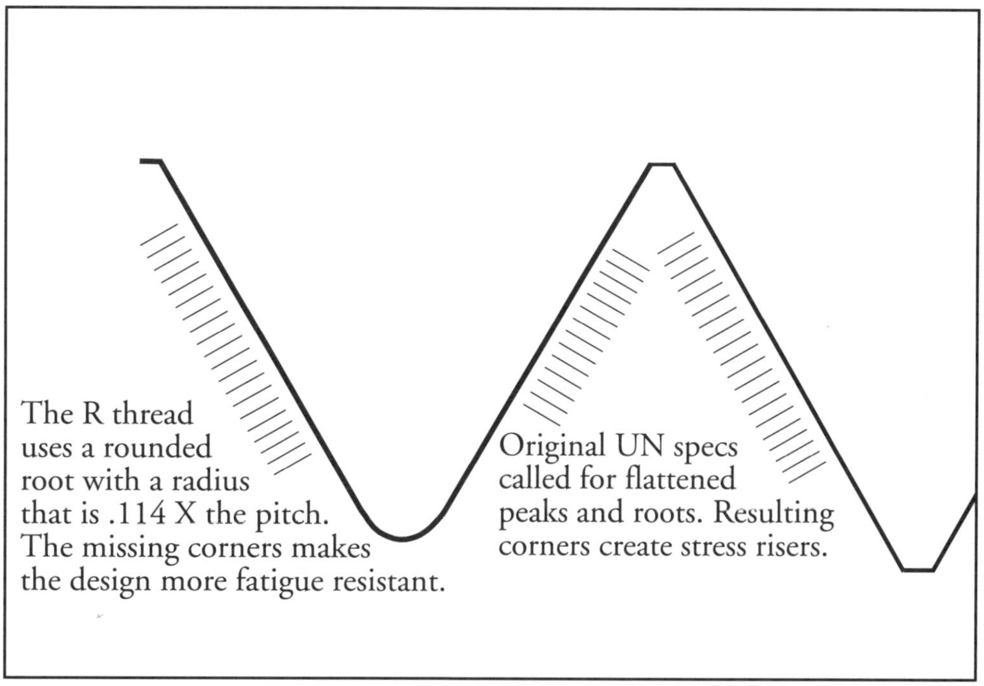

A notch, or two, at the base of the threads is nothing more than a stress riser, a place where the stress is concentrated. By rolling the threads and specifying a round root shape a bolt can be designed to withstand many more load and un-load cycles before it reaches the point of fatigue.

Whether it's new and ultra trick or old and very funky, the purpose of the hardware is to create a safe, neat, installation.

that particular group of bolts is manufactured from.

If you put enough load on a bolt it will change dimension, if only very slightly, and that change in dimension is known as the *strain*.

Further increases in stress will result in additional strain. This relationship between the amount of load and the resulting amount of dimensional change is not always linear, however. At lower levels of stress the bolt will "snap back" to it's original dimension when the stress is removed. Beyond a certain point though, the metal will have been stretched so far that it refuses to snap back. It has reached a point that exceeds the elasticity of the material.

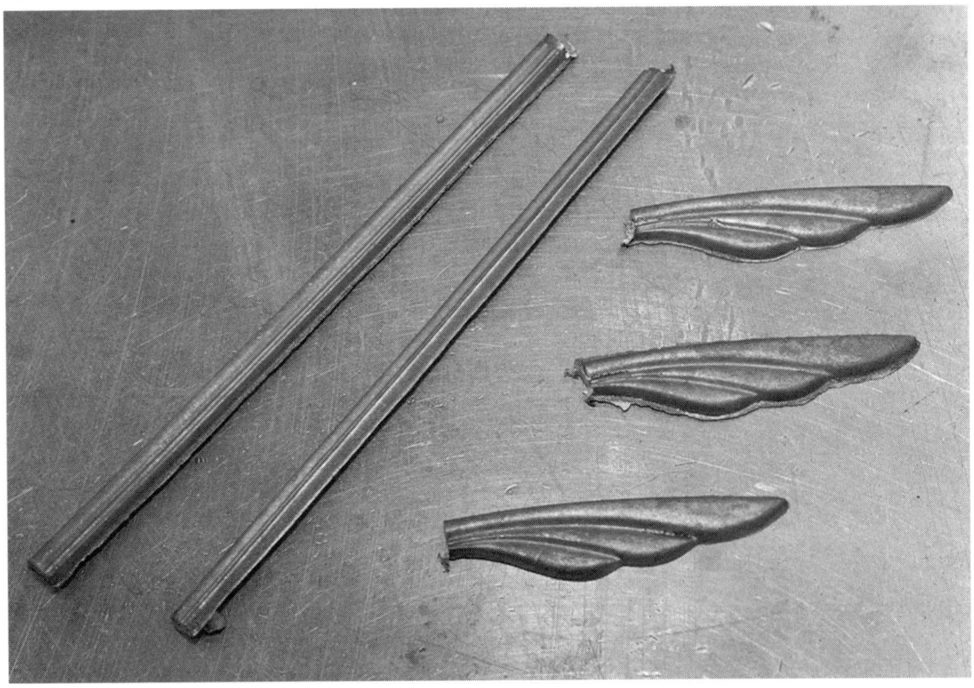

More hand-built hardware from the Steve Moal shop. These one-off castings will be plated and then placed across the dash of a very special roadster. The devil is in the details and that's what hardware is all about.

Engineers call this the bolt's yield point. The bolt has stretched so far that it won't snap back to it's original dimension. Generally, if you don't go past that first point of yield the bolt can be screwed out of the hole or out of the nut. And once out of the female threads the bolt may look just fine. A close inspection however, will reveal the fact that the bolt is now longer than it was originally. Though the change in dimension might be measured in thousandths of an inch, the bolt should be sent to the recycle bin and replaced with a new one.

Added increases in stress past the yield point for that bolt will stretch the bolt further until it can stretch no more. The Ultimate Tensile Strength is the point at which the bolt breaks. The charts for a particular group of bolts often list two figures. Typically, the first is the yield point while the second is the UTS.

When illustrated in two dimensions on graph paper the whole concept becomes easier to understand. At lower stress levels increases in stress create an increase in strain. The resulting graph is a nice straight line - until the line slanting uphill across the graph takes a hard turn to the right.

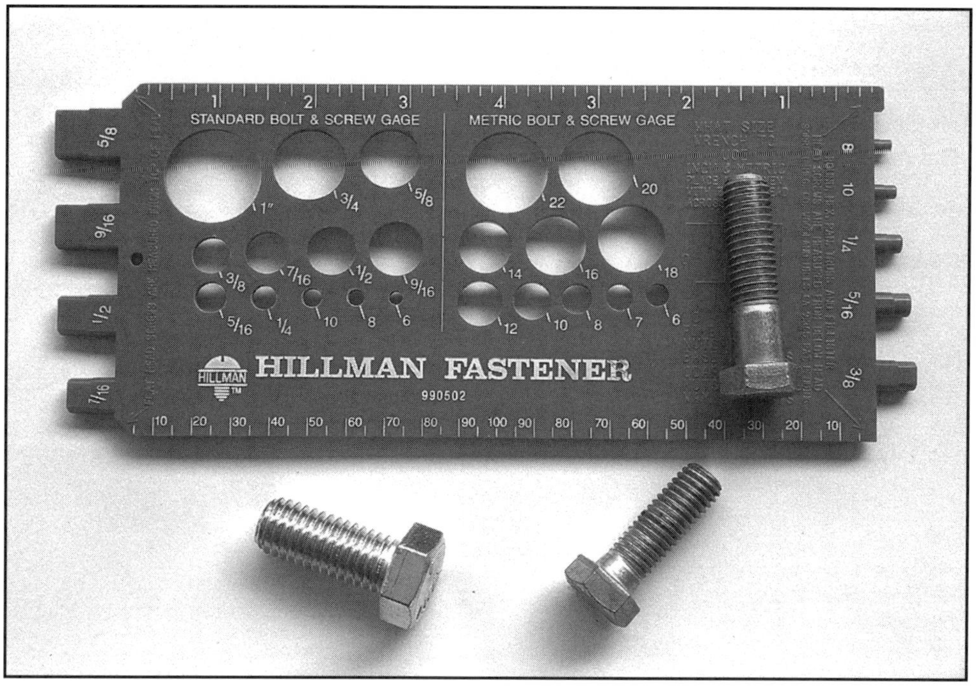

Most fastener companies and many supply houses have nifty gauges like this one that aid in identifying both Metric and Unified bolts.

The point at which the stress and strain graph "turns" is the yield point. This is the point at which the bolt will not come back to it's original dimension when the stress is removed. At the molecular level the metal has deformed and will continue to deform further with greater and greater amounts of stress, right up to the point of rupture.

The yield point is the one we've all sensed while tightening that bolt "just another quarter turn." It's the point where we feel the bolt give, just before the bolt or capscrew becomes a two-piece affair.

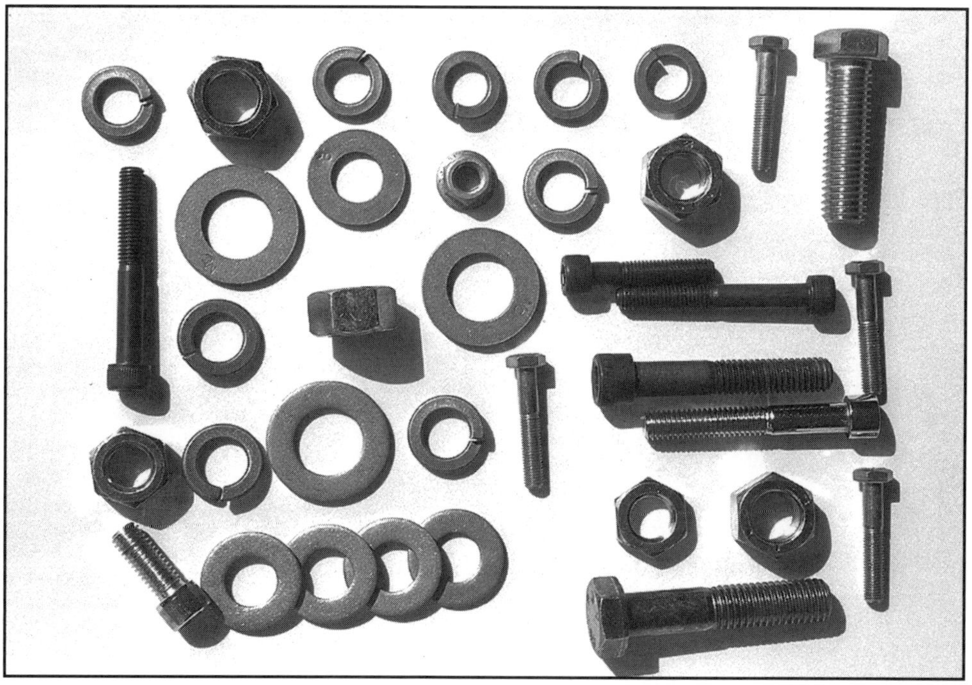

After learning a bit about fasteners you'll never consider a collection of stuff like this "junk." Because amongst all that junk are some Grade 8 jewels.

It's not enough to have a blown big block in a perfect Deuce. You also need class-A hardware and plumbing to hold the whole thing together.

Fatigue

The subject of stress leads to the related concept of fatigue. The idea that even if the bolt doesn't break when you torque it down, it might break 6 months later after a couple of million load-unload cycles. The coat hanger doesn't break the first time you bend it. No, it breaks after 10 or twenty cycles of bending back and forth.

High quality bolts are designed to resist fatigue through the use of good alloys, high-quality manufacture including heat treatment, and good design. A good bolt has carefully manufactured threads and the correct heat treatment applied during the best point in the bolt's genesis. It's important for example that the head be exactly perpendicular to the bolt's axis as even an error of just a few degrees causes aggravating bending within the bolt which in turn increases stress within the bolt enormously. It's also important that the threads blend smoothly into the unthreaded shank of the bolt so no stress risers are created.

Look for more on fatigue and how certain thread forms resist fatigue in Chapters Two and Three.

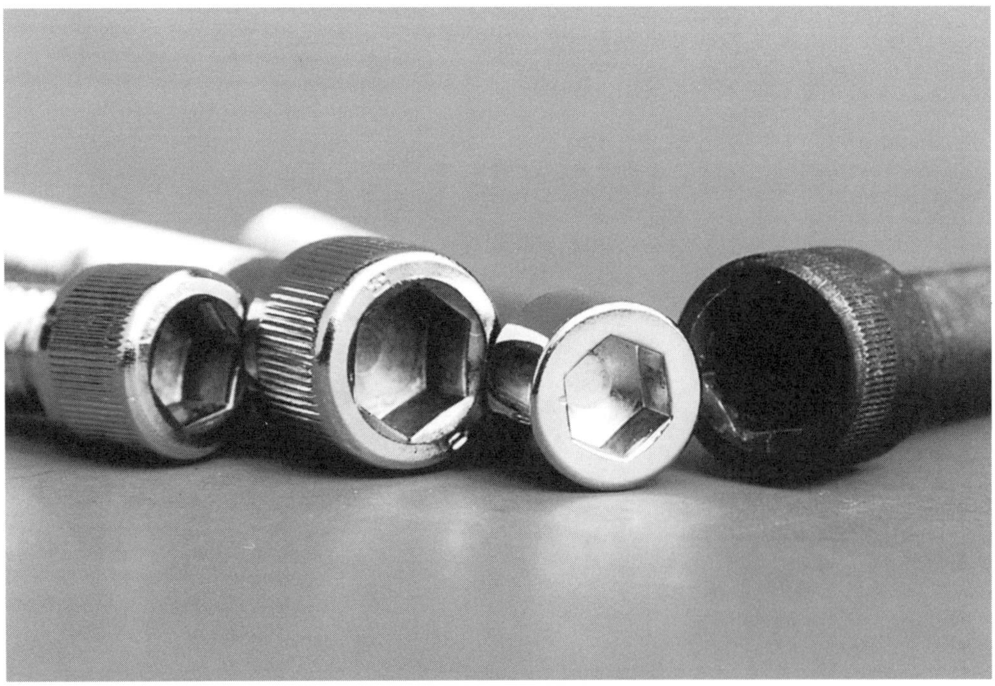

"Allen" bolts are generally rated as stronger than a Grade 8 bolt. But with decorative bolts you don't know for sure unless you ask (and trust) the supplier.

Polishing a bolt eliminates the marks that are used to identify the rating. Thus you are at the mercy of the supplier.

used for high quality tubing is also used to manufacture bolts. One of the most popular of these steels is designated as 4130 chrome-moly. The number, 4130, indicates the family of steel this particular alloy comes from and identifies the amounts of each alloy. All 4100 series steels, for example, contain chromium and molybdenum. The last two numbers indicate the amount of carbon added to the mix, .30% in this case.

Though we think of under-hood as the most hardware-intensive part of the car, the chassis is another area that requires specialized, quality hardware and fasteners.

Materials

Less expensive bolts are made from mild steel, steel with a low percentage of carbon (ignoring stainless and exotic bolts for now). Bolts of this nature are weak but also very malleable. By adding a higher percentage of carbon the strength of the material goes up, though there is also a reduction in the ductility. This is a costly trade-off when it comes to the bolts we use to build hot rods. Any good bolt needs to retain some springy-ness to be effective. Remember, most of these bolts and capscrews are loaded in tension and many must live through millions of load and un-load cycles.

Good bolts are commonly made from medium carbon steel with other additives that provide strength without making the material too brittle or glass-like. The alloy-steels may contain three or four percent nickel along with a small amount of manganese.

Perhaps the best known combination for gearheads is chromium and molybdenum, the material we call chrome-moly. The "super steel"

Nickel-chromium can also be combined to produce very useful alloys, often with small amounts of manganese and molybdenum. Depending on the heat treating and the specific amount of carbon, these steels can produce some ultra-high-strength bolts.

When it comes to heat treating, the timing is just as important as the specific temperature and quenching sequence. Consider that when a good bolt or capscrew is manufactured, the threads are rolled. This rolling operation forms the threads with great pressure (more on manufacture in Chapter Two). The pressure in turn compresses or "forges" the surface of the threads, making them much tougher than they would be otherwise. Now when you heat that forged material, the molecules are free to re-arrange themselves. This normalizing of the material essentially undoes the compressive layer formed during manufacture.

A good capscrew has a raised bearing surface just under the head.

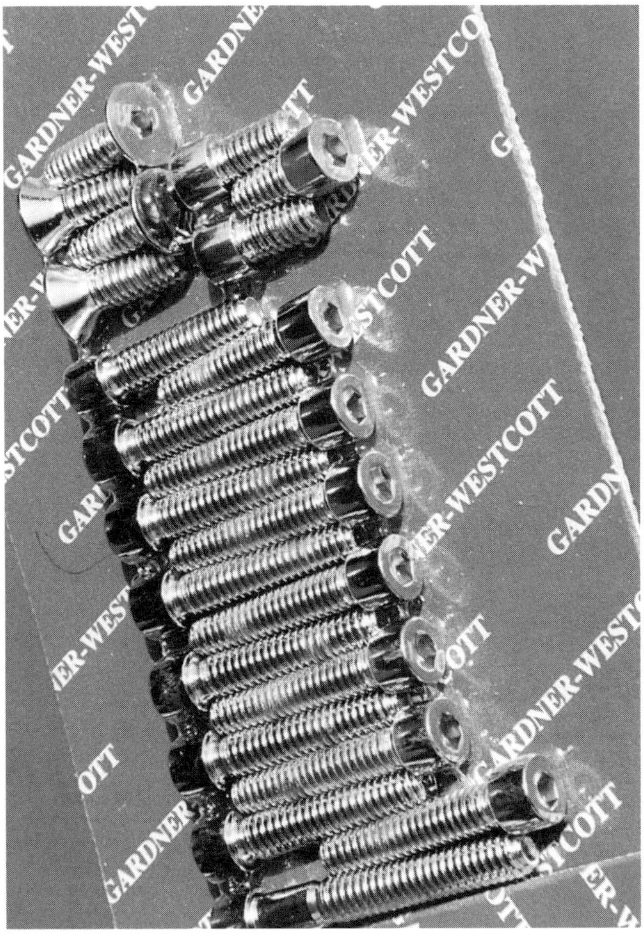

Gardner-Wescott makes a variety of decorative kits designed to fit one particular application.

Manufacturers often heat treat after the threads are formed, so that the thread-forming operation is done on non-heat treated steel. This means longer life for the tooling. In the case of some medium strength bolts, this is probably acceptable. But for high-strength fasteners, the heat treat is performed before the threads are formed, even if it does mean the manufacturers must use better tooling.

Q&A Walter Mullally from Gardner-Westcott.

Many of the bolts that hot rodders buy are purchased primarily for their aesthetic appeal. To ensure that we don't put form in front of function, we called Garner-Westcott, supplier of chrome and stainless bolts, to give us answers to commonly asked questions.

Walter, can you tell us a little bit about Gardner Westcott?

Basically we are an aftermarket nut and bolt supplier. We provide fasteners to the motorcycle and automotive industry. And while function is a big part of it, our fasteners are decorative. We're proud to say we've been in business for 27 years now.

You sell both chrome plate and stainless bolts?

Yes, we offer a full line of both chrome and stainless bolts. People say 'nothing shines like chrome but nothing lasts like stainless.'

Can you describe one of your typical chrome bolts. How good are the bolts you start with.

For our typical chrome bolt we start with a standard SAE Grade 5. We can also supply a Grade 8 chrome bolt to anyone who needs it. And the "Allen" bolts start out as Grade 8 or a little better than Grade 8 before we chrome plate them. Up to 5/8 inch diameter those bolts are 180,000 psi. minimum tensile strength.

We pride ourselves on our chrome bolts and nuts. You can screw them together without any problem at all. The only time we've had any problem is if the bolt was nicked during transit. All our nuts and bolts are guaranteed, so if there is any kind of problem we simply replace the bolt.

Do you have any trouble with hydrogen embrittlement.

No we don't. Some large customers request that their bolts be baked to eliminate any hydrogen, but we've just never had any trouble. I think the whole problem is overstated.

How strong is the typical stainless bolt?

Well, the stainless bolts we use have a high nickel content, that's why they don't rust. But they're not as strong as an alloy steel bolt. Most of what you buy is 304 and 316 stainless, it's all Grade 2 material. You can buy a true Grade 8 stainless and you'll know because you're paying a lot more for it. It's a different alloy and it will rust. When our customers need the strength we recommend the use of chrome plated bolts.

Do you recommend the use of anti-seize on stainless and chrome bolts?

On stainless, yes we do. We like to see paraffin used on the threads of the chrome nylon-collar type lock nuts. The plating process will dry out the nylon and it can get too hot during assembly. Actually, it's a good idea to use a lubricant on them all the time. Paraffin is a nice lube, it's not messy, it's easy to keep some in the tool box for those times when you need it.

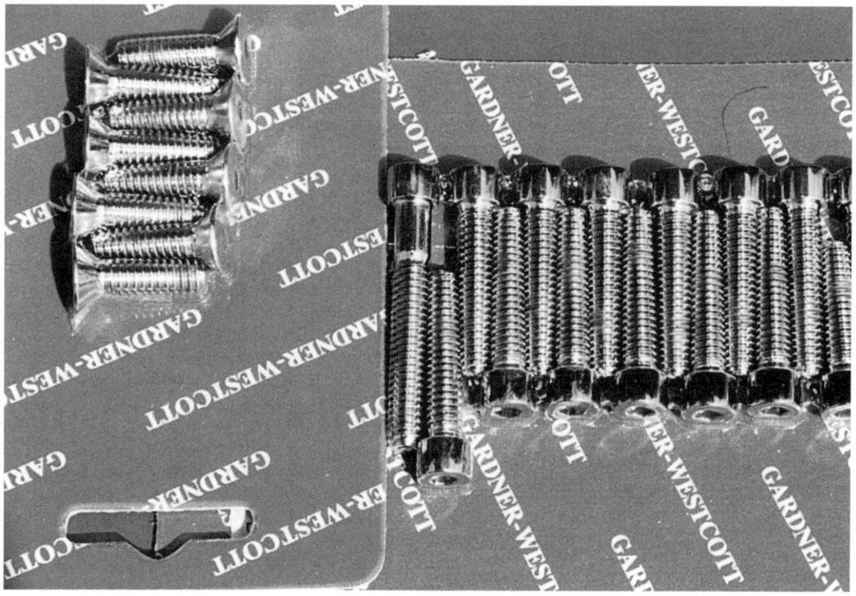

When it comes to decorative bolts, remember that stainless and chrome plated steel are not the same. Most of the Gardner-Wescott line are at least Grade 5 while most stainless bolts are the equivalent of about a Grade 2.

Chapter Two

Bolts and Capscrews

SAE, AN and All The Rest

A bolt is nothing more than a threaded fastener designed to screw into a hole or nut with matching female threads. In order to proceed with the discussion, we need to get a little nomenclature out of the way first. Technically a bolt is a fastener without a washer face under the head, while a capscrew has a washer face under the head.

More terms. The minor diameter of a bolt or capscrew is the diameter measured at the smallest

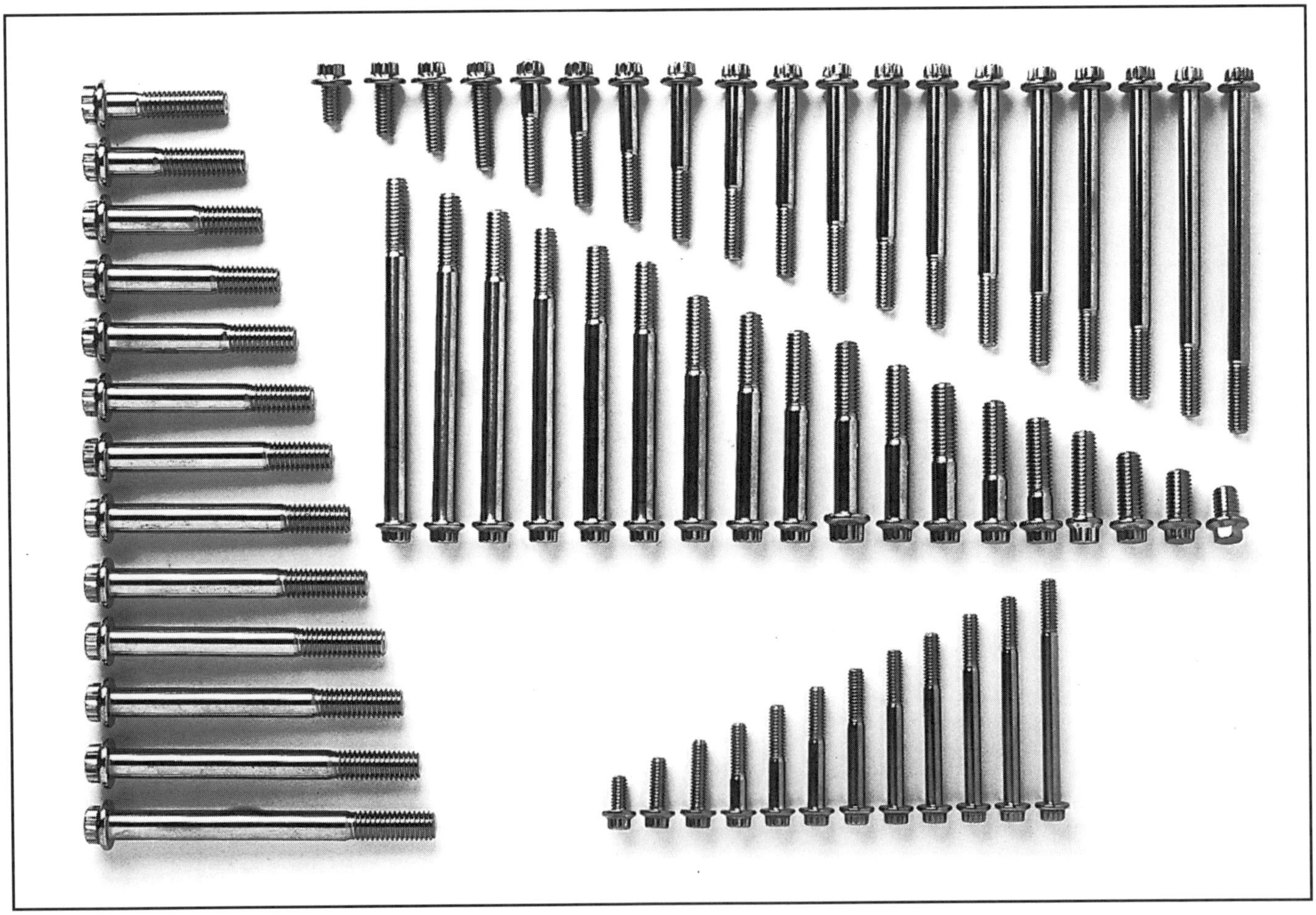

Stainless bolts are available in a variety of sizes, often in specific kits designed for one specific application. ARP

point, the bottom of the threads on either side. The major diameter, as you might expect, is the diameter measured at the largest point, the tops of the threads on either side. The shank is the unthreaded part of the bolt's shaft, the bearing surface is the raised and polished portion just under the head of a quality capscrew. The length is measured from the lower edge of the bearing surface, or the bottom of the head, to the end of the bolt. The grip length is the length of the unthreaded portion while the thread length is simply the length of the threaded portion of the bolt. Peak and root describe the point and the notch of a thread when viewed in cross-section.

How They Make a Bolt

Most quality bolts are made in a rolling or forming operation. The raw stock, known as "wire," is rolled through special dies that form the threads without any cutting. Though at first this might seem the wrong way to make a bolt the reasons bolts are made in this way are numerous and hard to refute.

First, cutting threads is very time consuming. Second, cutting leaves rough edges behind. Even the sharpest tooling will leave small tears in the surface of the metal. A quality rolling operation on the other hand actually leaves a smooth polished surface. Third, cutting threads means cutting across the grain of the bolt, making it much weaker. Rolling threads on the other hand encourages the grain to flow with the threads. Rolling the threads has the added advantage mentioned in Chapter One, the rolling operation compresses or forges the surface of the threads making them

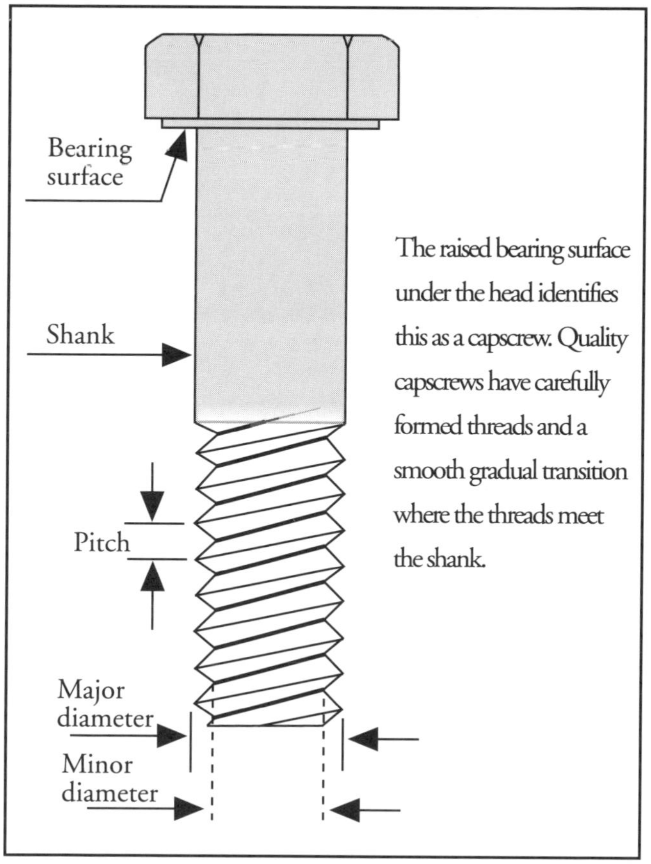

The major parts of a quality capscrew.

The invention of the lathe, a machine that relies on screw thread technology for its operation, made possible the production of the first identical fasteners at the beginning of the industrial revolution.

These big, nearly square threads are translation threads, designed to translate the turning of a screw into lateral movement.

much stronger. Finally, by rolling the threads instead of cutting them the manufacturers produce no scrap metal.

The tension that keeps the bolt tight can also be the bolt's undoing. Consider the threads as a ramp wound 'round an axis. When you tighten the bolt you are using mechanical force to move a load "uphill." Rotary motion of the head is converted to motion moving along the axis of the bolt. No matter how tight the bolt is, there will always be a tendency for anything on that ramp to slide downhill.

Talk about Threads

One of the earliest applications of thread technology came with the invention of the lathe. By using a translation thread, a tool could be moved at a particular rate while it worked on a rotating piece of metal or wood. In this case translation means converting the rotary motion of the screw to the linear movement of the tool stock.

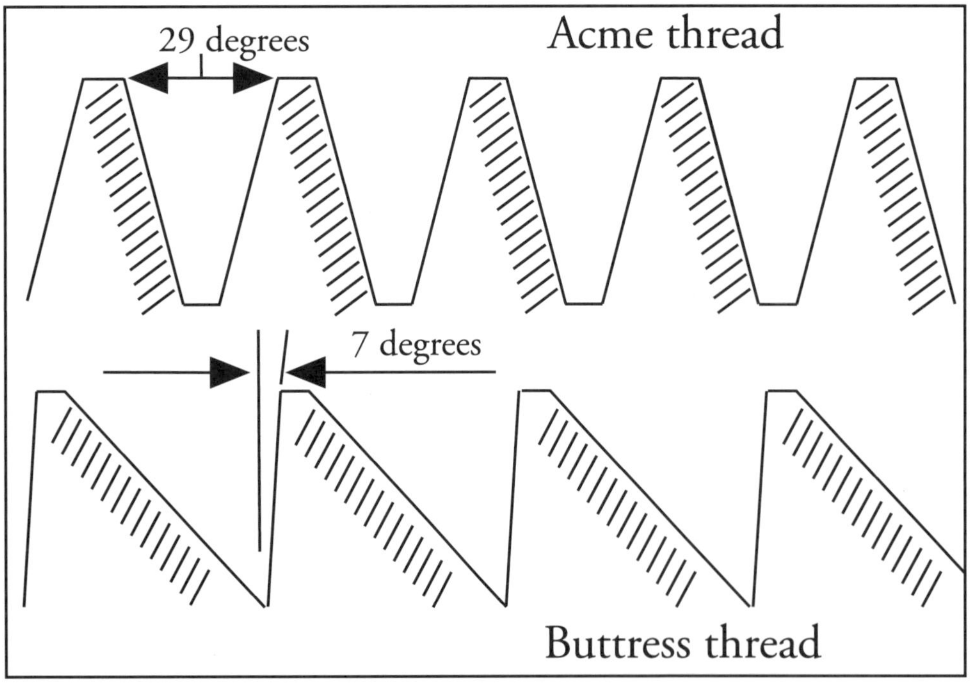

Not your typical Unified or metric threads. The Acme design is a common translation thread, while the Buttress thread is used on things like the screw in a stainless hose clamp.

Screw-thread technology was used in this way to create more screws, or bolts to be more specific. The earliest threads were not rolled, they were cut on lathes. These were the first "regular" fasteners with a specified pitch, thread profile, and diameter. Bolts that could be replaced with an identical part. It seems too simple to even wonder about today, but until the advent of standardized bolts you couldn't just run down to the hardware store to buy a new 5/16 UNC bolt to replace the one that fell out of your cotton gin.

The invention of standard bolts and nuts was one of the major advances of the industrial revolution. Without standardized fasteners it would be very difficult to build machinery that can easily and economically be assembled, and later disassembled and repaired.

Early engineers soon discovered that they needed a way to describe each and every bolt. They developed a nomenclature that would precisely describe the size and shape of the threads on each fastener they designed. Today we use pretty much the same terms to describe the threads on a bolt or capscrew that they did. Though a few of the basic terms were covered already, there are just a few more to consider so we're all "on the same page" when it comes to a discussion of bolts, capscrews and threads.

The pitch is the distance from one thread crest to another, which is nearly the same as the lead, defined as the distance the bolt or screw will move (along its axis) in one revolution.

The thread angle is the

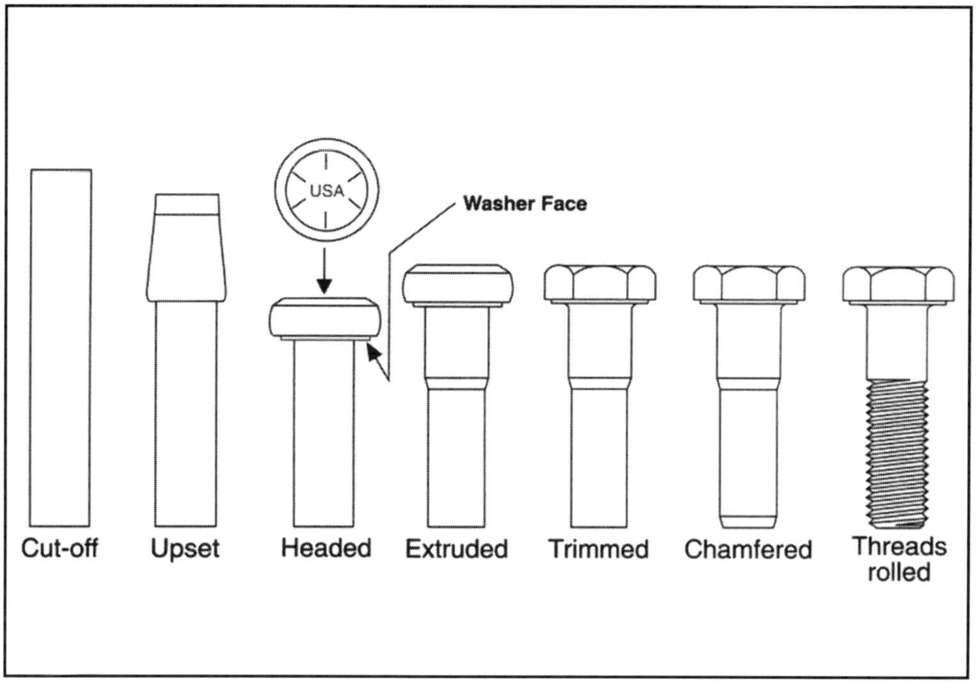

This diagram shows the various stages a bolt goes through in the genesis from "wire" to capscrew. Atlantic Fasteners

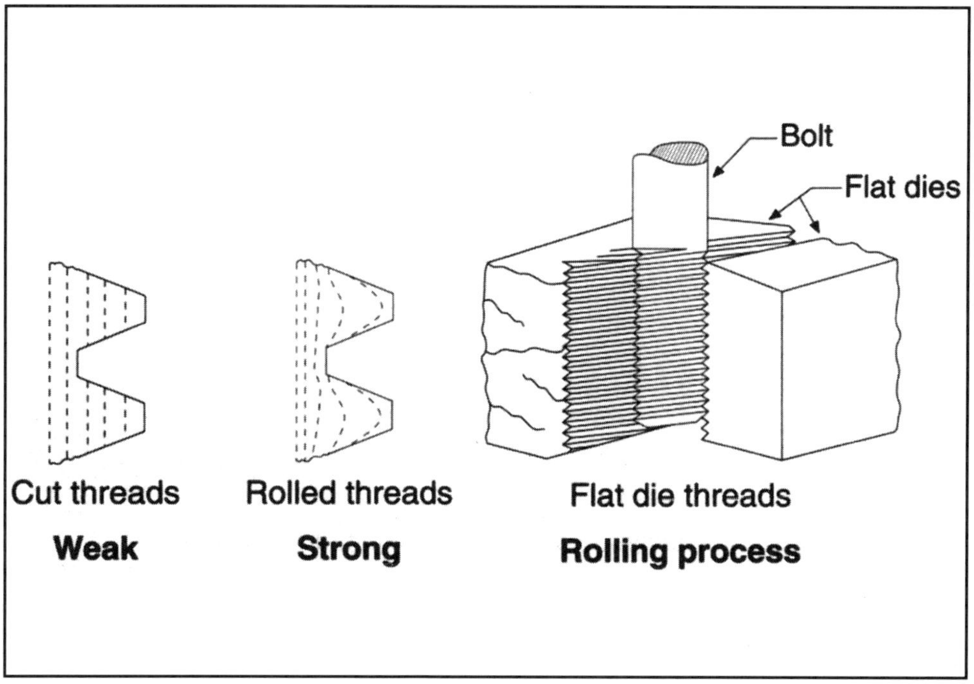

By rolling the threads with dies the manufacturer creates threads that are much stronger than those cut on a lathe. Correct alignment of the dies is critical to the manufacture of a great fastener. Atlantic Fasteners

The head of the bolt tells the story: Six radial dashes indicates a Grade 8 while three indicates a Grade 5. Quality bolts and capscrews should have a logo (called the manufacturer's headmark) so it can be traced back to the manufacturer. Avoid bolts that don't have a headmark.

angle of the threads when viewed in cross-section.

The root is the base of the thread, or the "notch" at the bottom of two adjacent flanks.

Speaking of flanks, the one that takes the load as the capscrew is tightened is known as the pressure flank.

The crest of the thread is the very top of each thread, the opposite of the root so to speak.

Despite this supposedly standardized nomenclature, there are different ways of describing the threads on a bolt or capscrew, depending on whether it's an "American" or metric part.

While American or Unified bolts are described as having 24 or 18 threads per inch, the metric system describes a bolt as having a pitch of a certain dimension, like 1.0 mm.

The problem with decorative bolts is the fact that the headmarks are usually polished off, making identification difficult.

Grading Systems and Specifications

Thread Specifications in the real world.

What we often call NC and NF or national course and national fine, are actually UNC and UNF. Or Unified national course and Unified national fine. This system came out of the confusion that arose during WWII when English mechanics tried to repair American Airplanes with Whitworth nuts and bolts. The ensuing troubles convinced the allies that

Thread Chart, Metric and Inch

Atlantic Fasteners

Most Common

Diameter (mm)	Pitch Coarse	Pitch Fine
1	0.25	
1.2	0.25	
1.6	0.35	
2	0.4	
2.5	0.45	
3	0.5	
4	0.7	
5	0.8	
6	1	
8	1.25	1
10	1.5	1 (1.25)
12	1.75	1.25 (1.5)
16	2	1.5
20	2.5	1.5
24	3	2
30	3.5	2
36	4	3
42	4.5	3
48	5	3
56	5.5	4
64	6	4
72		6
80		6
90		6
100		6

Not Popular

Diameter (mm)	Pitch Coarse	Pitch Fine
1.4	0.3	
1.8	0.35	
2.2	0.45	
3.5	0.6	
14	2	1.5
18	2.5	1.5
22	2.5	1.5
27	3	2
33	3.5	2
45	4.5	3
52	5	3
60	5.5	4
68	6	4
76		6
85		6
95		6

Special Applications

Diameter (mm)	Pitch Coarse	Pitch Fine
7	1	
11	1.5	1
15		1
25		1.5
26		1.5
28		2
39	4	3

Diameter (Inch)	Pitch Coarse	Pitch Fine
No. 0 (.060")		80
No. 1 (.073")	64	72
No. 2 (.086")	56	64
No. 3 (.099")	48	56
No. 4 (.112")	40	48
No. 5 (.125")	40	44
No. 6 (.138")	32	40
No. 8 (.164")	32	36
* No. 10 (.190")	24	32
No. 12 (.216")	24	28
1/4	20	28
5/16	18	24
3/8	16	24
7/16	14	20
1/2	13	20
9/16	12	18
5/8	11	18
3/4	10	16
7/8	9	14
1	8	14
1 1/8	7	12
1 1/4	7	12
1 1/2	6	12
1 3/4	5	
2 in.	4 1/2	
2 1/4	4 1/2	
2 1/2	4	
2 3/4	4	
3	4	

* Equivalent to 3/16

Metric bolts come in more than one series of coarse and fine thread while the Inch or Unified threads are more standardized.

Common Inch and Metric Steel Head Markings

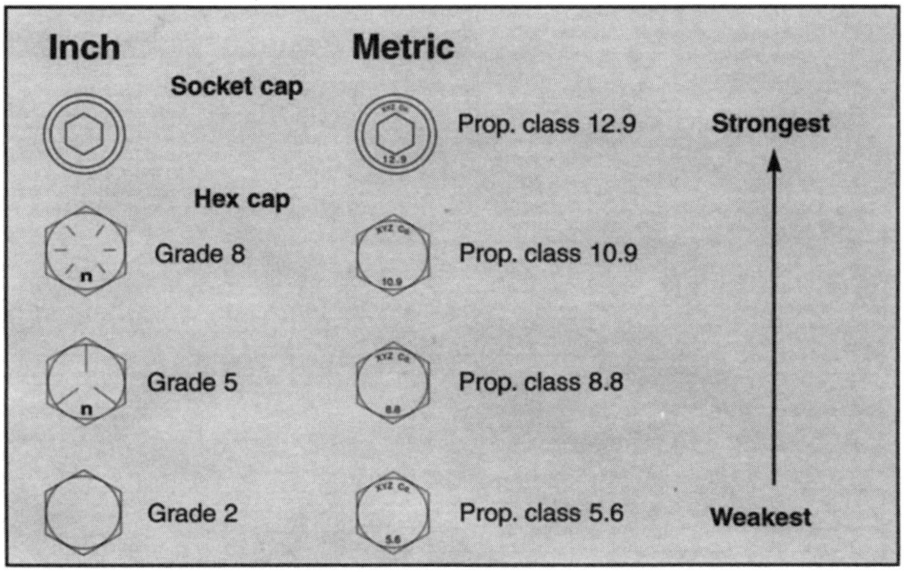

Arranged in order of equivalent strength.

Common Stainless Steel Hex Head Markings

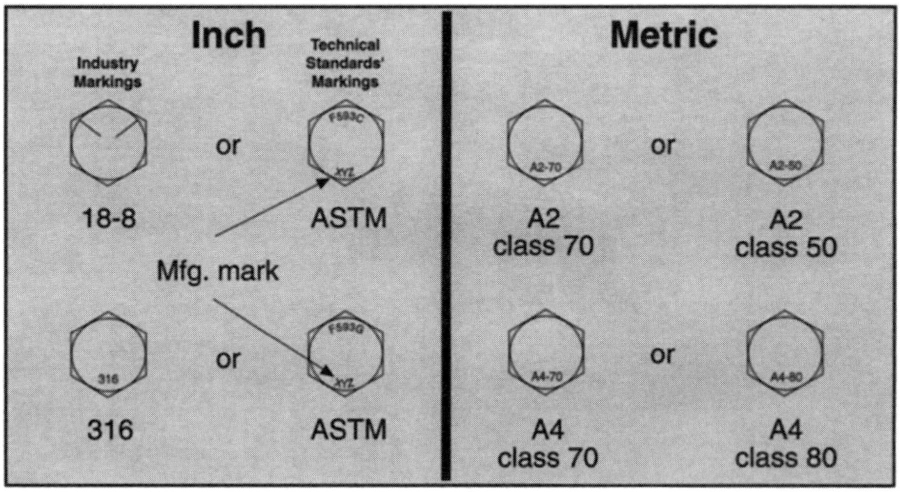

Inch

- **18-8** – which can be 302, 303 or 304 stainless – refers to 18% chromium and 8% nickel content.
- **316** is more corrosion resistant than 18-8 because it contains molybdenum, but in inch fasteners both have the same tensile strength.

Metric

- **A2** refers to metric 18-8.
- **A4** refers to metric 316.
- Class 50, 70 and 80 designate increasingly higher metric strength levels.
- A manufacturer's mark is required on metric M5 or larger diameters.

they needed some type of Unified thread form. The "Unified" system they settled on retained most of the then-current American standards and specifications.

The specifications called for an included angle of 60 degrees for both the coarse and fine threaded fasteners, all of which were measured in the well known inch system.

There has been some evolution of the thread specifications since those first specifications were written, but most of those have to do with the radius at the base of the thread. A sharp V-shaped notch at the base of the threads makes an ideal stress riser - a spot where the bolt is likely to fatigue and break. Even a flattened V includes two smaller notches, which again make ideal spots for the concentration of stress.

Because the original specifications for Unified threads allowed for a flattened V, there was enough room in those specifications for a improvement in the shape of the threads. Years earlier, engineers discovered that they could extend the fatigue life of a fastener considerably by simply "rounding" the root, or base of the threads. Obviously this rounding, specified as a particular radius, eliminated the stress risers found in a pure V or flattened V shape. Most of the better bolts and capscrews (including SAE Grade 8) now specify a "R" thread which simply spells out the specific radius at the bottom of the thread (see the illustration in Chapter One for a better explanation of the R thread).

The beauty of the R thread design is the way it combines a fatigue-resistant radiused root while staying within the basic confines of the UN specifications. Obviously, as the root of the capscrew threads gets more and more "rounded" the more likely it is that the crest of the female thread will interfere with that root. Despite this fact, the need for fatigue resistant bolts has driven industry to develop another thread form, the root diameter of which is larger than the R thread.

This thread form is known as the J thread, and must be matched up with female threads designed for the task, or those with a rather loose fit (see Tom Smith's comments in Chapter Three). While the specification for an R root is .108 to .144 X the pitch, the specification for the J root is .150 to .180 X the pitch. The J form is used in many aerospace bolts, and most (if not all) high quality connecting rod bolts.

The subject of root

Three random bolts. Left to right, a Grade 5, a 8.8 Metric bolt – roughly equivalent to a Grade 5-and a Grade 8. Note that all have the manufacturer's headmark.

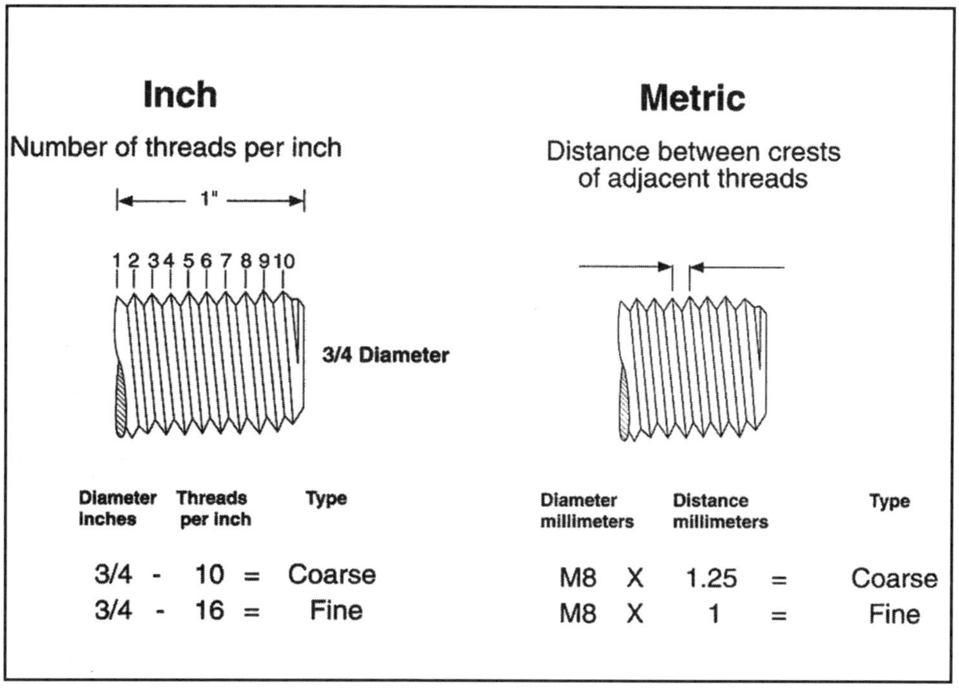

Though both inch and Metric fasteners come in coarse and fine threads, they are measured in very different fashions. Atlantic Fasteners

Common Grade Markings

Atlantic Fasteners

Identification Grade Mark	Specification	Fastener Description	Material	Nominal Size Range (in.)	Mechanical Properties		
					Proof Load (psi)	Yield Strength Min (psi)	Tensile Strength Min (psi)
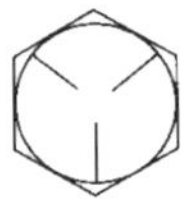	SAE J429 Grade 5	Bolts, Screws, Studs	Medium Carbon Steel, Quenched and Tempered	1/4 — 1 Over 1 — 1-1/2	85,000 74,000	92,000 81,000	120,000 105,000
	ASTM A449			1/4 — 1 Over 1 — 1-1/2 Over 1-1/2 — 3	85,000 74,000 55,000	92,000 81,000 58,000	120,000 105,000 90,000
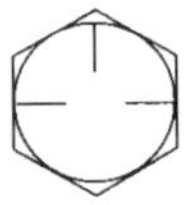	SAE J429 Grade 5.1	Sems	Low or Medium Carbon Steel, Quenched and Tempered	No. 6 — 5/8	85,000	–	120,000
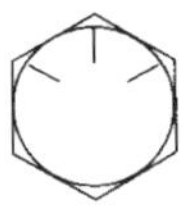	SAE J429 Grade 5.2	Bolts, Screws, Studs	Low Carbon Martensitic Steel, Quenched and Tempered	1/4 — 1	85,000	92,000	120,000
	ASTM A490 Type 1	High Strength Structural Bolts	Alloy Steel, Quenched and Tempered	1/2 — 1-1/2	120,000	130,000	150,000 min 170,000 max
	ASTM A490 Type 2		Low Carbon Martensitic Steel, Quenched and Tempered	1/2 — 1-1/2	120,000	130,000	150,000 min 170,000 max
	ASTM A490 Type 3		Atmospheric Corrosion Resisting Steel, Quenched and Tempered	1/2 — 1-1/2	120,000	130,000	150,000 min 170,000 max
	ASTM A354 Grade BB	Bolts, Studs	Alloy Steel, Quenched and Tempered	1/4 — 2-1/2 2-3/4 — 4	80,000 75,000	83,000 78,000	105,000 100,000
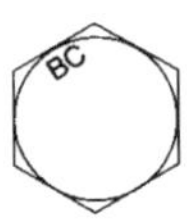	ASTM A354 Grade BC				105,000 95,000	109,000 99,000	125,000 115,000
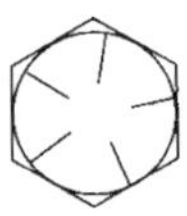	SAE J429 Grade 7	Bolts, Screws	Medium Carbon Alloy Steel, Quenched and Tempered	1/4 — 1-1/2	105,000	115,000	133,000
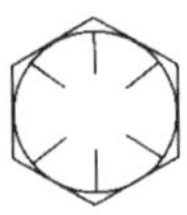	SAE J429 Grade 8	Bolts, Screws, Studs	Medium Carbon Alloy Steel, Quenched and Tempered	1/4 — 1-1/2	120,000	130,000	150,000
	ASTM A354 Grade BD		Alloy Steel Quenched and Tempered				

Common Grade Markings

Atlantic Fasteners

Identification Grade Mark	Specification	Fastener Description	Material	Nominal Size Range (in.)	Mechanical Properties		
					Proof Load (psi)	Yield Strength Min (psi)	Tensile Strength Min (psi)
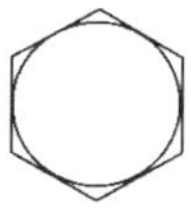 No Grade Mark	SAE J429 Grade 8.1	Studs	Medium Carbon Alloy or SAE 1041 Modified Elevated Temperature Drawn Steel	1/4 — 1-1/2	120,000	130,000	150,000
	ASTM A325 Type1	High Strength Structural Bolts	Medium Carbon Steel, Quenched and Tempered	1/2 — 1 1 -1/8 — 1-1/2	85,000 74,000	92,000 81,000	120,000 105,000
 No Grade Mark	ISO R898/1 Class 4.6	Bolts, Screws, Studs	Low or Medium Carbon Steel	M5 — M100	33,000	36,000	60,000
	ISO R898/1 Class 5.8			M5 — M24	55,000	57,000	74,000
 or 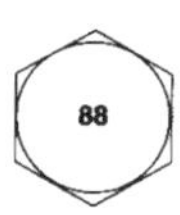	ISO R898/1 Class 8.8		Medium Carbon Steel Quenched and Tempered	M16 — M72	85,000	92,000	120,000
 or 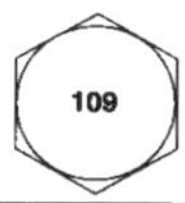	ISO R898/1 Class 10.9		Alloy Steel, Quenched and Tempered	M5 — M100	120,000	130,000	150,000

NOTES:

1. **ASTM Specifications:**
   - A 193—Alloy-Steel Bolting Materials for High-Temperature Service
   - A 307—Low-Carbon Steel Externally and Internally Threaded Standard Fasteners
   - A 320—Alloy-Steel Bolting Materials for Low-Temperature Service
   - A 325—High-Strength Bolts for Structural Steel Joints, including Suitable Nuts and Plain Hardened Washers
   - A 354—Quenched and Tempered Alloy Steel Bolts and Studs with Suitable Nuts
   - A 449—Quenched and Tempered Steel Bolts and Studs
   - A 490—Quenched and Tempered Alloy Bolts for Structural Steel Joints

2. **SAE Specification**
   J429—Mechanical and Quality Requirements for Externally Threaded Fasteners

3. **ISO Recommendations:**
   No. R898—Mechanical Properties of Fasteners—Part I —Bolts, Screws and Studs

4. Grade 7 bolts and screws are roll threaded after heat treatment.

shape brings up the topic of thread fit, often called the class of thread. Obviously there must be some clearance between the male and female threads or disassembly will be near-impossible. How much clearance there is between male and female threads is specified by the class.

Class 1 threads might best be described as a sloppy fit, while class 2 describes the most common fit found on standard automotive fasteners. Class 3 threads are more precise, with tolerances that are tighter than the other lower classes, while still allowing enough clearance that the fasteners can be assembled and disassembled without galling. Class 5 describes threads that are designed for an interference fit and are not meant to be disassembled.

In the nomenclature a bolt might be described as a 5/16 UNC 3A, three being the class of fit. The "A" following the 3 indicates a male fastener while a B indicates a female fastener.

Whitworth threads, a short treatise......

Though Whitworth threads might seem completely obsolete, a short examination is warranted, not only for what they can tell us about thread design, but also for those poor souls who restore and repair vintage English cars, bikes and aircraft.

As a young man I made my living as an auto mechanic. The only thing we hated worse than a Italian car was an English one. The Whitworth nuts and bolts that held these vehicles together were judged too weird to really worry about. Generally I could get an American wrench to fit the oddball bolt heads. And unless I lost a nut or bolt while working on the occasional MG or Triumph, there wasn't any need to delve into the intricacies of the threads, or note how they differed from the obviously superior American hardware.

The fact is Sir Joseph Whitworth did an admirable job when he designed the system in

Specialized sets of fasteners are available from a variety of sources for a wide range of applications. These oil-pan studs are from ARP.

These head studs feature threads that are rolled after heat treat. Studs should be installed "finger tight" and not jammed down into the bottom of the female threads. ARP

The Metric system

Though we like to think we're building American cars with American nuts and bolts, it's hard to avoid the use of at least some metric fasteners on our cars. The reasons are simple, the cars we call domestic, the ones we borrow components from, are often manufactured all or in part, overseas. Even if it really is an "American car" it probably contains some metric fasteners and fittings.

the middle of the nineteenth century. While the Unified National system initially allowed for notches at the root of the threads, the Whitworth system called for a specific radius from the very beginning. The rest of the basic specifications include a fifty five degree included angle instead of the 60 degree angle called for in the UN specifications. The Whitworth system seems at first much like our own with bolts sized in 1/16th inch increments, in coarse and fine threads. Differences however, include both the included angle already mentioned, and the actual pitch (or number of threads per inch) of the Whitworth fasteners.

New Whitworth nuts and bolts (which actually include British Standard Fine, BSCoarse and CEI) are available from sources like British Tools and Fasteners, or Coventry Spares. The men and women who restore English vehicles often find that because Whitworth and UN are fairly close, earlier owners have screwed a UN bolt in where a Whitworth came out. Meaning you may need HeliCoil repair kits, available from already mentioned sources.

High quality capscrews like these head bolts may be "waisted" along the shank in order to create a bolt that has uniform strength over its entire length. ARP

The beauty of the aftermarket is the wealth of very specialized fasteners, like these intended for Holley carburetors. ARP

Metric threads have features in common with our UNC and UNF thread forms. Like those truly domestic threads, the metric thread system uses an included angle of 60 degrees. Like most thread systems, these bolts and capscrews come in coarse and fine threads. Those features are where the similarities between the two systems end.

In the metric system thread pitch is expresses as the distance in millimeters from one crest to the next, instead of as the number of threads per some unit of measurement. Common pitch specifications include 1.0, 1.25 and 1.50 mm. One of the problems with the metric system is the fact that there are four slightly different metric "systems" though the ISO (International Standards Organization) specifications seem to be dominant. This is why a 8 mm bolt used on a truly imported car (say a Toyota), and the one used on a late model American car, may have different head sizes. Within a given metric size there are fine and coarse threads. An 8 mm bolt will commonly be available in 1.0 and 1.25 mm thread pitch. Any decent tap and die set (more later) will have a thread gauge, which is a good aid in identifying a particular bolt.

Another specialized high-performance application. High strength and (in some cases) longer wheel studs for competition use. ARP

The grade of a metric bolt is indicated with a two

Decimal Equivalents

Atlantic Fasteners

Drill Size	mm	Decimal Inches
—	0.10	.0039
—	0.20	.0079
—	0.25	.0098
—	0.30	.0118
80	0.34	.0135
79	0.37	.0145
1/64	0.40	.0156
78	0.41	.0160
77	0.46	.0180
—	0.50	.0197
76	0.51	.0200
75	0.53	.0210
74	0.57	.0225
—	0.60	.0236
73	0.61	.0240
72	0.64	.0250
71	0.66	.0260
—	0.70	.0276
70	0.71	.0280
69	0.74	.0292
—	0.75	.0295
68	0.79	.0310
1/32	0.79	.0313
—	0.80	.0315
67	0.81	.0320
66	0.84	.0330
65	0.89	.0350
—	0.90	.0354
64	0.91	.0360
63	0.94	.0370
62	0.97	.0380
61	0.99	.0390
—	1.00	.0394
60	1.02	.0400
59	1.04	.0410
58	1.07	.0420
57	1.09	.0430
56	1.18	.0465
3/64	1.19	.0469
55	1.32	.0520
54	1.40	.0550
53	1.51	.0595
1/16	1.59	.0625
52	1.61	.0635
51	1.70	.0670
50	1.78	.0700
49	1.85	.0730
48	1.93	.0760
5/64	1.98	.0781
47	1.99	.0785
—	2.00	.0787
46	2.06	.0810

Drill Size	mm	Decimal Inches
45	2.08	.0820
44	2.18	.0860
43	2.26	.0890
42	2.37	.0935
3/32	2.38	.0938
41	2.44	.0960
40	2.50	.0980
39	2.53	.0995
38	2.58	.1015
37	2.64	.1040
36	2.71	.1065
7/64	2.78	.1094
35	2.79	.1100
34	2.82	.1110
33	2.87	.1130
32	2.95	.1160
—	3.00	.1181
31	3.05	.1200
1/8	3.18	.1250
30	3.26	.1285
29	3.45	.1360
28	3.57	.1405
9/64	3.57	.1406
27	3.66	.1440
26	3.73	.1470
25	3.80	.1495
24	3.86	.1520
23	3.91	.1540
5/32	3.97	.1562
22	3.99	.1570
—	4.00	.1575
21	4.04	.1590
20	4.09	.1610
19	4.22	.1660
18	4.31	.1695
11/64	4.37	.1719
17	4.39	.1730
16	4.50	.1770
15	4.57	.1800
14	4.62	.1820
13	4.70	.1850
3/16	4.76	.1875
12	4.80	.1890
11	4.85	.1910
10	4.91	.1935
9	4.98	.1960
—	5.00	.1968
8	5.05	.1990
7	5.11	.2010
13/64	5.16	.2031
6	5.18	.2040
5	5.22	.2055

Drill Size	mm	Decimal Inches
4	5.31	.2090
3	5.41	.2130
7/32	5.56	.2188
2	5.61	.2210
1	5.79	.2280
A	5.94	.2340
15/64	5.95	.2344
—	6.00	.2362
B	6.05	.2380
C	6.15	.2420
D	6.25	.2460
1/4	6.35	.2500
E	6.35	.2500
F	6.53	.2570
G	6.63	.2610
17/64	6.75	.2656
H	6.76	.2660
I	6.91	.2720
—	7.00	.2756
J	7.04	.2770
K	7.14	.2810
9/32	7.14	.2812
L	7.37	.2900
M	7.49	.2950
19/64	7.54	.2969
N	7.67	.3020
5/16	7.94	.3125
—	8.00	.3150
O	8.03	.3160
P	8.20	.3230
21/64	8.33	.3281
Q	8.43	.3320
R	8.61	.3390
11/32	8.73	.3438
S	8.84	.3480
—	9.00	.3543
T	9.09	.3580
23/64	9.13	.3594
U	9.35	.3680
3/8	9.53	.3750
V	9.56	.3770
W	9.80	.3860
25/64	9.92	.3906
—	10.00	.3937
X	10.08	.3970
Y	10.26	.4040
13/32	10.32	.4062
Z	10.49	.4130
27/64	10.72	.4219
—	11.00	.4331
7/16	11.11	.4375
29/64	11.51	.4531

Drill Size	mm	Decimal Inches
15/32	11.91	.4688
—	12.00	.4724
31/64	12.30	.4844
1/2	12.70	.5000
—	13.00	.5118
33/64	13.10	.5156
17/32	13.49	.5312
35/64	13.89	.5469
—	14.00	.5512
9/16	14.29	.5625
37/64	14.68	.5781
—	15.00	.5906
19/32	15.08	.5938
39/64	15.48	.6094
5/8	15.88	.6250
—	16.00	.6299
41/64	16.27	.6406
21/32	16.67	.6562
—	17.00	.6693
43/64	17.07	.6719
11/16	17.46	.6875
45/64	17.86	.7031
—	18.00	.7087
23/32	18.26	.7188
47/64	18.65	.7344
—	19.00	.7480
3/4	19.05	.7500
49/64	19.45	.7656
25/32	19.84	.7812
—	20.00	.7874
51/64	20.24	.7969
13/16	20.64	.8125
—	21.00	.8268
53/64	21.03	.8281
27/32	21.43	.8438
55/64	21.84	.8594
—	22.00	.8661
7/8	22.23	.8750
57/64	22.62	.8906
—	23.00	.9055
29/32	23.02	.9062
59/64	23.42	.9219
15/16	23.81	.9375
—	24.00	.9449
61/64	24.21	.9531
31/32	24.61	.9688
—	25.00	.9842
63/64	25.00	.9844
1"	25.40	1.0000

or three-digit number found on the head. Three of the most common Gradings are 8.8, 9.8 and 10.9. Though the ratings are given in newtons per square millimeter they can be converted to an approximate SAE grading as follows. An 8.8 is roughly equivalent to a SAE Grade 5, while a 10.9 is roughly the same as a SAE Grade 8 with an Ultimate Tensile Strength of 150,000 psi (see the SAE section below for more on the grading systems).

Like the bolts and capscrews we think of as American, the metric capscrews are available with internal heads or as a socket headed capscrew. Unlike the SAE bolts and capscrews, all metric "bolts" have a washer surface under the head and thus can be considered capscrews.

The SAE Grading System

As hot rod builders and shade-tree mechanics, most of us are familiar with SAE graded fasteners. These are the well-known Grade 5 and Grade 8 bolts we get from Gardner-Wescott, the local industrial supply house or the local hardware store.

SAE bolts come in various strengths. These bolts carry the radial dashes on the head that most of us have learned to identify. Three dashes is a Grade 5 while six identify the bolt as a Grade 8, a bolt many of us consider "as good as it gets."

As we explained, bolts are measured in pounds per square inch of tension or stress. The ultimate tensile strength or UTS is the point at which the bolt breaks. The other specification given for quality bolts is the yield point, or point at which the bolt will no longer bounce back to its original dimension once the stress is removed.

A SAE Grade 2 bolt, often called a hardware-store bolt, is rated at 74,000 psi UTS up to a size of 3/4 inch. This same bolt has a yield strength of 57,000 psi.

Moving up the scale, a Grade 5 bolt, the point at which good, heat treated bolts start, is rated at 120,000 psi UTS and has a published yield point of 92,000 psi. Grade 5 bolts are considered good enough for most general purpose automotive use, engine covers, and light double-shear duty.

What many of us consider the ultimate bolt, the Grade 8 bolt, is rated at 150,000 psi and 130,000 psi yield strength. These can be used in heavy duty double-shear applications, assuming the shank is the correct size for the hole it's being inserted into (more on this later). Properly manufactured

The aftermarket supplies more and more kits designed to answer a specific need, be it special connecting rod bolts or intake manifold bolts or stainless capscrews like these. ARP

Grade 8 fasteners use the "R" thread root to minimize the effects of fatigue.

There is more to a bolt or capscrew than the ratings in psi. Until recently, there were allegations that SAE specifications had no real meaning, that no one was doing effective inspections or quality control. But to quote Frank Akstens from the Industrial Fasteners Institute: "SAE stuff does get inspected. The Fastener Quality Act is now in force, as of December of 1999. That law says the fasteners must meet specifications for which they were ordered." The new law forces manufacturers to maintain a certain level of testing and inspecting. There is a hot line number (1 800 424 2980) so a user can turn in an offending manufacturer to the government. The new law means that manufacturers will have to keep better paper work on their products.

Frank Akstens goes on to explain that, "Grade 5 and 8 have a manufacturer's identification marking on the head along with the radial dashes. This makes it easier to trace the bolt back to the manufacturer. Something like 'LE' for Lake Erie Screw Corporation. Grade 2 fasteners do not need dashes and do not need a manufacturer's mark." The manufacturer's mark makes them accountable and increases the likelihood that the bolt you buy is the bolt you think it is.

Another problem with SAE rated fasteners isn't a problem as long as we're aware of the limitations that these fasteners carry with them. These bolts and capscrews should be used only for tension applications.

SAE graded bolts don't do a good job in shear applications. The first reason is the wider latitude used for the specifications governing the diameter of the unthreaded portion of the shank. This simply means that the bolt or capscrew may be a very sloppy fit in the bracket or shock absorber mount. The second reason SAE bolts are better suited to tension loads is the fact that there is no specification for the length of the unthreaded portion, so the threaded part of the bolt is generally way too long, meaning either the threaded portion will be used in a shear application (in which case the threads may chew up the hole or bracket) or that much of the threaded portion will have to be cut off. Unlike the SAE bolts, higher quality bolts like those manufactured to AN specs can be counted on to have an unthreaded portion of a very specific length determined in part by the bolt's diameter.

SAE fasteners have taken a lot of heat in the past few years. Yet, for building street rods, not competition cars or aircraft, Grade 5 and 8 are perfectly adequate for most of the situations we encounter. At least one big California street rod

This is only a small sampling of the threaded fasteners available to the hot rodder. It helps to set a standard early in the project as to which bolts (grade 5, or 8 or?) you will use for general assembly. which for engine dress up and which for the chassis.

HeliCoils and Thread Repair

Story by Mark Zimmerman, photos by Jeff Hackett

Most threads are stripped through continued over-torquing. The other common problem is under-torquing, which causes the fastener to move about in the hole until the threads are literally eroded away. The introduction of dirt between the fastener and the thread are culprits as well. Spark plugs and drain plugs are common examples of this. Of course, plain old carelessness in the form of cross-threading and jamming a fine threaded bolt into a coarse threaded hole also accounts for a fair number of stripped threads.

Occasionally a bolt that went in fine comes out with some or most of the threads dangling from it. This is usually the result of dissimilar metals (steel or stainless steel into aluminum or cast iron) being assembled without adequate lubrication. Any time you install a steel or stainless steel bolt into aluminum or cast iron, it should be lubricated with a molybdenum-based anti-seize compound.

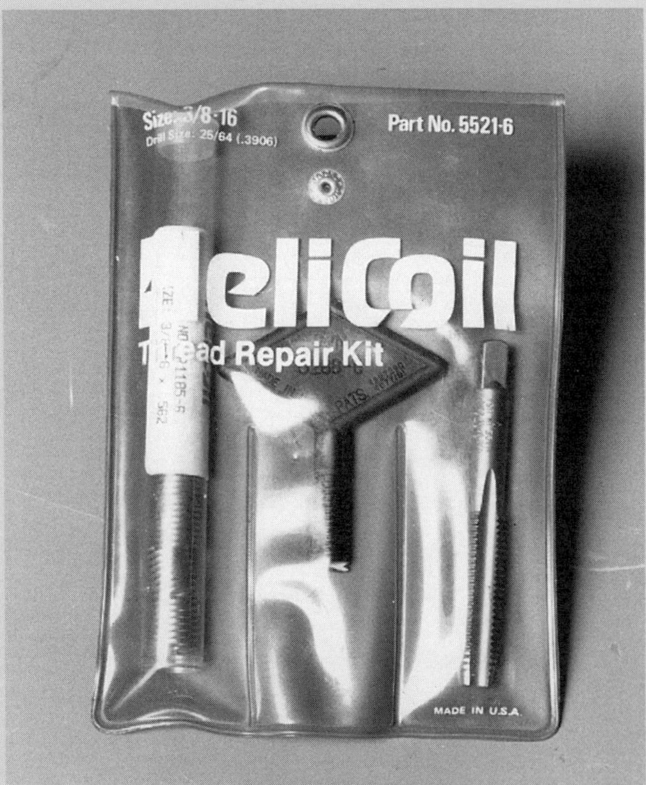

The basic HeliCoil set consists of the coils, the special tap, and the insertion tool.

The Fix

Now that you have at least a cursory knowledge of the reasons behind stripped threads, its time to learn how to repair them. The first and most obvious solution that may come to mind is simple: re-drill the hole and re-tap it to the next-over size. Fine idea if you have the room to do it. In many instances, it may well be possible to enlarge the hole, say from 6mm to 8mm or 1/4" to 5/16", and thread the hole accordingly. The problem is that this doesn't always work.

A better and more permanent repair is a HeliCoil-type insert. Its also the only way, short of welding up the hole and starting from scratch, to repair a stripped spark plug hole.

HeliCoil kits are available at most industrial supply shops and many auto parts stores. The kit consists of a dozen or so spring steel inserts, a purpose-ground tap, and a mandrel for installing the inserts. You supply a drill bit of the correct size (the appropriate size is listed on the package), a 3/8" drill, and a steady hand.

Normally, drilling out the stripped hole presents little, if any, problem. Make sure the drill bit is positioned true to the hole, use a moderate speed and pressure, and you'll find the bit will basically guide itself. In some cases, especially with small holes, you can use a tap handle to turn the bit. Remember, you're not removing much material. Once the hole is drilled and the chips removed, the hole is tapped like any other using the supplied tap and the proper lubricant. Most industrial suppliers carry a variety of cutting oils under names like Thread-Eze or Kool-Kut that are worth picking up if you plan to do any serious threading.

Now that your hole is drilled, tapped, and cleaned, its ready to accept the HeliCoil insert. The insert is first threaded into the mandrel and, if you've done everything just right up to this point, it can be screwed in without further ado. When the uppermost thread is about half a turn below the surface, *stop* turning and remove the mandrel. Break off the drive tang by giving it a sharp blow with a hammer and a punch. The tang can then be removed with a magnet or a pair of tweezers.

The neat thing about this kind of repair is that you can use the same style, size, and pitch of fastener as the original, and usually the repair can be accomplished in place. The exceptions are spark plugs and drain plugs.

HeliCoils and Thread Repair

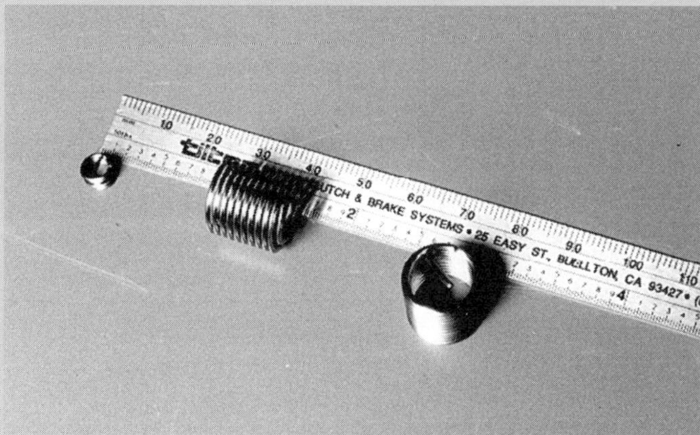

The coils themselves are available in nearly every known diameter and length.

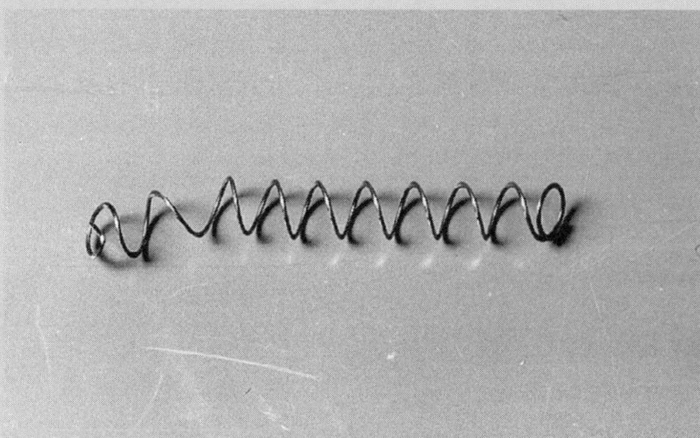

Don't worry, if you mess up, the HeliCoil can always be removed.

These two pieces present a unique problem because the chips created during the cutting operation have nowhere to go other than the bowels of the engine.

HeliCoils come in a variety of pitches, diameters, and lengths. In a pinch one that's slightly long can be cut down to the correct height. Once you've bought the installation kit, the coils themselves are cheap. Prices vary, but expect to pay somewhere between $25 and $50 for a standard kit such as 3/8" or 8mm/1.25mm. The spark plug kit is about double.

The Alternatives

There are several alternatives to the HeliCoil. However, there are only two that I would recommend. The first is Loctite's Thread Restorer. This is an epoxy-like compound that can be mixed on the spot and used to repair any non-critical fastener up to 3/8 inch in diameter. The operative phrase here is *non-critical.* If you plan on using it temporarily to repair a stripped 1/4 inch bolt on a valve cover, fine. But if you are going to use it to repair an 3/8 inch bolt from a brake caliper, no way.

The second alternative is called a Timesert. Rather than using a coiled wire to re-thread the hole, the Timesert is a one-piece steel shell. The installation process is similar to that of the HeliCoil except that the top of the hole is chamfered with a special tool to accept a matching chamfer on the Timesert. Another special tool is used to screw the Timesert into its hole. As its drawn tight it expands the bottom of the insert slightly, thus locking it firmly in place.

Timeserts are sold as individual kits or you may purchase a master set containing the most commonly used sizes. The major disadvantage to using Timeserts is the relative scarcity of suppliers. They are also slightly more expensive than HeliCoils and marginally harder to install.

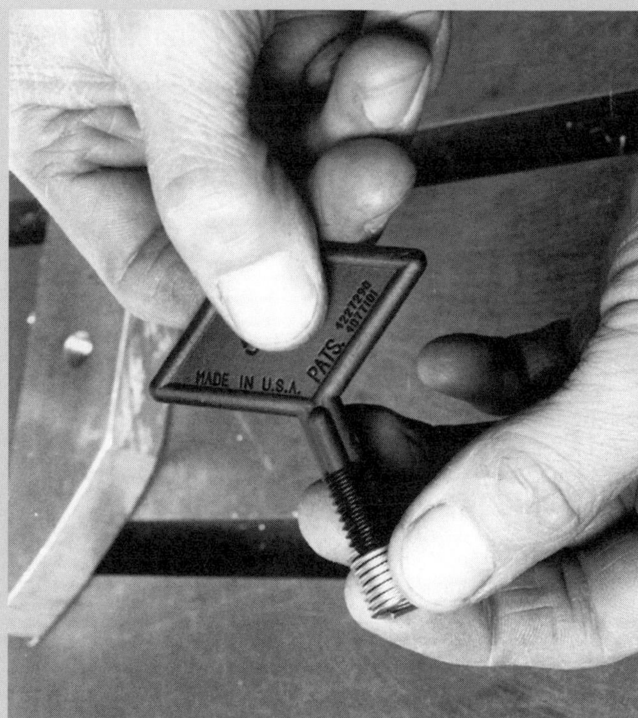

The HeliCoil is screwed onto the installation tool then threaded into the hole.

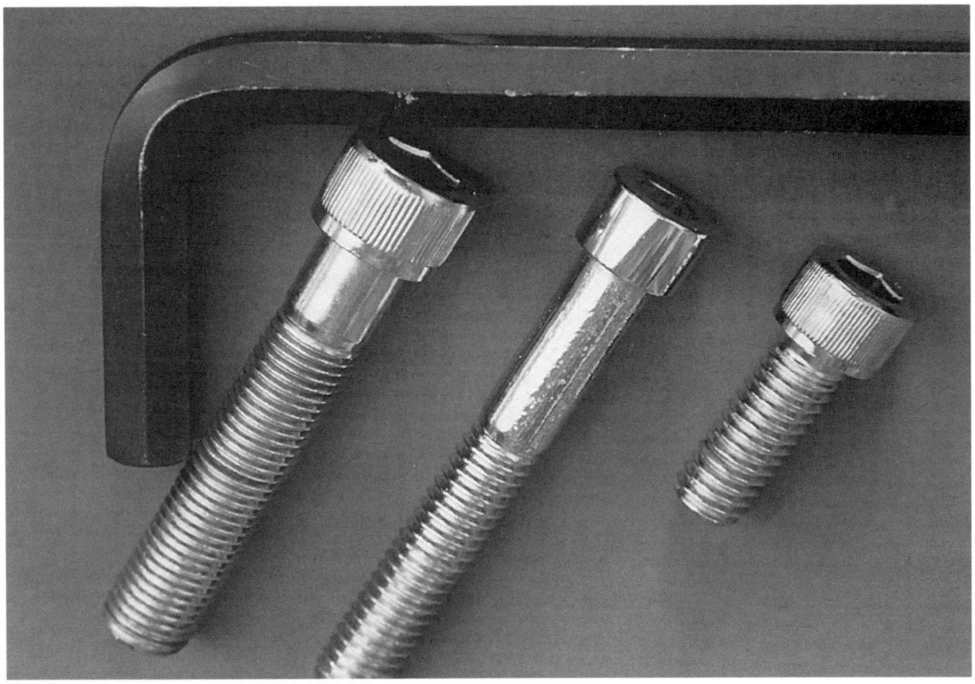

Chrome plated socket headed cap screws come in both smooth and knurled heads.

shop, SO-CAL, uses SAE Grade 5 for nearly the entire car. Grade 8 are substituted for heavily loaded bolts and high tech bolts are used occasionally, but mostly for aesthetic reasons.

Troubles with quality arise in the case of chrome and polished bolts, which by their nature have no marking on the head. In these cases you have to judge the bolt by the manufacturer and the individual store where you shop.

In any case, you should use discretion in choosing your bolt suppliers. Ask them where the supply comes from. If they don't know then look for a new supplier. Be certain the fasteners are made in the US of A by a quality manufacturer. Avoid like the plague anything that promises to be "better than Grade 8."

Though we think most of the bolts that hold our cars together are in tension, a surprising number are actually loaded in single or double shear.

Army Navy

The next upgrade in fasteners is supplied by Air Corps/Navy system, commonly abbreviated AN. Many hot rodders have come in contact with brake and hydraulic hoses sized as a "dash three" or "dash four." Or the 37 degree fittings used on stainless brake lines, the fittings which are often preceded by the two letters, AN.

This set of specifications was devised to provide a better grade of hardware, primarily for aircraft. Today, these AN specified fasteners are often used by anyone looking for a bolt or capscrew of higher quality and precision than that provided by the SAE system.

The dash three, or –3 sizing makes sense if you consider the 3 as the numerator, over 16. Thus –3 is actually a bolt 3/16th inch in diameter while a –4 is 4/16 or 1/4 inch in diameter.

AN Bolts and Capscrews

The AN bolts and capscrews that most readily replace the SAE items are called airframe bolts. These fasteners come in all the sizes we are likely to use in our shops and though they are available in many lengths, the *threaded* length is always double the bolt's diameter. Thus, these fasteners do not have all the extra threads seen on many SAE bolts and capscrews. The unthreaded portion of the bolt, or shank, is held to a much closer tolerance than with the other, more common, system. These AN bolts and capscrews then can be used in either tension or shear applications.

All AN 3 through AN 20 bolts come with UNF threads and a class three fit. Material choices include carbon steel rated at 125,000 psi for UTS and 75,000 psi for yield, and also a CRES (corrosion resistant), or stainless material with the same ratings as the carbon steel. The AN 3 though 20 airframe fasteners are also available in an aluminum alloy, though the rating is only 62,000 psi for the UTS.

For coarse thread applications you have to use the related MS (Military Standards) 20074 series bolts. Like the AN fasteners, these come in a wide variety of lengths, are manufactured to tight specifications and mimic the AN specifications in nearly every way.

While you can't buy these AN and MS pieces at the local hardware or supply house, you will be able to find them through the local airport, or through one of the aircraft supply houses. The advantages in using these AN bolts include the vast array of lengths available, all with unthreaded shanks manufactured to a tight tolerance. For anyone building a race car, these bolts can be ordered with the head already drilled for safety wire.

Yet, for most of us building street cars, the good old SAE Graded bolts, particularly the Grade 5 and the Grade 8 are more than adequate. And when we need something better, like a special connecting rod bolt, the aftermarket has a whole raft of high-strength fasteners designed for that specific job.

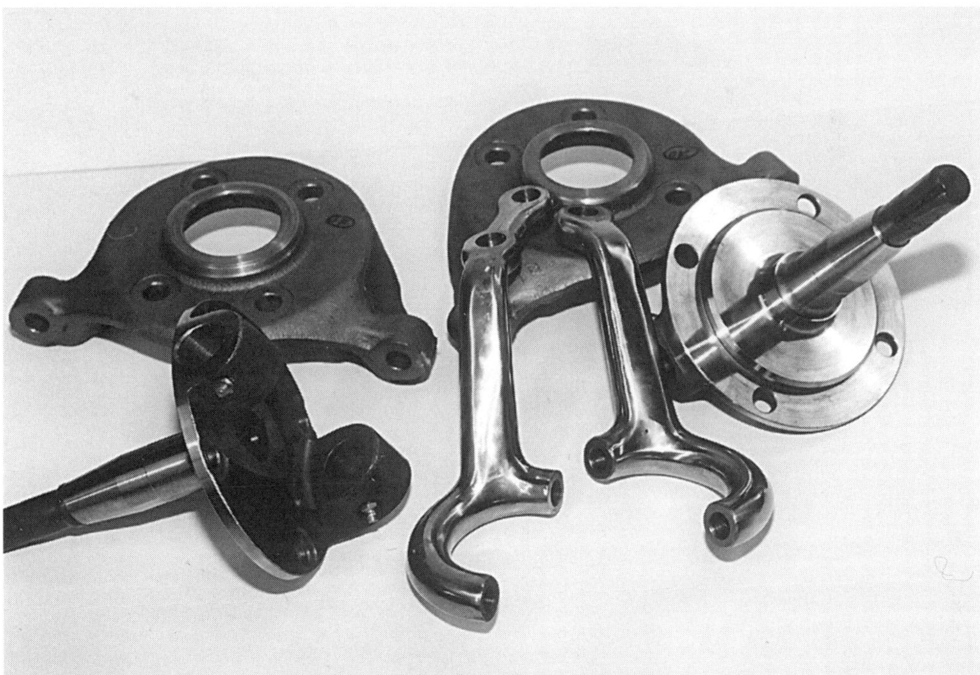

From the standpoint of safety, the front suspension components are among the most important on the car. Look for well-known brand names and forged steel, and screw it together with only the best fasteners.

Chapter Three

Specialized Fasteners

With Fatigue Fighting Threads

Special tasks require special equipment. In the automotive world the bolts that receive the worst abuse are probably the rod bolts, especially on true "hot rod" engines.

As Tom Smith from ARP explains in his interview, the rod bolts are the most important bolts in the engine. They are highly loaded and very, very important to the life of the engine.

These bolts require more than just a good material. In order to avoid fatigue they must be

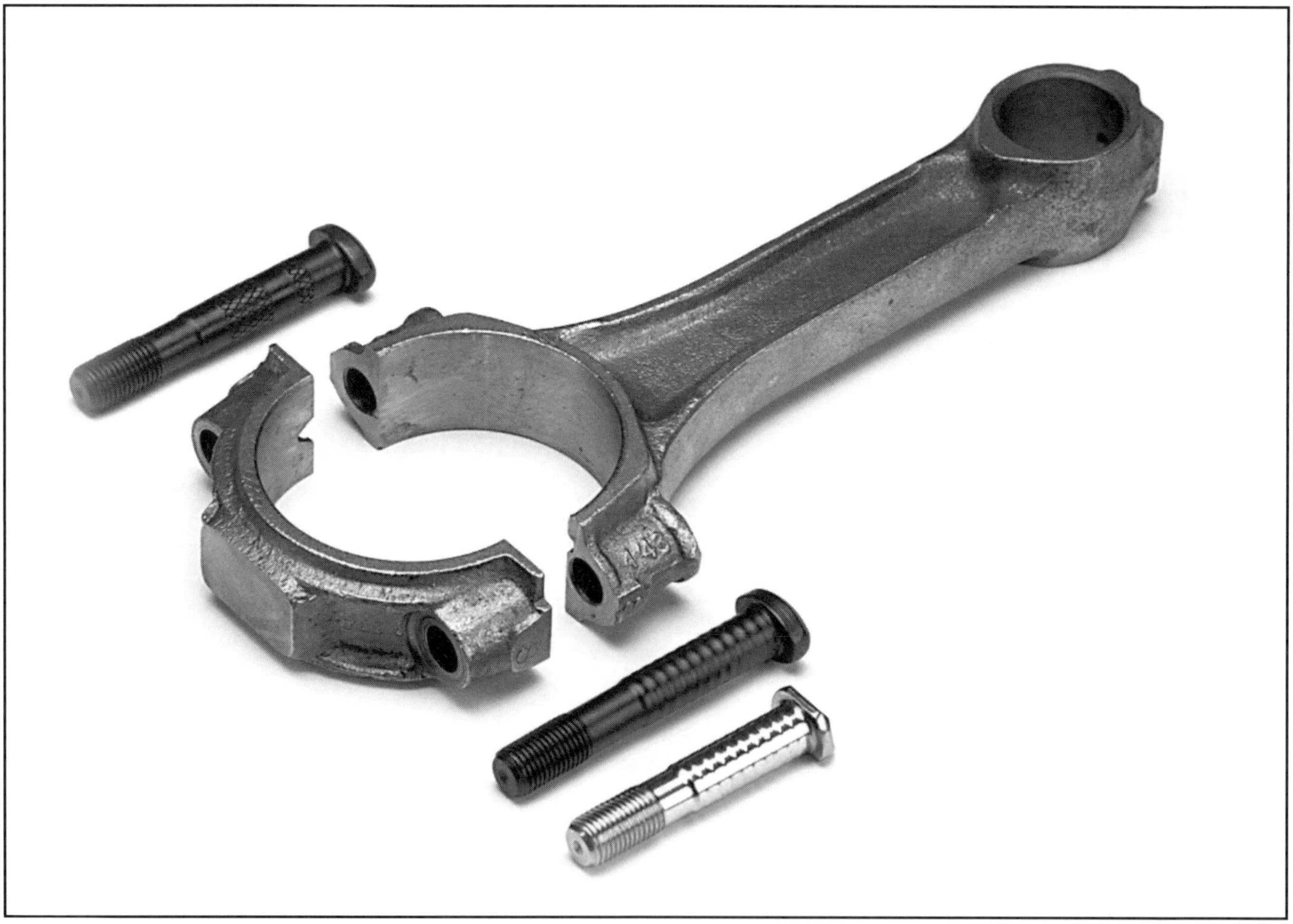

The connecting rod bolts are probably the hardest working bolts in the entire car. ARP offers three levels of bolt for use in various street and competition applications.

carefully designed and manufactured. Stress risers must be eliminated through the careful rolling of the threads and by heat treatment before the threads are formed. This combination of exotic alloys, careful design and manufacture has its rewards, bolts that are rated at 220,000 psi and more.

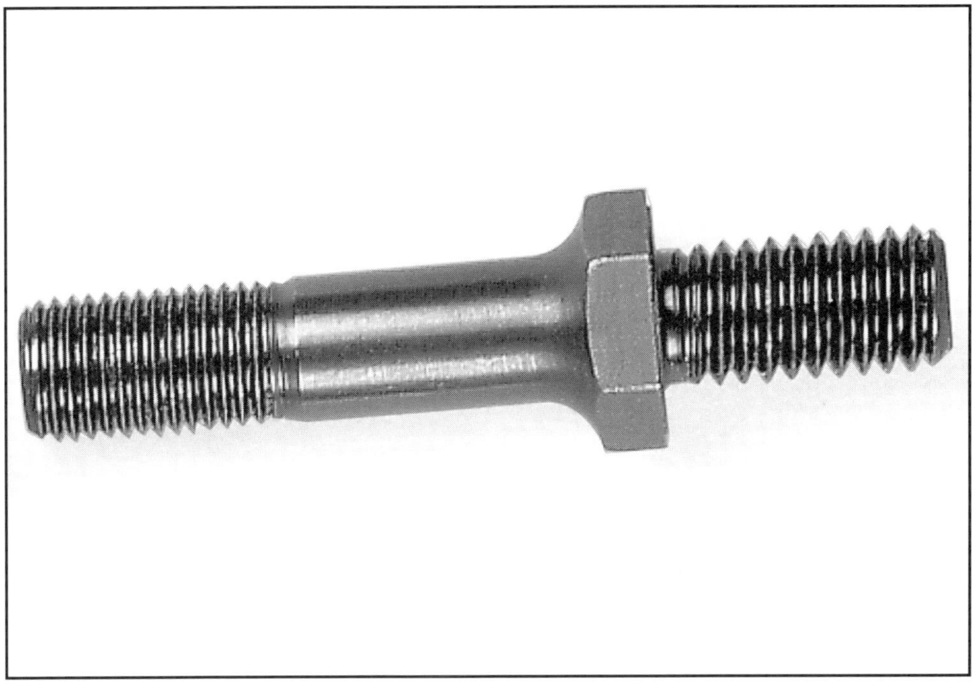

Nearly any bolt or capscrew in the engine can be upgraded with something better, including the rocker arm studs. ARP

Hydrogen Embrittlement

Most of us have heard of hydrogen embrittlement, yet how many of us really understand the term? Essentially, hydrogen atoms work their way into the atomic matrix that makes up the bolt or nut. The hydrogen will tend to congregate at the most highly stressed areas of the bolt and cause a weakening of the material and ultimately the bolt itself.

The various plating processes, from cadmium to chrome, often introduce the fastener to hydrogen, thus the concern in some quarters regarding the possible weakening of chrome-plated bolts. Because hydrogen is a gas, it can, and often is, "baked off" following any plating process (for more on this topic see the interview with Tom Smith farther along in this chapter).

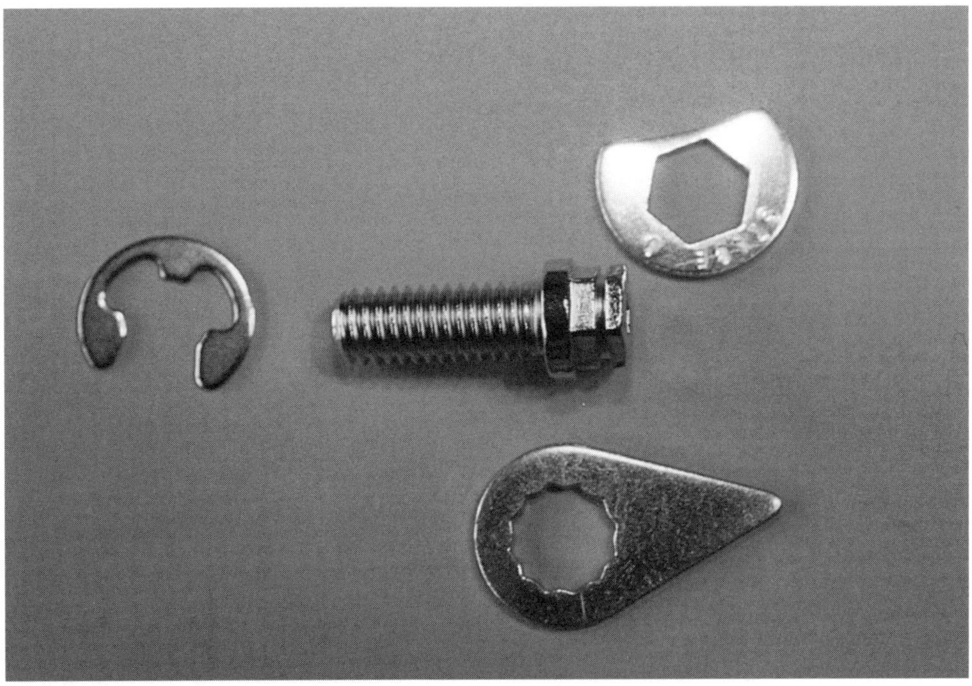

Header bolts have a nasty habit of backing out of the hole, a problem solved through use of these specialized locking fasteners from Stage 8.

Allen bolts

Universally known as "Allen" bolts, (Allen is actually a trade name) these Socket Headed Cap Screws are the preferred fastener for many hot rodders. The small head can be an advantage in many situations and these fasteners are reputed to be extremely durable, though most people use them for their apparent precision and that intangible feel of "machinery" they lend to anything they touch.

These header studs feature a bullet nose and come with washers, and nuts with a serrated face. ARP

Many bolt books state that all SHCS bolts are at least 170,000 psi for UTS. In other words, better than a Grade 8 bolt. Unfortunately, this is no longer true. Like all the other hardware you buy, you now have to be careful where, and from who, you buy your SHCS bolts. In particular, the chrome plated variety are often only about a Grade 5, but you don't know unless you ask. The other problem that comes along with these nifty fasteners is the relatively long threads, which may have to be shortened with a die-grinder or hacksaw.

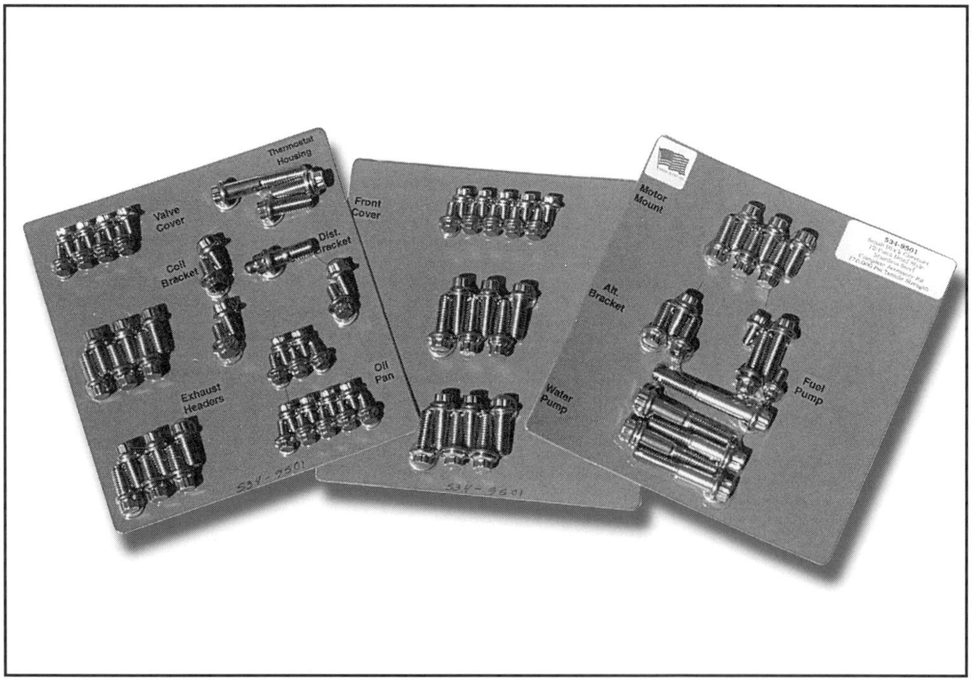

Twelve point bolt kits, designed for specific engines, are available in both steel and stainless steel. ARP

The small head, which many see as an advantage, can be a problem as well. The small size means it's hard to use the full strength of the bolt to clamp things together. And if you use a standard stamped washer under the head it will deform later leaving you with a loose bolt. The answer is to use a hardened and ground, or Grade 8, washer under the head of the SHCS bolt.

The only thing better

than an SHCS is one with a button head. These little rounded heads look like rivets. The button head however, allows for only a very shallow female socket, meaning you can't get a good grip with the wrench. So don't use the button heads when you need serious clamping pressure.

The only people who like these socket headed cap screws more than hot rodders are custom Harley-Davidson builders. Which means any good Harley-Davidson dealership or aftermarket shop will have a great selection of these bolts.

The ring gear is under constant load and unload cycles and as such requires very good bolts to secure it to the carrier. ARP

Chrome bolts

They say chrome is king, but when it comes to a chrome plated bolt, there are a few things you should know. First, chrome plating a bolt weakens it slightly (see the notes on hydrogen embrittlement above). Compensation may be provided if the manufacturer started with a high quality bolt. The other problem is the fact that these bolts have no marking on the head, so there is no easy way to judge their quality. For this reason it's extra important that you purchase the bolts from a supplier you trust to provide good quality fasteners. (For more on chrome bolts see the interview in Chapter One.)

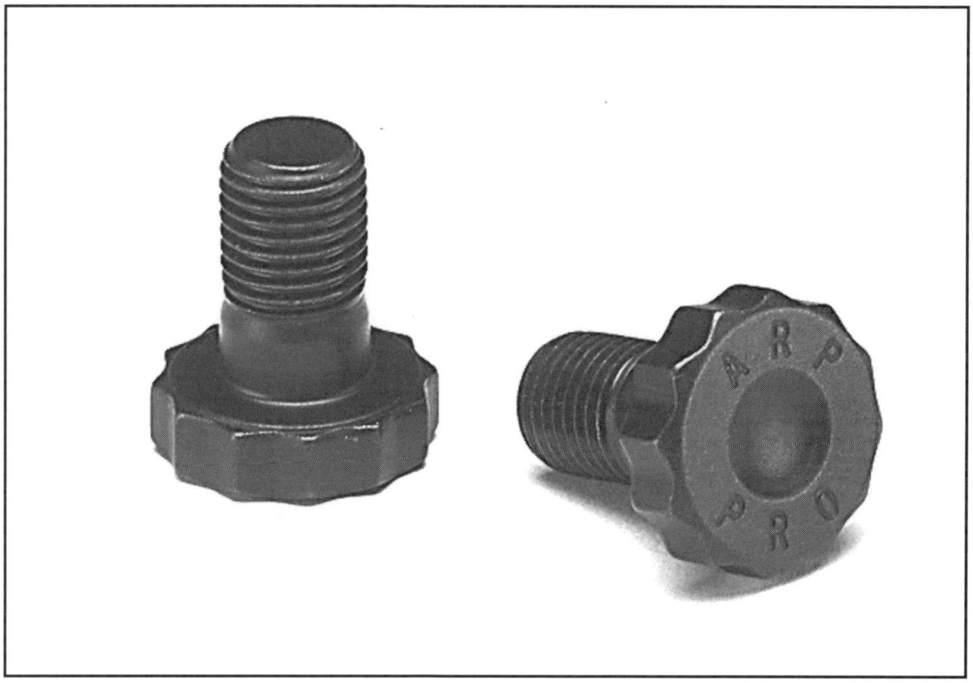

Designed to withstand the tremendous shock loads generated on launch, these special ring gear bolts are made from 8740 Chrome-moly and are rated at 190,000 psi. ARP

You can have your own

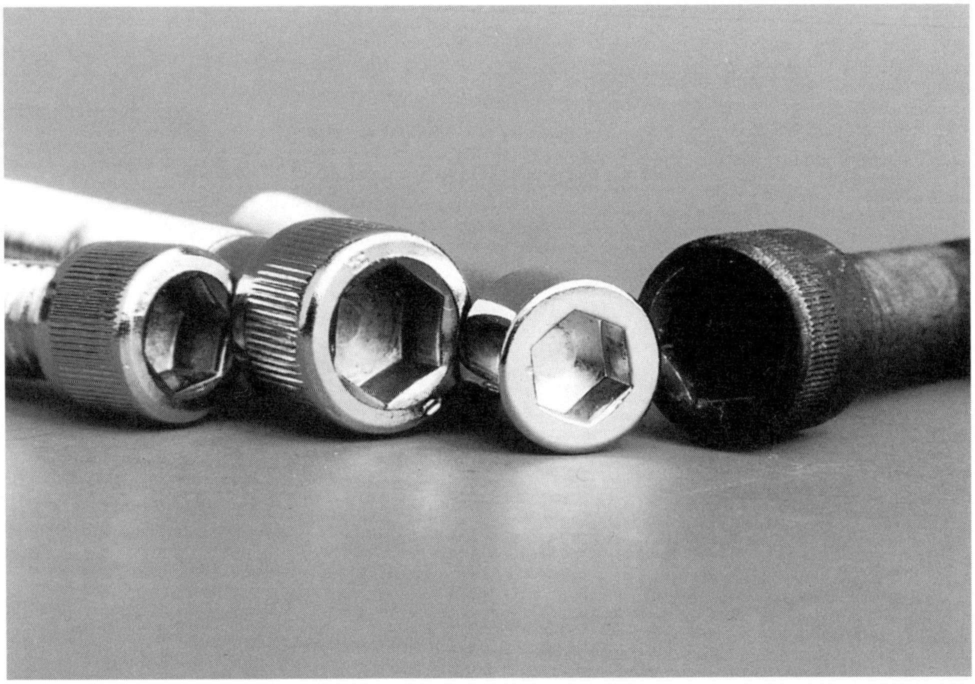

"Allen" bolts come in strengths as high as 180,000 psi though many decorative SHCS are only about a Grad 5.

bolts chrome plated, but considering the availability of already-chromed bolts, it's not a good trade off. While the nickel and chrome plating aren't very thick, the process does add to the dimensions of the threads, meaning that shiny bolt you just had plated might stick when it goes into the hole (or more likely, when you try to screw it out). If you do have a bolt chrome plated, be sure to mask off the threads so they don't grow in size.

If in doubt about any bolt or nut, it's a good idea to chase the threads with a tap or die. If the die or tap is doing much cutting, there's a problem and the best approach is to look for a replacement.

Button-head SHCS look great but the head isn't as deep as a conventional SHCS, so the wrench doesn't go in as far. All this means the button-heads can't be tightened to the same degree as the standard SHCS.

The use of chrome plated SHCS can be filled with frustration. Anyone who has used these bolts soon discovers that rust often develops down inside the head, due to the fact that the chrome plating process just can't get plating down into those crevices. The answer is to use the little chrome caps that snap into the socket, paint the inside or the heads, or put a dab of clear silicon on the end of the wrench the first time the bolt is used.

Because the chrome can flake off the fastener, even a good one, and cause it to bind in the hole, a good anti seize should be used on chrome bolts. Loctite products also do a good job of preventing metal to metal contact and can also be used to prevent galling of chrome nuts and bolts. Most of these bolts are Grade 5 or Grade 8, which means you want to be sure they don't gall and break off in the hole. Because they're so tough, they're also hard as hell to drill out and extract.

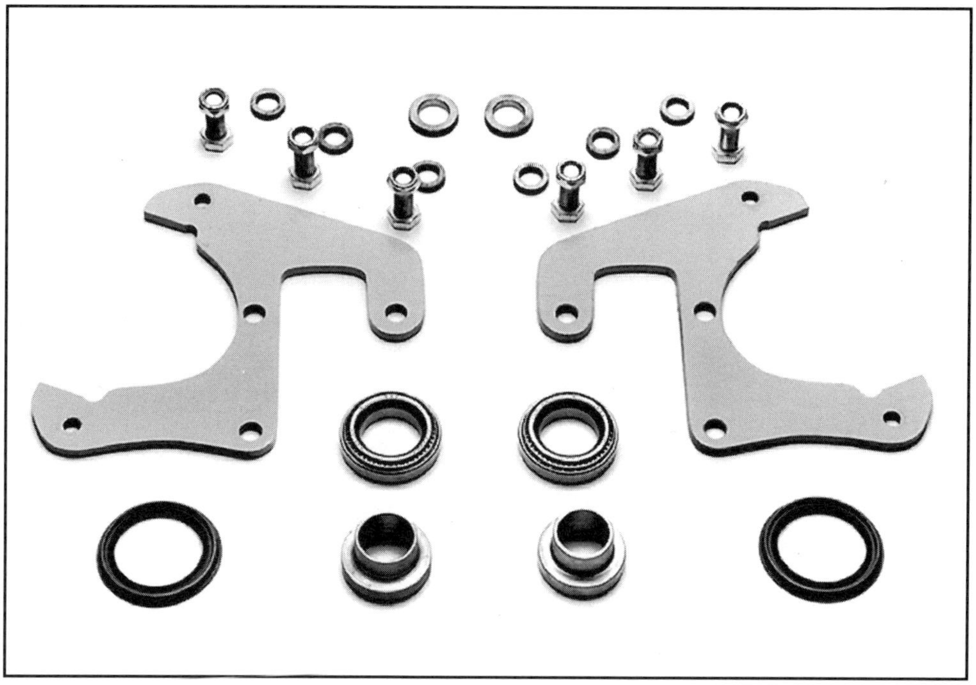

The better kits from the aftermarket come with their own hardware and fasteners - especially in cases like these brake caliper mounting kits where the strength of the fastener is so important. Chassis Eng.

Dzus-Fasteners

As a kid growing up in the late Fifties, my friends and I simply thought of Dzus fasteners as very, very cool. We didn't ponder the engineering or cleverness that went into their design. We were responding rather to their simplicity and the fact that they were nearly always found in association with very fast cars, Bonneville cars in particular.

Often called Dzus buttons, these quarter-turn fasteners are available in a number of styles and shank lengths.

William Dzus is the man who designed those early "buttons" that so fascinated me and my jean-clad peers. His genius was in designing a fastener for panels that would allow quick and easy disassembly with nothing more than a screw driver. A fastener with enough spring in it that the fastener wouldn't come unscrewed. The spring also provided the right degree of isolation to the panel so vibration and the resulting stress cracks were minimized.

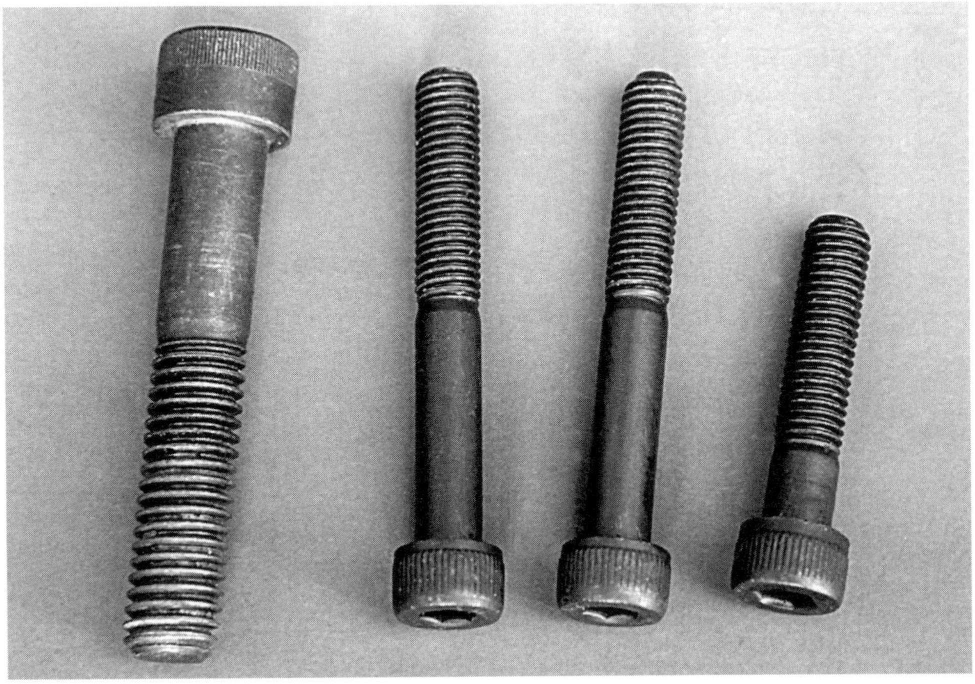

These industrial looking SHCS are probably rated at 180,000 psi, but you don't know until you check the headmarks (though hard to read, SHCS have them too).

As Jim Petrykowski from Metal Fab outside Minneapolis explains, "The Dzus fastener has three things going for it: It only takes a quarter turn to completely engage the fastener, it resists vibration because it's spring loaded, and when used on sheet metal it is very strong."

Today the "Dzus" fastener is made by hundreds of companies in thousands of variations. Most of these however break down into a few styles. Some come with a dimpled support plate and some actually eject the male fastener after it's turned and released from the wire underneath.

All fasteners of this type use spring loaded wire, welded or riveted to the lower panel, as the other half of typical Dzus fastener. Some use a straight screwdriver slot, some use a Phillips head and some are designed like a wing-nut with their own built-in handle.

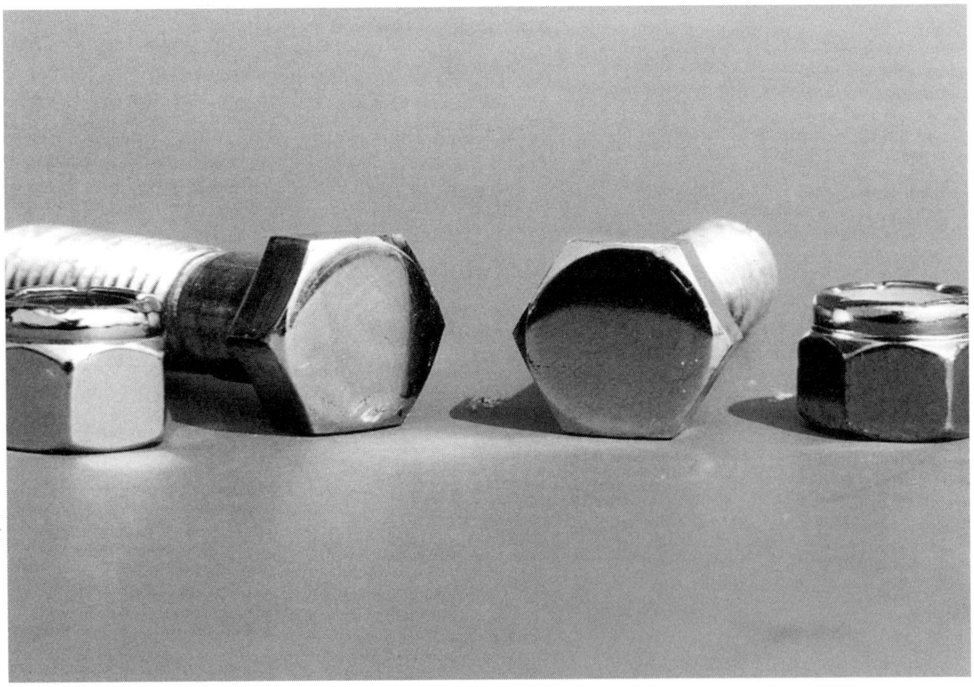

Chrome-plated nuts and bolts can suffer from hydrogen embrittlement, though the larger problem with these fasteners is the inability to judge their strength based on external markings.

Those that feature some kind of slotted receptacle for a screwdriver or tool are flush or nearly flush with the surface. Which is why they were developed initially for aircraft and later used on Bonneville cars. These quarter-turn fasteners come in various lengths to compensate for thinner or thicker sheet metal and fiberglass.

Despite the cleverness of the design, these fasteners are not terribly strong either in tension or shear, when compared to a more conventional nut and bolt combination. They also don't do well locating a panel because of the sloppy nature of the fit. Where you need more strength another style of quick acting fastener (most of which require more than a quarter turn) should be used. And where location is critical, pins or some other method can be used to locate the panel and thus reduce the shear load on the quarter-turn fasteners.

What Makes a True Super Bolt

Among the best known of the aftermarket companies making very high quality fasteners for the automotive aftermarket is ARP. Not just good bolts, ARP manufactures some of the toughest connecting rod bolts you can buy. For a little insight into what makes an ARP bolt special we talked with longtime ARP employee Tom Smith.

Tom, tell us a little about ARP.

Our founder came from an aerospace fastener company. But his hobby was racing and he saw first hand that many of the engines that broke, broke because of fastener failure. In fact, we are MS 20250 certified, which means we can make aerospace fasteners. That is not our bread and butter, however. The automotive aftermarket is our main market.

Tell us how a good bolt is manufactured?

We start with seam and defect free wire, aerospace quality material. Most fasteners get cold headed. That means they forge the head from the same piece of wire the bolt is made from, so it's all one piece. The heat treat is next. We do our own heat treating. Anything over 2 inches long is individually racked. They are hung vertically in a screen which allows for a more consistent quench than if they were stacked on top of each other. The screen also holds them straighter so they don't twist like they would if they were laying in a heap.

After heat treating they are sand blasted to remove scale. Then they get shot peened, which gives the part some compressive stress and extra strength. Then comes finishing, grinding OD diameters, undercuts if there are some. Fatigue rated bolts get fillet rolled, this puts a cold work in the radius under the head,

The thread rolling is next. It's one of those situations where if the little things aren't right you don't end up with a good bolt or capscrew. They call it a "match." There are two or three dies in a thread rolling machines and they must be lined up perfectly to create a match. If you're the slightest bit out of match or the bushings that the dies run on are worn you get seams or laps in the threads. Those imperfections in the threads will prevent the bolt from passing the fatigue tests. They're stress risers, where the bolt

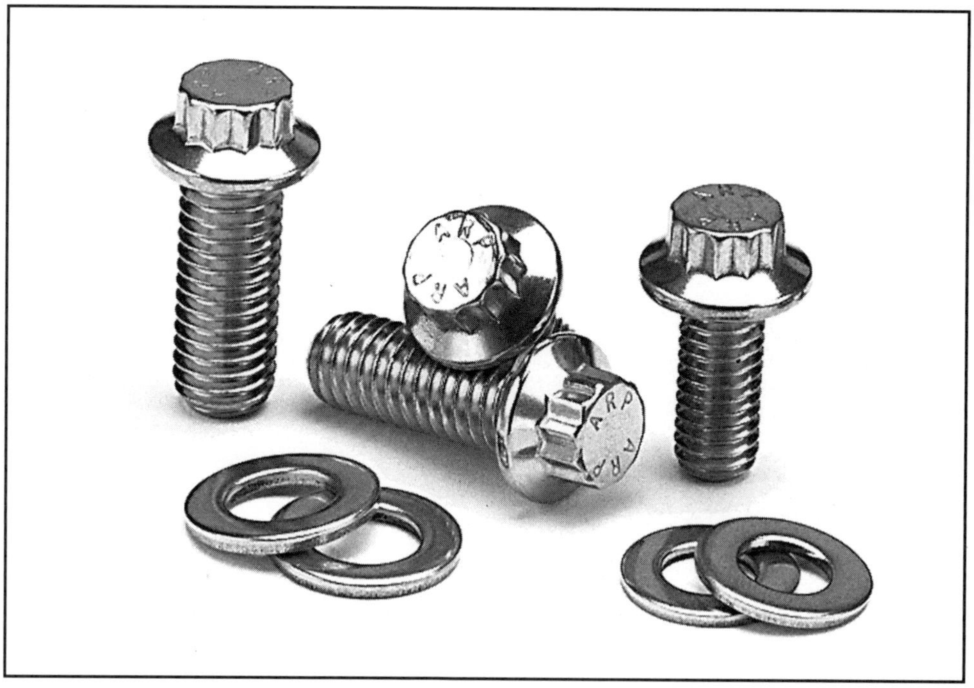

Most stainless bolts are not very strong. Exceptions include many of the selections in the ARP catalog.

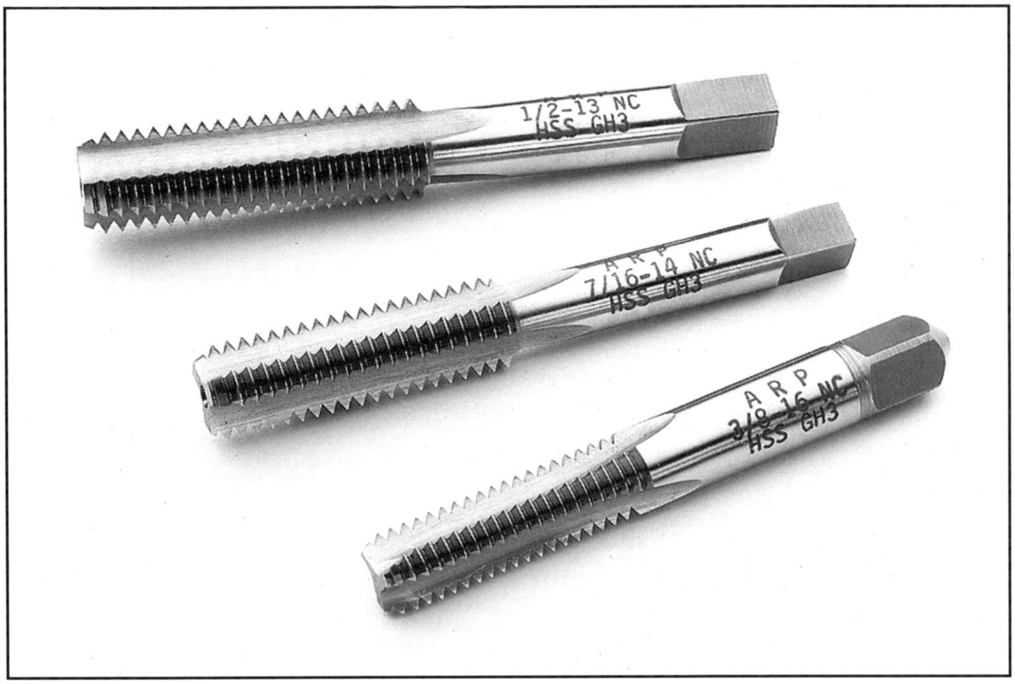

You can't get accurate torque readings or clamp loads unless the threads are clean. These thread chasers are designed to clean threads, not cut them, before engine assembly. ARP

will break. By keeping laps and seams out of threads you get a better fatigue life. We do testing in-house, we are able to do it as the machine runs. We might pull out every thousandth bolt and do actual fatigue testing on that bolt. That way if there is a problem developing with a thread rolling machine we discover it right away. It's a better way of testing than just grabbing random samples at the end of a run.

How many cycles do you run on fatigue testing?

We run them to failure, but they must pass 250,000 cycles minimum.

Our bolts all meet the 8879 specification for thread roll. That's an old aerospace standard. It means no laps, no seams and a radiused runout where the last thread meets the unthreaded portion of the shank. On commercial bolts they use the same root radius, as the root meets the shank, as they do with the complete thread. We put in a radiused root, a nice smooth transition from the threaded section into your shank or undercut diameter. Again, we do this so you don't have a stress riser there. We like to think that we go the

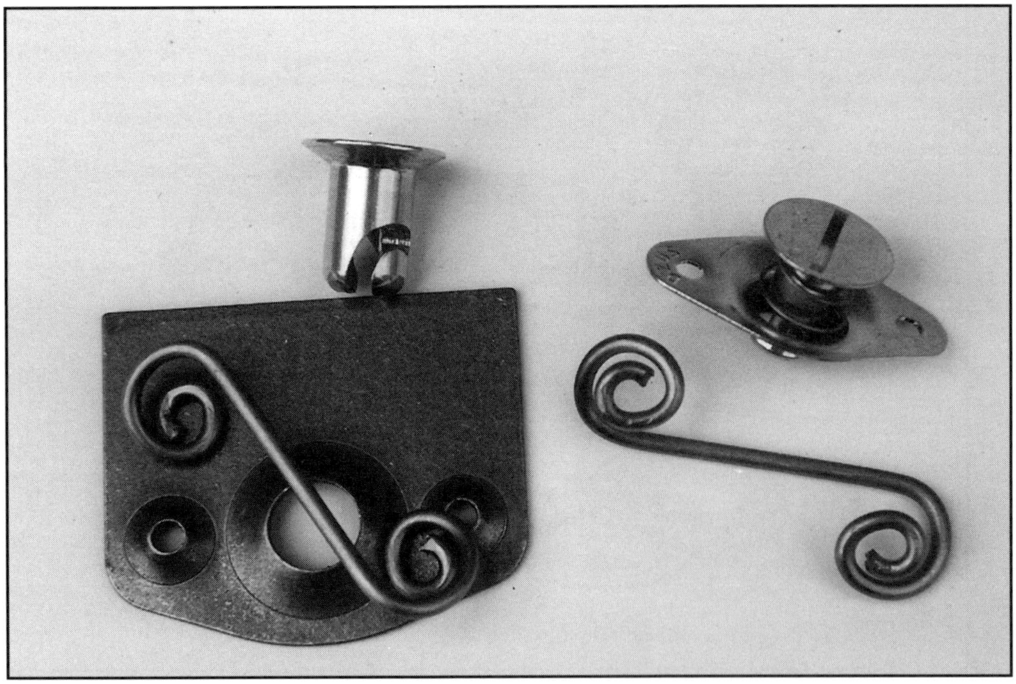

Head styles include slotted and hex. Some pop out completely while other styles stay with the panel.

extra step to make a really good fastener.

What about the thread form, do you use the R and J thread form?

Yes, Any fatigue rated fastener is a J form, a controlled root radius. All of our fits are class 3A. Now the internal threads are 3B on any CNC block, or the female threads in a standard GM block for example. A bolt with a J root form will always fit in a class 3 female thread. It's a little tighter fit and is especially nice if the block is old and it's been assembled and disassembled a number of times.

What about torque values, how accurate are they? How is the torque value affected by the different lubricants and coatings in use?

Torque is a crap shoot. It gets you close. We don't manufacture our own bolt lubes so we went to a company that makes special lubes. Now we carry our own moly lube and thread sealer. We set our torque specifications with the use of our specific lube. That's how you have to do it. If you change the lube the torque will change too.

And there are still variables. The finish on the mating surface where the nut comes up against the connecting rod cap, for example, how rough is that surface? That's why, for a connecting rod, we recommend you measure the stretch instead of the torque. You eliminate all the variables that way. Stretch equals preload. At a given stretch, 75% of the yield, you will consistently get the same clamping load. That helps a guy be confident that the bolt is pre-loaded to the optimum value, and that the con rod will stay round, the clamp-

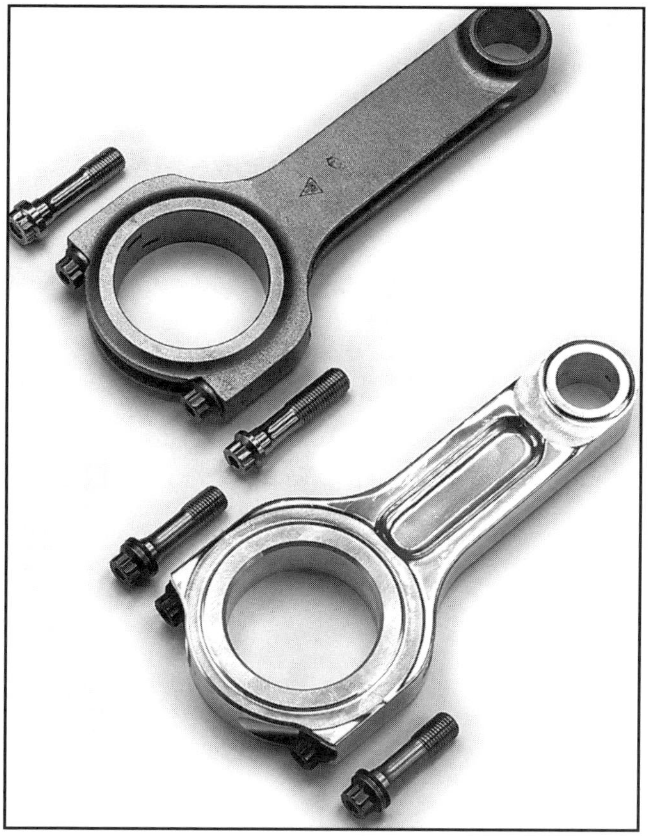

A number of aftermarket competition connecting rods come with high performance heat treated bolts from ARP.

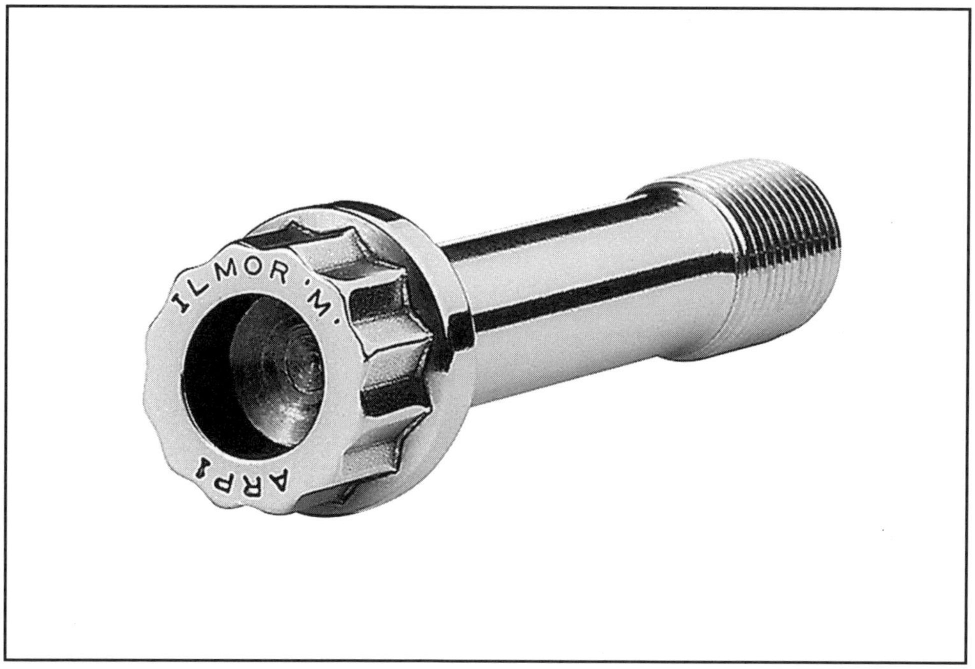

Probably not what you want in the small-block you drive on the street, these "formula One" con-rod bolts are designed to withstand use at 18,000 RPM. ARP

Taps and Dies

It might seem that with a good tap and die set the owner can cut male and female threads in any material. After reading this fine book however, you've realized that good threads are rolled and not cut. You also now know that cutting more threads on a fastener in order to make it fit a particular situation undoes all the careful design and manufacture that went into that capscrew. All of which is not to say you shouldn't have a set of taps and dies in the tool box, because you should.

There are just too many times when that special bolt you are screwing into a hole goes in a little hard and you want to run a die over it to see if it's clean and whether or not it's been tightened past the point of yield. Sometimes it's a situation where the bolt itself was too long, so you've cut a half inch off the end, and ground the edges to create a taper, but in order to ensure it will neatly and cleanly engage the female threads, it helps to run a die over the part of the threads that were cut and ground. The nice thing about the tap and die set you buy from Sears or the Snap-on dealer is the fact that it contains a thread gauge, which is a great aid in trying to positively identify the size of a particular bolt. This is especially nice these days when many of our hot rods include a

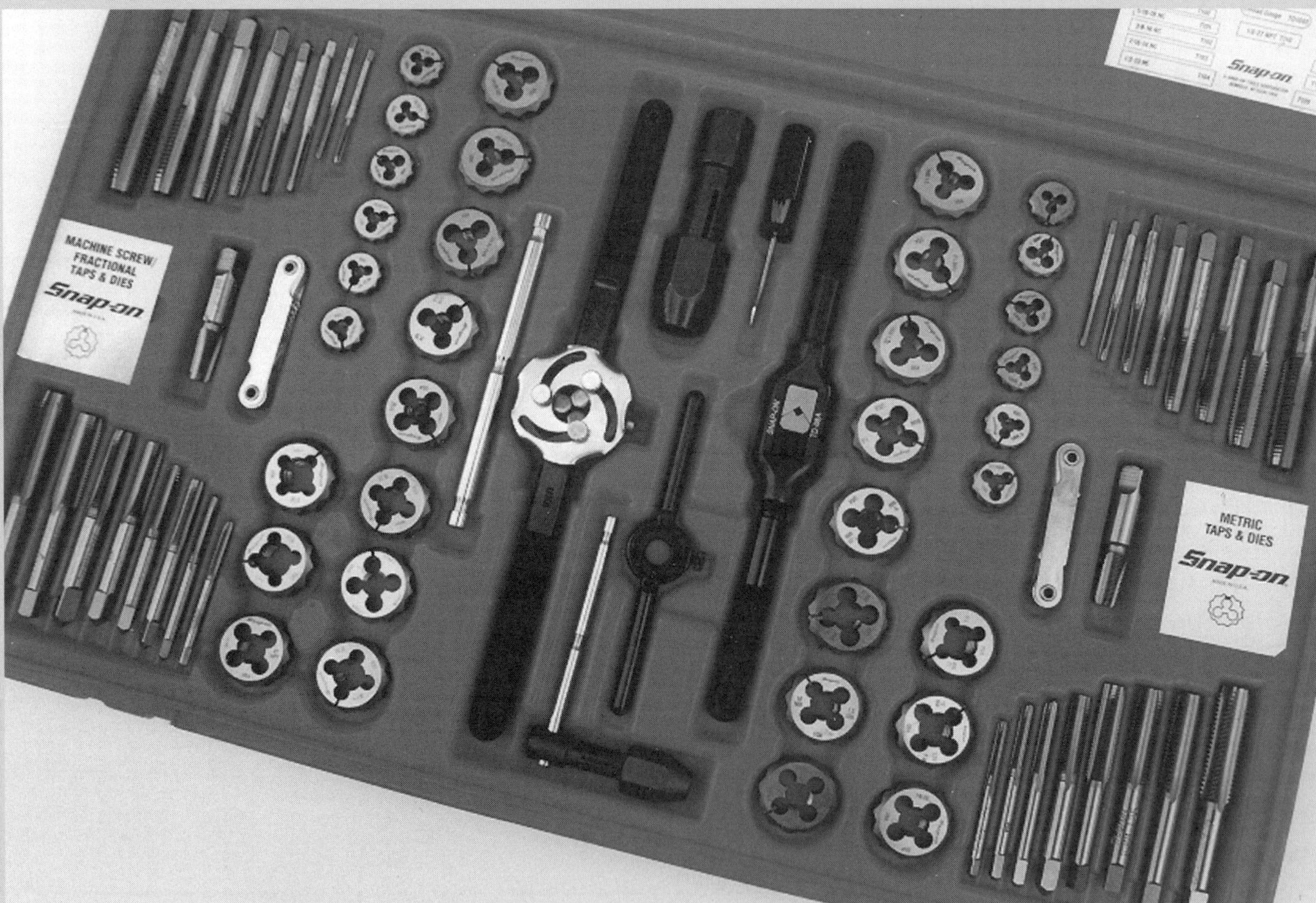

Every good tool box should include a set of taps and dies, for cleaning threads on critical bolts and tapping that occasional hole in a non-critical application.

Taps and Dies

A good tap and die set will include a thread gauge, a handy tool to have and a good way to identify a particular bolt.

Like taps, the dies are tapered and must be started from one end - and will be used more for cleaning than for cutting threads.

mix of American and metric bolts. In fact, the taps themselves are often useful in this same capacity.

There may even be times when fabrication of a small part requires tapping the female threads. Anyone who has tapped a hole knows that it's not nearly as easy as it seems on paper.

Do it Right

Correctly tapping a hole requires some common sense. To paraphrase a line from an old Jimmy Stewart movie, "The worst thing about common sense is the fact that it's not very common at all." So in case you're like the rest of us, short on common sense, here are the guidelines for tapping a decent hole.

Use the right size drill for the initial hole, most tap and die sets include a chart of tap and clearance drill sizes. This way you start out with a hole of the correct dimension. Don't cheat and make the hole a little smaller in an effort to create deeper and stronger threads. A hole too small is sure to result in a tap that's broken off in the hole.

Drill the hole straight. This means using a drill press or lathe to drill the hole, not that wobbly old 3/8 inch hand drill.

Taps and Dies

Understand that the taps that came with your small hand set are probably taper taps, which makes them easy to start. This will result in a tapped hole with no threads in the bottom. If the application requires threads all the way to the bottom of the hole, you will need to find a bottom tap, created for just that task. Or you can grind the taper off a tap to make your own bottom tap.

Use lubricant when cutting the threads. WD-40, though better than nothing, isn't a particularly good lubricant for the tap. Instead of the aerosol can sitting on the bench, find some genuine tapping lubricant available from many good hardware stores and industrial supply houses. Note that aluminum requires a different lubricant for the tap than steel or cast iron.

The drill press you used to drill the hole can also be used to start the tap in the hole straight, the hardest part of the hole process. At least use a good T handle on the tap and be sure the tap is positioned straight up and down as you apply modest pressure and begin turning the handle. Bench mounted tap stands can be used to securely hold the part and ensure that the tap, turned with the handle that is part of the fixture, is kept perpendicular to the work. Similar, though smaller, hand tapping fixtures are also available for this task.

If you take a minute to read the instructions

Tap Size	Drill Size	Probable % Thread
0-80	3/64	71-81
M1.6 x .35	1.25 mm	69-77
1-64	53	59-67
M2 x .4	1/16	72-79
1-72	53	67-75
2-56	50	62-69
2-64	50	70-79
M2.5 x .45	2.05 mm	69-77
3-48	5/64	70-77
3-56	46	69-78
4-40	43	65-71
4-48	42	61-68
M3 x .5	40	70-79
5-40	38	65-72
5-44	37	63-71
M3.5 x .6	33	72-81
6-32	36	71-78
6-40	33	69-77
M4 x .7	3.25 mm	74-82
8-32	29	62-69
8-36	29	70-78
10-24	25	69-75

Tap Size	Drill Size	Probable % Thread
10-32	21	68-76
M5 x .8	4.2 mm	69-77
12-24	16	66-72
12-28	15	70-78
M6 x 1	10	76-84
1/4-20	7	70-75
1/4-28	3	72-80
5/16-18	F	72-77
5/16-24	I	67-75
M8 x 1.25	6.7 mm	74-80
3/8-16	5/16	72-77
3/8-24	Q	71-79
M10 x 1.5	8.4 mm	76-82
7/16-14	U	70-75
7/16-20	25/64	65-72
M12 x 1.75	10.2mm	69-74
1/2-13	27/64	73-78
1/2-20	29/64	65-72
M14 x 2	15/32	76-81
9/16-12	31/64	68-72
9/16-18	33/64	58/65
5/8-11	17/32	75-79

Tap Size	Drill Size	Probable % Thread
5/8-18	37/64	58-65
M16 x 2	35/64	76-81
3/4-10	21/32	68-72
3/4-16	11/16	71-77
M20 x 2.5	11/16	74-78
7/8-9	49/64	72-76
7/8-14	13/16	62-67
M24 x 3	53/64	72-76
1-8	7/8	73-77
1-12	59/64	67-72
1-14	15/16	61-67
1-1/8—7	63/64	72-76
1-1/8—12	1-3/64	66-72
M30 x 3.5	1-3/64*	75
1-1/4—7	1-7/64*	76
1-1/4—12	1-11/64*	72
1-3/8—6	1-7/32*	72
1-3/8—12	1-19/64*	72
M36 x 4	1-1/4*	82
1-1/2—6	1-11/32*	72
1-1/2—12	1-27/64*	72

***Reaming Recommended**

Most tap and die sets will include a chart like this one indicating the right size drill to use before you begin tapping.

Taps and Dies

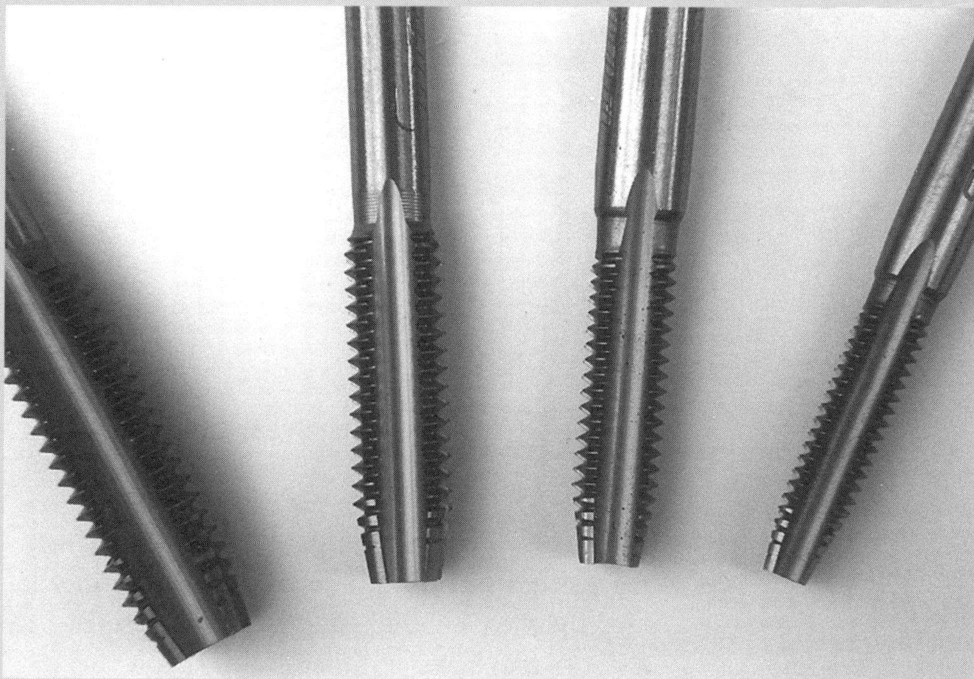

Most tap and die sets provide taper taps for easy starting. These do not cut good threads to the bottom of a blind hole. For that you need a bottom or plug tap.

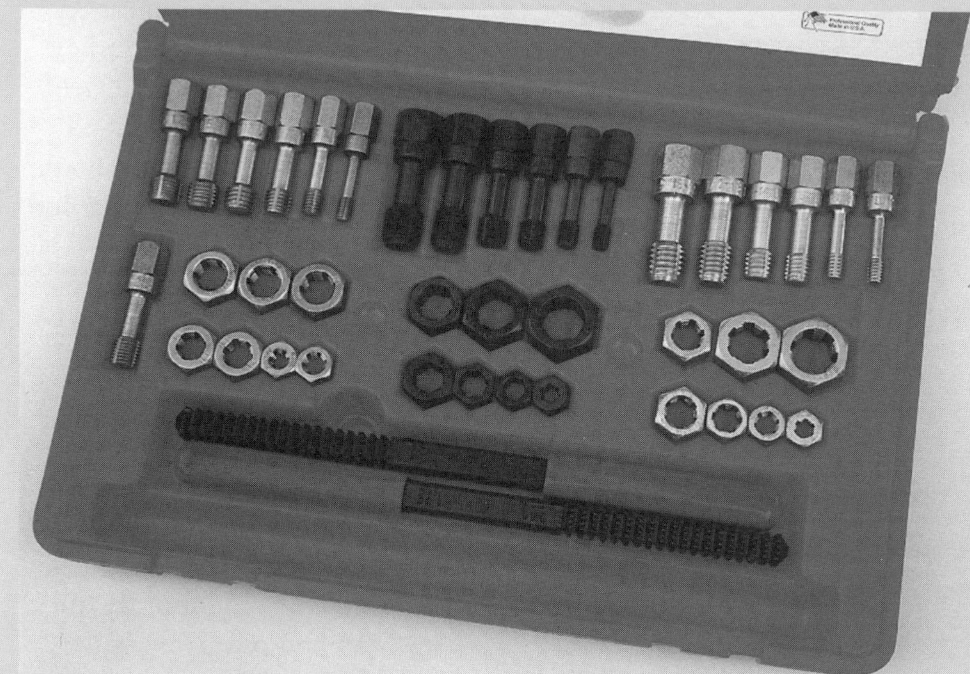

What looks like a tap and die set from Snap-on is actually a thread-repair kit designed to re-shape the damaged threads without cutting them.

that came with that Acme tap set, you will find that they recommend turning the tap a maximum of one-half turn before reversing the direction. When you turn it back the other way you will feel a light "snap." That snap is the tap breaking off the little curlicues of metal that were raised in the preceding half turn. When the bottom of the hole fills with filings you will have to unscrew the tap and blow the chips out the hole.

Anytime you feel binding in the tap, stop and slowly work the tap out of the hole by turning it first one way, then the other. Failure to follow this cautionary step can result in a tap that breaks off in the hole.

Compared to threads cut at a factory these homemade threads aren't very good. So make the hole and the threads a little longer if possible as a means to increase the total amount of contact between the male and female threads. Finally, unless you're a machinist don't try to cut threads in structural parts, they just aren't good enough.

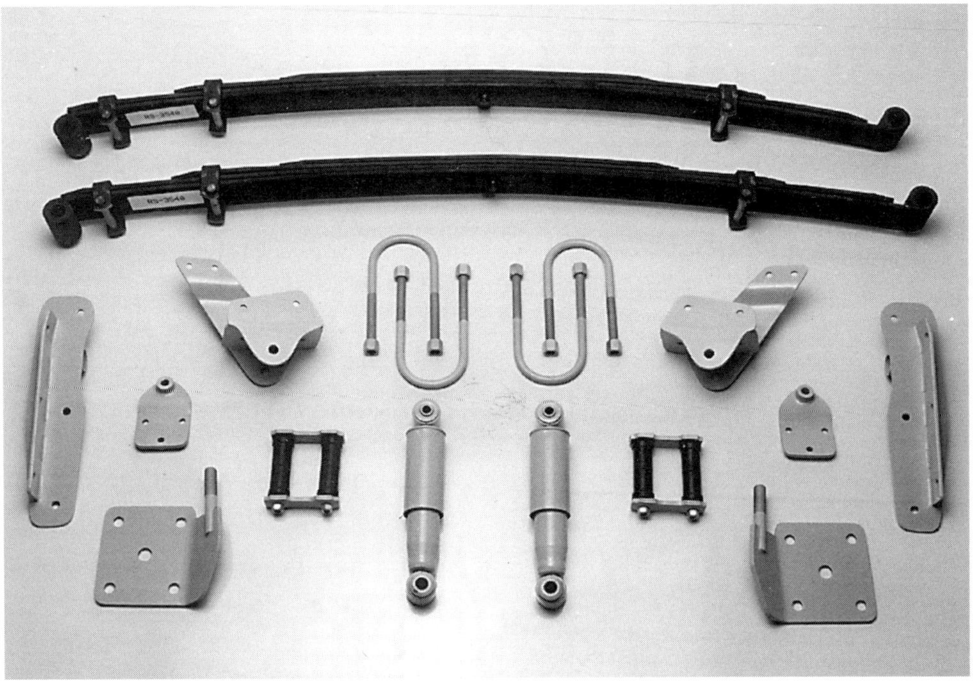

Specialized bolts, like the U-bolts seen here, should come with the kit you buy from the aftermarket. That way you know the fasteners are the right size and strength. Chassis Eng.

ing load is exactly the same on both sides of the connecting rods.

Seventy-five percent of yield is the safest for the bolt, and the builder knows that he has that by using a stretch gauge. And he can log the original length of each fastener before it's tightened. Then when he goes back at the end of the season he can check to be sure the bolts have all returned to their original length. Now he knows they haven't exceeded yield. When you're racing you might miss a shift and exceed the inertial load for the cap of one connecting rod, so the fastener may have exceeded yield. If you check the no-load length of those bolts when the engine is disassembled there is no chance of using a defective fastener. If one of the fasteners is longer than it was, indicating it's gone past the yield point, the builder should replace the bolt and should check the sizing of that rod as well.

Think about the load on the calipers, and the caliper mounting bolts, when you hit the brakes hard at 80 mph. Now be sure to use the bolts that came with the caliper kits. ECI

How do you set the torque or stretch specifications for a given bolt?

We just did some Duesenberg rod bolts. You start by taking the weight of the con rod, less the cap, and half the bearing shell. Add the weight of the piston and pin. Now figure the stroke and the max RPM to determine the inertial load on the cap. Let's say that the inertial

A Guide to Common Coatings

Atlantic Fasteners

Coating or Finish	For Use On	Degree of Corrosion Resistance	Characteristics
Anodizing	Aluminum	Excellent	Acid electrolytic treatment for aluminum, frosty-etched appearance. Hard oxide surface gives excellent protection.
Black chromate	Zinc-plated or cadmium plated steel	Added corrosion protection on cadmium and zinc-plated surfaces.	Black, semilustrous. Chemical dip. Used for decorative outdoor purposes. Can be lacquered.
Brass plate, lacquered	Steel, usually	Fair	Brass electroplated finish which is then lacquered. Recommended only for indoor decorative use.
Bronze plate, lacquered	Steel, usually	Fair	Has color similar to 80% copper, 20% zinc alloy. Electroplated, lacquered finish. Only recommended for indoor decorative use.
Cadmium plate	Most metals	Excellent	Bright silver-gray, dull gray, or black electroplated finish. For decoration and corrosion protection (especially marine applications).
Clear chromate finish	Cadmium and zinc-plated parts	Very good to excellent	Clear bright or iridescent chemical conversion coating applied to zinc or cadmium-plated surfaces for added corrosion protection, coloring, and paint bonding. The colored coatings usually have greater corrosion resistance than the clear.
Dichromate	Cadmium and zinc-plated parts	Very good to excellent	Yellow, brown, green, or iridescent colored coating same as clear chromate.
Olive drab, gold or bronze chromate	Cadmium and zinc-plated parts	Very good to excellent	Green, gold, or bronze tones same as clear chromate.
Chromium plate	Most metals	Good (improves with increased copper and nickel undercoats)	Bright blue-white, lustrous electroplated finish. Has relatively hard surface. Used for decorative purposes.
Copper plate	Most metals	Fair	Electroplated finish. Used for nickel and chromium-plate undercoat. Can be blackened and relieved to obtain Antique, Statuary, and Venetian finishes.
Copper, brass, bronze, misc. finishes	Most metals	Indoor, very good	Decorative finishes. Applied to copper, brass, bronze-plated parts to match colors. Color and tones vary from black to almost the original color. Finish names are: Antique, Black Oxide, Statuary, Old English, Venetian, Copper Oxidized.
Lacquering, clear or color-matched	All metals	Improves corrosion resistance. Some types designed for humid or other severe applications.	Used for decorative finishes. Clear or colored to match mating color or luster.
Lead-tin	Steel, usually	Fair to good	Silver-gray, dull coating. Gives good lubrication to tapping screws. Applied by hot-dip method.
Bright nickel	Most metals	Indoor excellent. Outdoor good if thickness is at least 0.0005 in.	Electroplated silver finish. Used for appliances, hardware, etc.
Dull nickel	Most metals	Same as bright nickel	Whitish cast. Can be obtained by mechanical surface finishing or using a special plating bath.
Passivating	Stainless steel	Excellent	Chemical treatment. Removes iron particles and produces a passive surface.
Zinc or Manganese Phosphate	Steel	Very good	Antichafing properties used on sliding or bearing surfaces. Black manganese-iron phosphate coating with nondrying petroleum oils containing corrosion inhibitors.
Colored phosphate coatings	Steel	Superior to regular phosphated and oiled surfaces.	Chemically produced color coating will increase corrosion resistance. Available in green, red, purple, blue, black, etc.
Rust preventatives	All metals	Varies with function of oil	Vary in color, and film thickness. Usually applied to phosphate and black oxide finishes. Used to protect parts in transit or prolonged storage.
Silver plate	All metals	Excellent	Decorative, expensive. Excellent electrical conductor.
Electroplated tin	All metals	Excellent	Silver-gray color. Excellent corrosion protection for parts in contact with food.
Hot-dip tin	All metals	Excellent	Silver-gray color. Same as electroplated, but thickness is harder to control, especially on fine-thread parts.
Electroplated zinc	All metals	Very good	Bright—blue-white gray coating. For corrosion protection of steel parts.
Electrogalvanized zinc	All metals	Very good	Use where bright appearance is not wanted. Dull grayish color.
Hot-dip zinc	All metals	Very good	For maximum corrosion protection. Dull grayish color. Use where coating thickness is not important. Corrosion resistance is directly proportional to the coating thickness.
Hot-dip aluminum	Steel	Very good	For maximum corrosion protection. Dull grayish color. Use where coating thickness is not important. Corrosion resistance is directly proportional to coating thickness.

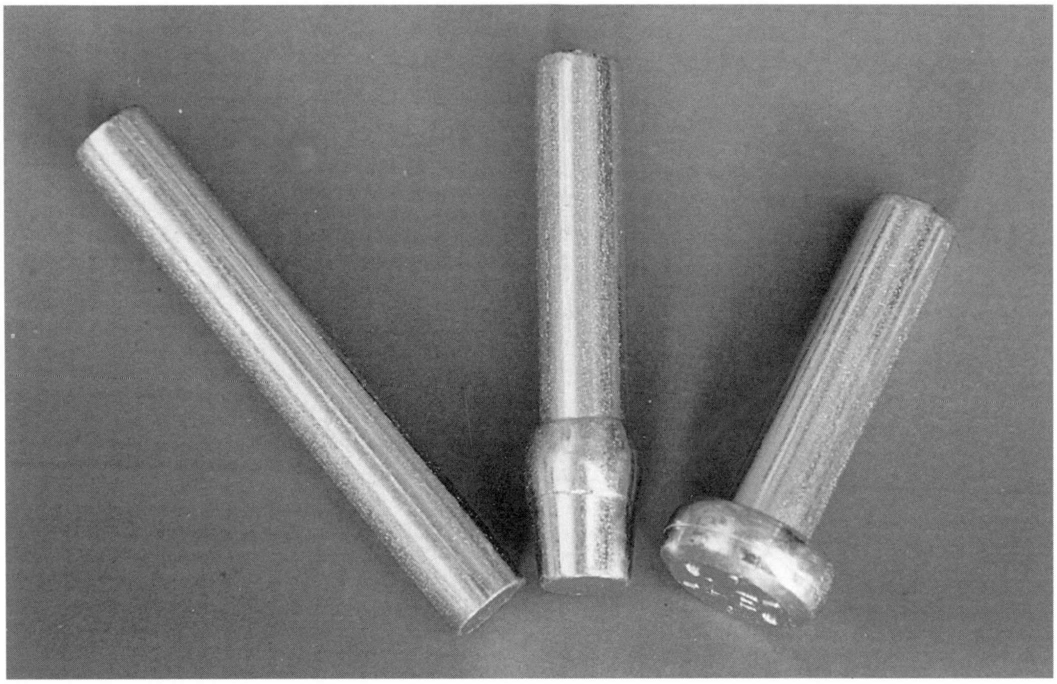

A photo series showing the steps involved in the manufacture of a quality bolt. Left to right: first the wire is cut to length. Then the cold-heading starts, accomplished in a number of separate steps.

load is 10,000 pounds. We try to design a bolt that will have 10,000 lbs. per fastener for a total of 20,000, so it's twice as strong as it needs to be.

Now you take that load and determine how strong that bolt should be, then determine the material it should be made from. Then we make a bolt or take one from stock. We tensile it, it gives us a yield strength and peak, Let's just say it's a 7/16 inch fastener and it yields at 20,000 lbs. We want 75% of that for pre load. Now, 15,000 is 75% of the yield. How much torque does it take to achieve that, we do that in a load cell.

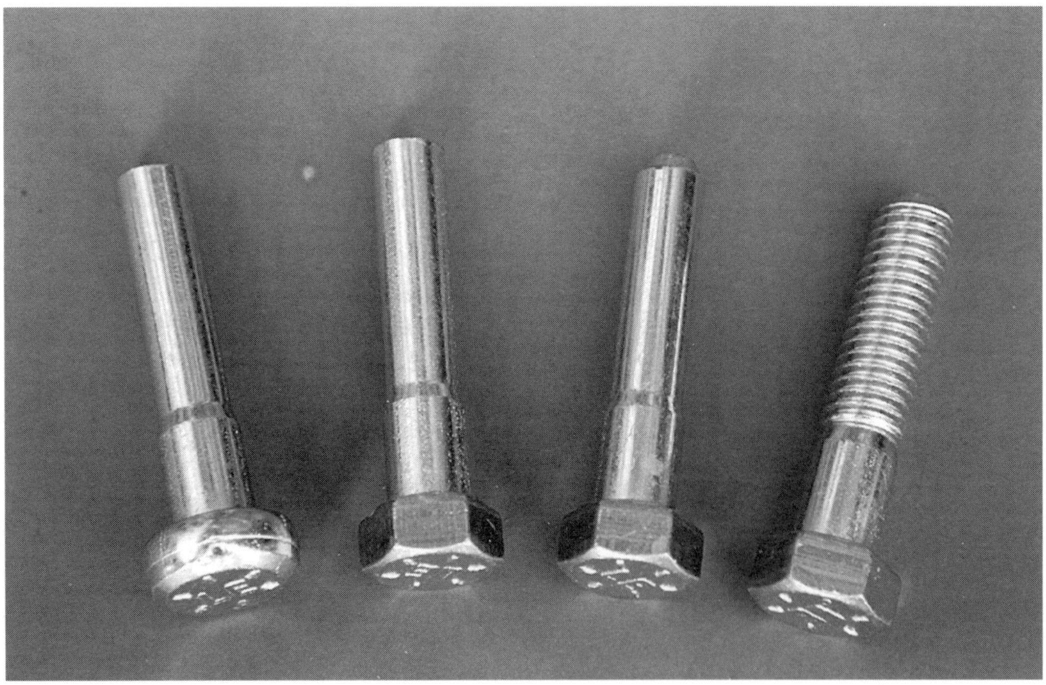

The final steps in the manufacture of a bolt: necking down the shank, cutting a taper on the end and then rolling the threads.

Now that it's pre-loaded, how much stretch does it have. If, for example, the stretch was .0075 inches at the correct pre-load, we can stretch it to .095inch and then loosen it and there should be no change in length, no evidence that we exceeded yield. Then to be absolutely sure, we can put it back in and stretch it to .0105 inch and then take it out and it should show evidence of yield, it should be slightly longer than it was originally.

We figure that with a connecting rod bolt, we can't be too careful, If you loose the con rod bolt everything goes. We go that extra mile, to aerospace standards or better. We do it all in-house, right down to the black oxide or polished finish.

What about the idea that a bolt that's under-torqued won't last as long, in terms of fatigue life, as one that is tightened to 75% of yield?

If the clamping load is more than the load the bolt will be subjected to, the bolt will never feel any additional tension. If, however, it's under clamped it will feel more of the load

And there are harmonics to worry about. With insufficient pre-load the bolt will want to back out, to come loose. As it gets loose it feels more and more fatigue. If for some reason one connecting rod bolt isn't tightened, it will unscrew itself and drop into the pan, then pretty soon the other one will break. When they pull the engine apart, they find one broken bolt and one complete one, lying in the pan. People always assume that one broke first and the other backed out, but it's the other way around.

We like to see people use a stretch gauge because it 's so much more accurate. A stretch gauge is real cheap insurance, they're only about 100 dollars. Most of the aftermarket bolts now have a little dimple so you can accurately use a stretch gauge.

Is your heat treating always done before thread rolling?

Yes, we do our heat treat before extruding the threads. That way you get a nice thread shape. Heat treating is a personal thing, each company does it a little differently, We heat the bolts to 2000 degrees and then cool them to 300 degrees very, very fast. That makes them very strong but also very brittle, you've lost the ductility. To get the ductility back we put them into a draw furnace and draw them down to an acceptable range.

There's more to making a good fastener than just handing a print and a set of specifications to a job shop. We've got the testing equipment and experience to make bolts that only a very few companies do.

Long-time employee Tom Smith has been with ARP long enough to know what goes into making a quality fastener - and why each step is so important. ARP

Chapter Four

Nuts and Washers

Split-ring and Self-locking

We've said it before, the best bolt in the world isn't worth a damn without matching female threads. Those threads commonly take the form of a nut, or threads tapped into a casting. In some cases an insert is installed into a part or a casting and takes the part of the tapped threads.

In the case of a capscrew and nut, the strongest union is provided if the male and female components have fine threads (all other factors being equal), because this way you get a

Seems the focus is always on the bolts, studs and capscrews. Yet, none of them are any good without a matching set of female threads. Like capscrews, nuts come in a bewildering array of styles and strengths. ARP

larger root diameter and there is more physical contact between the threads.

The threads cut into a casting are often coarse. As explained earlier, the coarse threads are better suited to those "coarse" materials and help to compensate for the difference in strength between the material the bolt is manufactured from and the material the casting is made from.

Nuts

Nuts break down into those that are self-locking and those considered free-running. True experts in the field tend to give little consideration to free-running nuts for a couple or reasons. First, many of the bolt and nut combinations are used in shear or double-shear. In which case the nut bears little load and is primarily responsible for holding the bolt in place. These situations beg for some kind of self-locking nut. Second, even when the bolt and nut combination is used in compression rather than shear, there generally isn't a good reason not to use a good self-locking nut. These self-locking nuts are especially helpful when screwing together semi-fragile parts, like fiberglass panels, where you don't want the bolts terribly tight for fear of cracking the fiberglass.

Free-running nuts

Some of what are technically free-running nuts are manufactured specifically for a particular task. Connecting rod nuts and the nuts that cap cylinder head studs come to mind. These nuts either "came with the car" or are purchased specifically for a particular application.

When it comes to a quality bolt or capscrew, most of us have access to Grade 8 bolts from an industrial supply house or a hot rod or motorcycle shop (tractor and implement shops are sources as well). So you've got a high quality capscrew and you want a matching, high quality nut. Well, you can't buy a Grade 8 nut.

What you can buy are L-9 nuts from Sharp Enterprises, with a UTS of 180,000 psi. ARP makes a variety of high-quality nuts as well. Available in most common American sizes are hex nuts rated at 180,000 psi, and another set of twelve-point nuts with the same ratings available

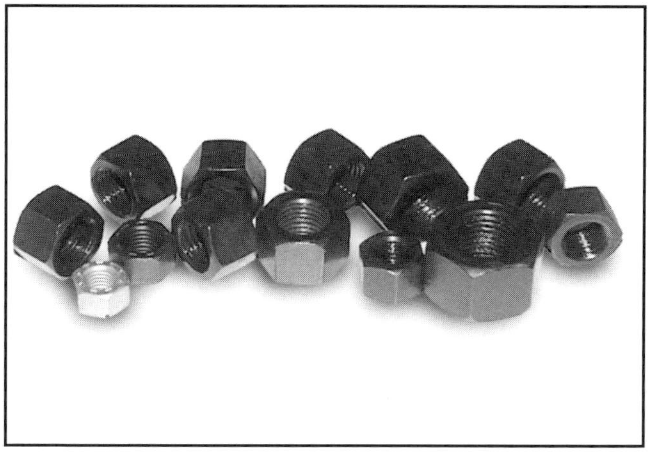

These high-test nuts are black-oxide coated and rated at 180,00 psi (better than Grade 8). ARP

Lock-nuts with a Nylon collar are one of the most popular and durable types of lock nut. This style is available in chrome plate as well as in stainless.

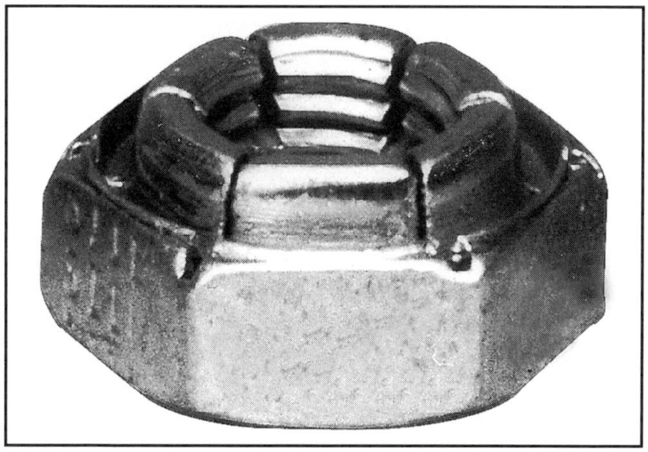

All-metal lock nuts like this feature a "crimped" collar that must be distorted and pushed apart by the threads on the bolt. Lock-nuts of this type are very useful in high-heat applications.

Hex Nuts and Hex Jam Nuts

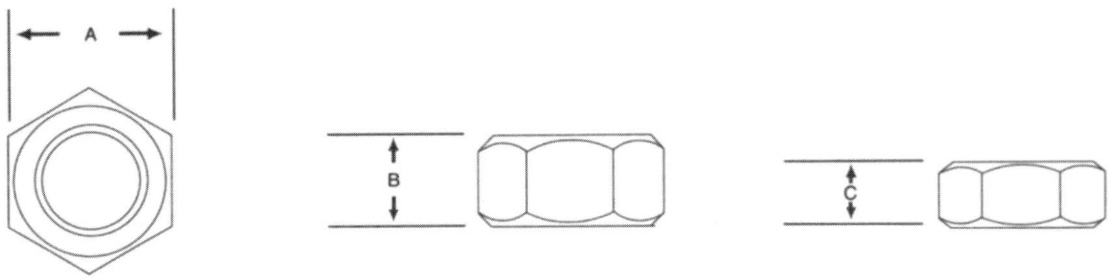

Basic Major Diameter of Thread	Width Across Flats (A)			Thickness Hex Nuts (B)			Thickness Hex Jam Nuts (C)		
	Basic	Max.	Min.	Basic	Max.	Min.	Basic	Max.	Min.
1/4	7/16	.438	.428	7/32	.226	.212	5/32	.164	.150
5/16	1/2	.500	.489	17/64	.273	.258	3/16	.195	.180
3/8	9/16	.562	.551	21/64	.337	.320	7/32	.227	.210
7/16	11/16	.688	.675	3/8	.385	.365	1/4	.260	.240
1/2	3/4	.750	.736	7/16	.448	.427	5/16	.323	.302
9/16	7/8	.875	.861	31/64	.496	.473	5/16	.324	.301
5/8	15/16	.938	.922	35/64	.559	.535	3/8	.387	.363
3/4	1-1/8	1.125	1.088	41/64	.665	.617	27/64	.446	.398
7/8	1-5/16	1.312	1.269	3/4	.776	.724	31/64	.510	.458
1	1-1/2	1.500	1.450	55/64	.887	.831	35/64	.575	.519
1-1/8	1-11/16	1.688	1.631	31/32	.999	.939	39/64	.639	.579
1-1/4	1-7/8	1.875	1.812	1-1/16	1.094	1.030	23/32	.751	.687
1-3/8	2-1/16	2.062	1.994	1-11/64	1.206	1.138	25/32	.815	.747
1-1/2	2-1/4	2.250	2.175	1-9/32	1.317	1.245	27/32	.880	.808

in both American and metric sizes.

One good way to lock a nut in place is with a second nut. Specific "jam" nuts, thinner than a standard nut, are provided for this purpose by many hardware manufacturers. The smaller size helps to reduce their bulk and weight, important for competition situations.

Self-locking nuts

More commonly used than a jam nut to ensure the nut and bolt don't come "undone," self-locking nuts are available in a variety of styles. One of the most common is the Nylock-type of lock nut that combines a six-point nut with a nylon collar. Nylock is a trade name, so maybe it's better to term these nylon-collar nuts. In any case, the nylon collar has no threads, so as the nut is screwed onto the bolt the bolt threads must force (but not cut) their way through the collar, which is sized to have an I.D. slightly smaller than the outer diameter of the bolt. As the bolt threads its way through the nylon, friction is created between the metal male and female threads. Added to this is the friction between the nylon collar and the bolt threads. The combination works well and resists vibration as well as anything else.

Nylon-collar nuts are available in standard steel as well as chrome and stainless. Experts often suggest that

Available in sizes from 1/4 inch to 1/2 inch, these general purpose washers are good for medium duty work, like attaching accessories to the engine. Can be purchased in stainless or steel with black oxide coating. ARP

The better washers are hardened and ground, or Grade 8. The Grade 8 are generally better as they're made from a better alloy in addition to being a little heavier.

some kind of lube be used so the friction and resulting heat of assembly doesn't melt or deform the nylon collar. Anyone who has used stainless or chrome fasteners on a regular basis knows the importance of using anti-seize on the threads so the stainless doesn't gall and the chrome is less likely to flake off and jam the nut on the bolt.

What these lock nuts aren't good at is enduring high heat situations. For securing things like headers and exhaust manifolds, turbo housings and the like, a better choice is an all-metal lock nut.

Like the nylon-collar lock nuts, the all-metal variety are really two nuts in one. The bottom, or larger part, of the nut is your typical free-running metal nut. The upper section of the nut is distorted in one of two ways to create friction on the threads of the bolt. Some of these nuts feature an upper section with radial lines cut down part way into the nut. [See Illustration] The upper part of the nut is then "crushed" at the factory so the resulting area has a smaller I.D. than the rest of the nut. The variation on this theme uses an upper nut section that is intentionally deformed into an elliptical pattern. In either case, the bolt must force its way up through this upper section of the nut, creating friction both between the lower nut threads and the bolt, and between the mis-shaped threads and the male threads.

In most cases these all-metal nuts can be reused many times. The only caveat is to be sure the nuts and bolts are well matched. If, for example, the bolt is of much higher quality and strength than the nut, it could essentially cut threads in the upper part of the nut instead of forcing the metal to conform to the shape of the bolt.

There are also a group of self-locking nuts with a built in "plug" or pellet of nylon. These work much like the nylon-collar nuts though the amount of contact between the nylon and the threads is reduced as compared to a nylon-collar design. Generally considered to be less effective as a self-locking nut than other designs already mentioned, these pellet nuts are better suited to industrial situations than the assembly of a prized automobile.

Flanged nuts help to spread the load and eliminate the need for a washer. They can also be welded to a frame rail where a body-mounting bolt comes through, for example, so you can screw the bolt in without the need to hold the nut at the same time. Note the shape, the two nuts on the right are self-locking.

Castellated nuts

Nuts that look like a castle, and other slotted female fasteners, aren't really locking nuts in the true sense of the word. These nuts are meant to be used with a male partner ventilated with a hole. A cotter pin inserted into the hole passes through the "turret" of the nut. What actually keeps these nuts in place is the friction between the male and female threads. The cotter key is just a means of keeping the nut on the ball joint or tie-rod end if the whole thing becomes loose. To ensure these nuts never come loose you can either use a special slotted and self-locking nut, or put some Loctite on the threads.

Inserts

(Sec the side-bar in Chapter Two for more on HeliCoils).

One of the most common inserts is the HeliCoil, a very nifty wire-type insert made from stainless wire, wound to make threads. Once again, HeliCoil is a trade name, and these wire-type inserts are available from a number of companies.

To me a HeliCoil is a good way to repair damaged threads, though there are situations where an insert is used with a new assembly. This occurs most frequently when the base metal doesn't lend itself to threads good enough to be used again and again. An assembly made from aluminum, for example, that will be disassembled on a regular basis, might have wire-type inserts instead of female holes tapped directly into the aluminum. Inserts are used here because the stainless steel wire will stand up to frequent threading and unthreading of the male fastener better than will the aluminum.

Inserts also come in a "tube" type. Think of a thin to medium sized metal tube, with 3/8 inch threads on the outside and 1/4 inch threads on the inside. The person wishing to repair the threads in a casting, or provide for stronger threads than the aluminum will tolerate, could drill and tap a hole for the 3/8 threads, screw in the insert (often with a special tool) then lock it in place with small pins. When finished they have a nice 1/4 inch steel or stainless steel female thread in the aluminum casting.

These inserts come in thin and thick walled versions. The thick walled tube-type inserts have a size difference of two while the thin-walled inserts have a size difference of only one thread size, i.e. the insert might be 5/16 on the outside and 1/4 inch on the inside.

The key to satisfactory insert use is much like the guidelines for tapping holes. You have to start with a hole that's drilled strait, one of the correct

Much like washers, lock-washers come in standard, heavy duty and Grade 8. Though lock washers are extremely common, most experts feel a good lock-nut does a better job.

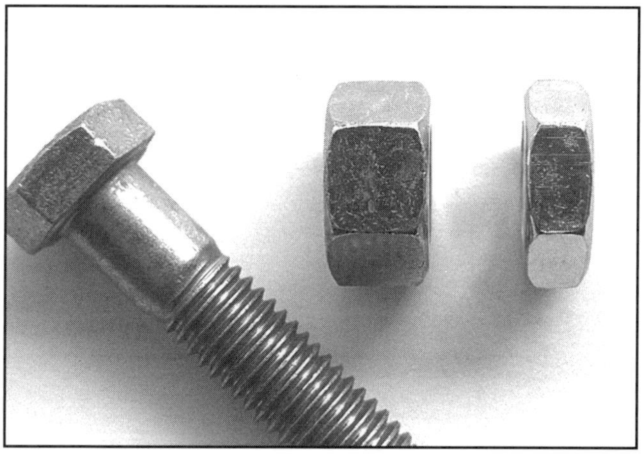

Free-running nuts come in standard sizes as well as the thinner variety seen here, used as jam nuts.

Inserts come an a variety of styles and sizes. On the left a Timesert (or tube-type insert) with a HeliCoil (wire-type) on the right. Both styles of insert are manufactured by numerous companies under their own trade names.

Type B Plain Washers

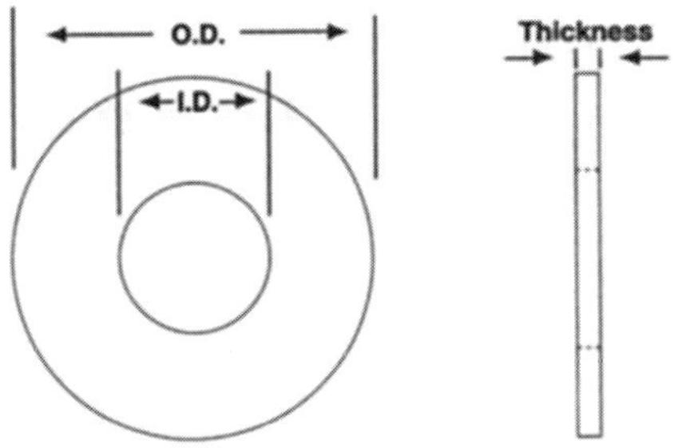

Atlantic Fasteners

Size of Bolt (inches)	Series	I.D. (inches)			O.D. (inches)			Thickness		
1/4	Narrow	.281	+.015	−.005	.500	+.015	−.005	.063	+.071	−.056
	Regular	.281	+.015	−.005	.734	+.015	−.007	.063	+.071	−.056
	Wide	.281	+.015	−.005	1.000	+.015	−.007	.063	+.071	−.056
5/16	Narrow	.344	+.015	−.005	.625	+.015	−.005	.063	+.071	−.056
	Regular	.344	+.015	−.005	.875	+.015	−.007	.063	+.071	−.056
	Wide	.344	+.015	−.005	1.125	+.015	−.007	.063	+.071	−.056
3/8	Narrow	.406	+.015	−.005	.734	+.015	−.007	.063	+.071	−.056
	Regular	.406	+.015	−.005	1.000	+.015	−.007	.063	+.071	−.056
	Wide	.406	+.015	−.005	1.250	+.030	−.007	.100	+.112	−.090
7/16	Narrow	.469	+.015	−.005	.875	+.015	−.007	.063	+.071	−.056
	Regular	.469	+.015	−.005	1.125	+.015	−.007	.063	+.071	−.056
	Wide	.469	+.015	−.005	1.469	+.030	−.007	.100	+.112	−.090
1/2	Narrow	.531	+.015	−.005	1.000	+.015	−.007	.063	+.071	−.056
	Regular	.531	+.015	−.005	1.250	+.030	−.007	.100	+.112	−.090
	Wide	.531	+.015	−.005	1.750	+.030	−.007	.100	+.112	−.090
9/16	Narrow	.594	+.015	−.005	1.125	+.015	−.007	.063	+.071	−.056
	Regular	.594	+.015	−.005	1.469	+.030	−.007	.100	+.112	−.090
	Wide	.594	+.015	−.005	2.000	+.030	−.007	.100	+.112	−.090
5/8	Narrow	.656	+.030	−.007	1.250	+.030	−.007	.100	+.112	−.090
	Regular	.656	+.030	−.007	1.750	+.030	−.007	.100	+.112	−.090
	Wide	.656	+.030	−.007	2.250	+.030	−.007	.160	+.174	−.146
3/4	Narrow	.812	+.030	−.007	1.375	+.030	−.007	.100	+.112	−.090
	Regular	.812	+.030	−.007	2.000	+.030	−.007	.100	+.112	−.090
	Wide	.812	+.030	−.007	2.500	+.030	−.007	.160	+.174	−.146

Grade 8
Extra Thick Washers

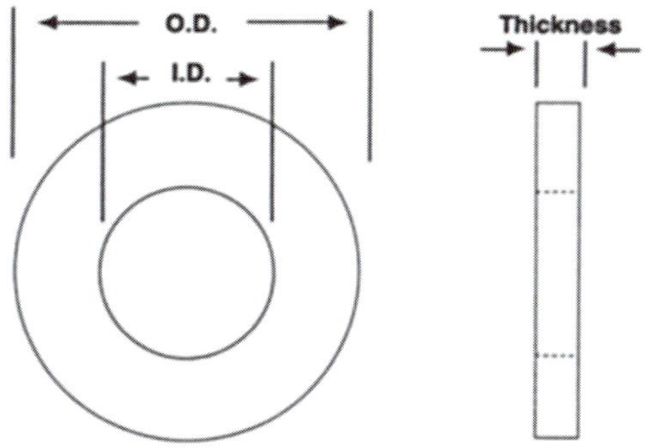

Atlantic Fasteners

Size of Bolt (inches)	I.D. (inches)	O.D. (inches)	Thickness Gauge
1/4	.281 ± .003	.625 ± .005	.086 ± .007
5/16	.344 ± .003	.688 ± .005	.086 ± .007
3/8	.406 ± .003	.813 ± .005	.108 ± .008
7/16	.469 ± .003	.922 ± .005	.108 + .008 − .007
1/2	.531 ± .005	1.063 ± .015	.199 ± .009
9/16	.594 ± .005	1.188 ± .015	.199 ± .009
5/8	.688 ± .005	1.313 ± .015	.250 + .014 − .010
3/4	.813 ± .005	1.469 ± .015	.250 + .014 − .010
7/8	.938 ± .005	1.750 ± .015	.250 + .014 − .010
1	1.125 ± .005	2.000 ± .015	.250 + .014 − .010

diameter for the intended insert. The tap used to cut the threads needs to be sharp, and should be "cleared" often to get all the chips off the threads and the flutes between the cutting areas As with any tapping operation, lubrication of the tap is a good idea.

Washers & Lock-washers

They might seem too simple to discuss, yet there are enough different types of washers that this book needs to consider at least a cursory discussion of the various types and their uses.

Flat washers are not all created equal. The ones from the hardware store are stamped out of flat, mild steel with I.D. and O.D. diameters that might best be called "generous." The plating is cheap zinc or cadmium that resists corrosion for the full period of time that the washers sit in the hardware store bin. If you use a cheap hardware-store washer under the head of a high-strength bolt, the washer may deform under the head of the bolt, resulting in a loss of clamping pressure and torque.

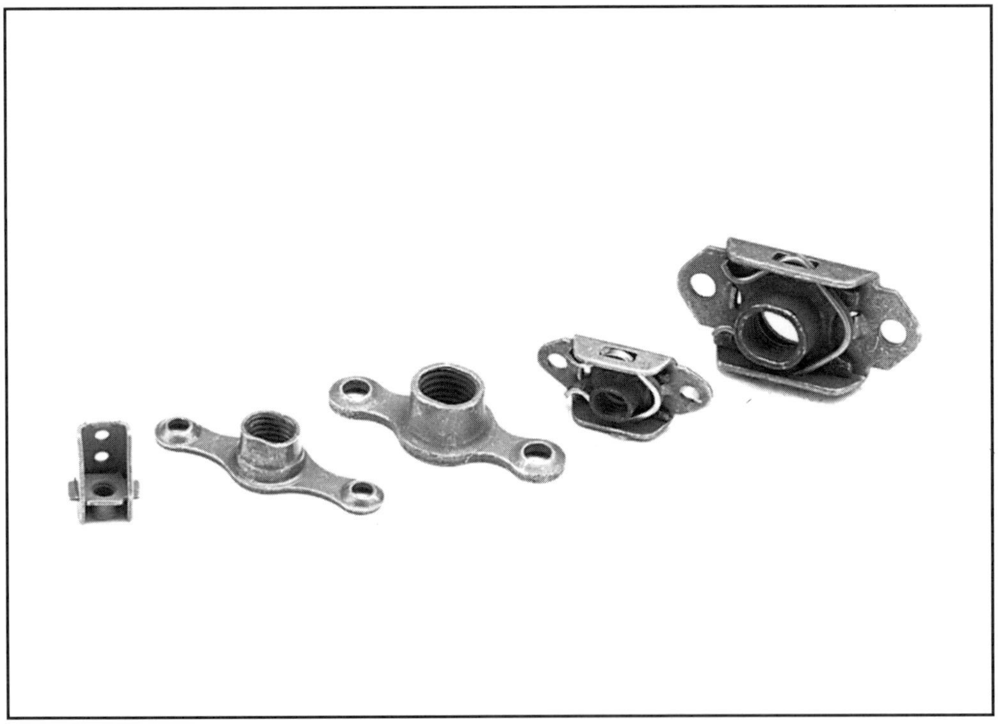

Plate nuts like these can be welded or screwed in place to eliminate the need for a conventional nut. Made from alloy steel with cadmium plating. ARP

Better, more precise washers are available from a variety of sources. Chrome plated and stainless washers can be found for sale at the local hot rod or motorcycle shop where you bought much of the dress-up hardware for your project. The chrome washers are generally much thicker than the cheap ones described above and probably started out as a ground washer before the plating was applied.

If you're doing serious clamping, especially with small headed bolts like a SHCS, it's essential to use a high quality washer. Though both "hardened and ground," and Grade 8 washers are much better than the hardware store variety, the Grade 8 have an edge in strength. This is because, as one of the engineers at Atlantic Fasteners reports, "Grade 8 washers are made from alloy steel and are harder than a hardened and ground washer, which is made from 1010 carbon steel. Grade 8 washers have the same hardness as a SHCS."

Sharp Enterprises offers standard, hardened and "L-9" washers in a variety of sizes. ARP can provide what they call their "special purpose" washers, in sizes from 3/8 to 9/16 inch I.D. including many metric sizes. These are available in different thickness, with or without a chamfer on the I.D. to clear the radius under the bolt head.

Most of the above also offer fender washers, those oversize washers with the large O.D. relative to their I.D. dimension.

Lock washers

Builders of competition cars and also aircraft seldom use lock washers. Yet, they are as common as billet wheels on hot rods. The washers themselves break down into a number of styles from serrated to the common split-ring lock washer.

A properly torqued bolt or capscrew is in tension when correctly installed. This tension keeps friction between the thrust flanks of the male and female threads. A good locking device does its job primarily by maintaining this friction between male and female threads.

Not everyone feels that the tried and true split-ring lock washer actually does a good job of maintaining the tension in a bolt or capscrew. For those who can't break an old habit, higher quality Grade 8 split ring lock washers are available from a variety of sources, including Sharp Enterprises. Remember to use a flat washer between the lock washer and the work surface.

"Star" type lock washers are available as well. These seem to work on the theory that if you can really lock the head or the nut in place against the "load" that you can prevent that head or that nut from turning and thus loosening. These seem to be especially common in light load situations, when the bolt or bolt and nut are holding panels in place for example, or when the bolt is screwed into a fairly soft material. Another good use of a star washer is under the head of a bolt when that bolt needs to make a good electrical connection. Think about the battery ground cable that's attached to the engine block. Or a light housing with a separate ground wire that is run to the body.

Of course what makes a star washer a good choice under a wire terminal – the fact that it bites into the metal on either side – means that it will bite into and through the paint on that freshly painted fender.

In the end we need to remember that not all washers, or self-locking nuts, are created equal. When it comes to locking a nut in place a lock washer is better than nothing, and a lock nut is generally better than that.

A twelve point nut provides twelve places where the wrench or socket gets a grip, which makes it easy to tighten the nut. There's also an aesthetic consideration. The nuts shown are rated to 180,000 psi. ARP

Special purpose washers are available from ARP in a variety of sizes and thickness, with or without I.D. chamfer to allow clearance for the radius under the bolt head.

Chapter Five

Torque Talk

How Tight is Tight

Torque seems at first a simple enough concept. And the idea of tightening the cylinder head bolts to a certain value makes all the intuitive sense in the world. How else are we to get the bolts tight enough? More important, how else do we make sure the bolts are all tightened to the same value, to the same degree of tightness? So we've all been taught to use the torque specifications found in most service manuals and a good torque wrench on all critical nuts and

A torque wrench is the most common way of measuring the tightness of a fastener. What we're really after, however, is a particular clamping load. ARP

bolts. Some technical manuals even include a chart that gives recommended torques for nearly any bolt, based on the size.

The torque specification is really just a means of achieving a certain clamping pressure. The problem with torquing a bolt – and achieving the correct clamping pressure - comes with what might be called the "variables." As Frank Akstens from the Industrial Fastener Institute explained, "The Air Force did a study on torquing some years back. They looked at the things that affect the actual clamping pressure. The Air Force found a couple of hundred variables. Of course the basic chemistry of the metal is a major factor. Stainless, for example, wants to gall when it's screwed into stainless. Heat is produced and the nut can become welded to the bolt, you think it's tight because it feels tight, but it's not."

The two most common ways to ensure the bolt doesn't back out of the hole is with a split-ring lock washer or a "Nylock" type of self-locking nut.

"The other major factor is the coating and plating on the bolt.

There are torque tables with a suggested value for a given bolt. Let's say it's a 1/4 – 20, the torque recommended in the table might work. But maybe the bolt was zinc coated and the zinc was put on with electrolysis, so it went on a little thick. Now the bolt screws into the hole

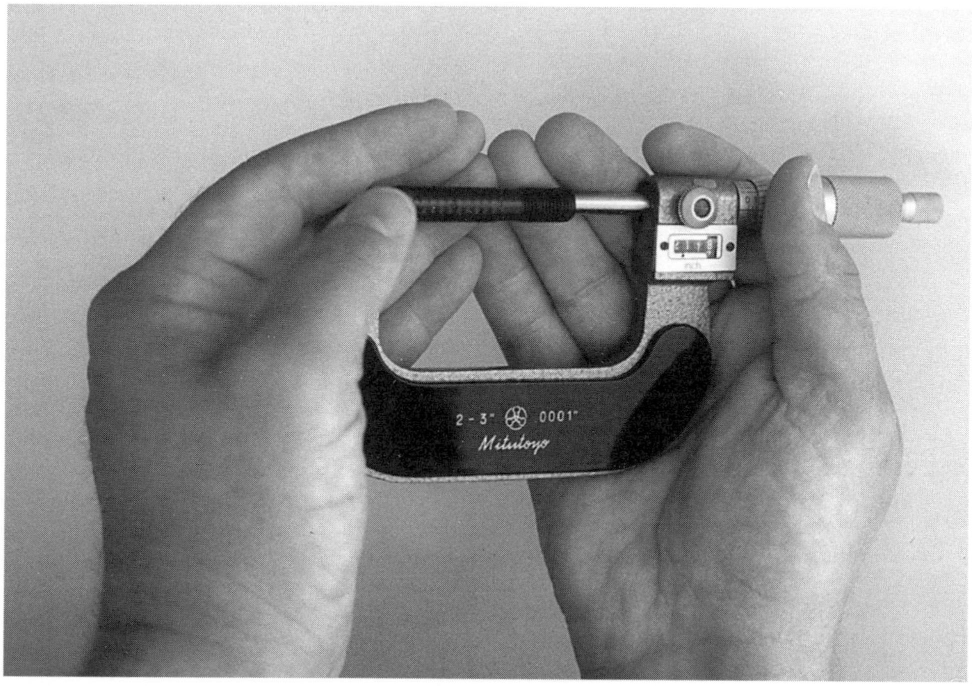

Engine builders often measure the length of critical bolts, like connecting rod bolts, before assembly. Then carefully measure them again when the engine is pulled apart for repair or rebuilding. If the length has changed the bolts have exceeded their yield point and should be replaced. ARP

We always think of the bolts that hold our cars together as being loaded in tension. Yet, a closer examination reveals a relatively large number that are loaded in single and double shear.

extra tight. What you think is torque is actually friction so the clamping load is much less that you thought. Maybe you can't even get the bolt tight enough to get the correct clamping load."

Frank brings up the major points affecting what might be called the net torque, or clamping pressure, created by a given reading on the torque wrench.

Understand first that we are dealing with tension bolts here. In most of these cases we are tightening the bolts in order to create a certain clamping force. One of the biggest problems Frank identifies is friction.

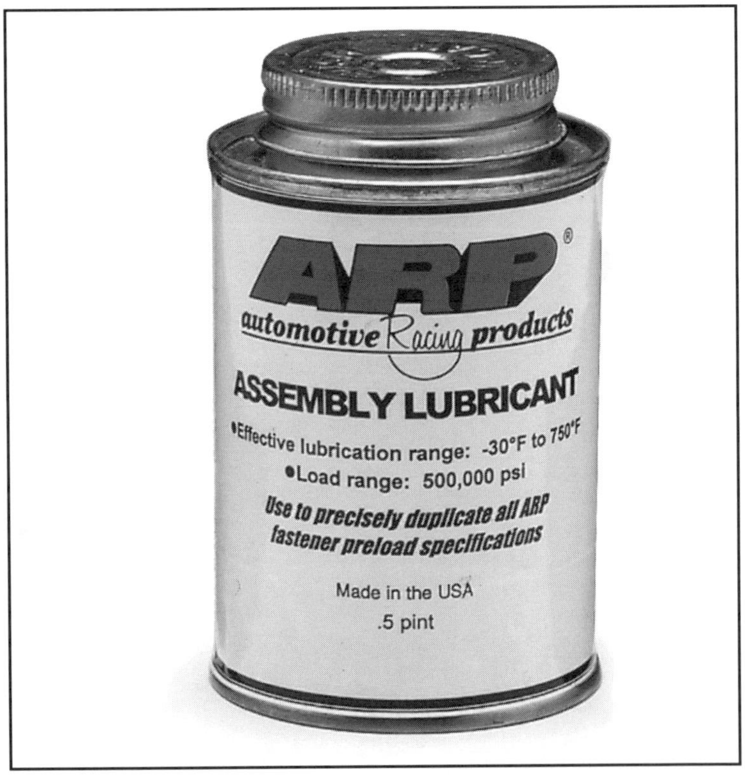

The use of lube or anti-seize on the threads will reduce friction between the threads. This means the clamping load achieved at a given torque setting can increase dramatically. For critical applications ARP recommends using their lube and their torque specifications. ARP

When you tighten a bolt there are two forces set up inside that bolt, One is tension (assuming a tension joint application) which is trying to make the bolt longer. The other is the "torsional" load created by the twisting motion of the wrench (technically there is no such thing as a torsional load, it's actually a combination of compressive and tensile loads)

The tension within the bolt, properly called the stress as discussed in Chapter One, is a desirable thing. After you've removed the wrench from the tightened bolt, there should be remaining stress within the bolt. This stress is what keeps the head clamped against the engine block and the fender in place against the frame. The "torsional" stress will disappear after the wrench is removed from the head of the bolt.

The trouble here is the fact that as you tighten the bolt to say, 80 foot pounds, you don't know how much of that turning force is being used to overcome friction between the threads and how much of it is actually clamping the parts together.

A booklet on torque from Atlantic Fasteners contains a good example. At the back is a recommended torque chart of the type that Frank describes (reproduced here with permission). For a 5/16 – 18 bolt the chart specifies a torque of 17 ft. lbs. for a plain bolt and 13 ft. lbs for a plated bolt. In other words, the plated bolt will achieve the same clamp load as the unplated bolt at only 13 ft. lbs. Instead of 17 ft. lbs. And the reason is simple. Because there is less friction more of the turning energy is actually converted into clamping the parts together rather than overcoming friction between the threads.

For situations where you can get at both ends of a bolt, a stretch gauge is a more accurate way of measuring the tension on a bolt. This way you bypass inaccuracies that result from dirty threads or the wrong thread lube. ARP

The formula for tightening in foot pounds is pretty simple: Torque = D x P x K/12, where D is the diameter of the bolt, P is the clamp load objective established by the engineer and K is the coefficient of friction. The K value can vary widely depending on the bolt finish and the lubricant. An uncoated but lightly oiled bolt, for example, has a K of .20 while a Zinc plated bolt has a K of .15 and a bolt with

Friction between the threads can eat up more than half the indicated torque, meaning the bolt is only half as tight as you thought it was. Make sure the threads on critical bolts are clean and free of nicks. ARP

nickel-base anti-seize has a K of roughly .05 (all figures from Atlantic Fasteners).

What this means is that for a 1/2 inch bolt and a desired clamp load of 10000 pounds, using an oiled bolt, the torque is 83.3 ft. lbs. The same scenario, with the same desired clamp load, using a bolt with nickel-base anti-seize, requires only 20.8 ft. lbs.

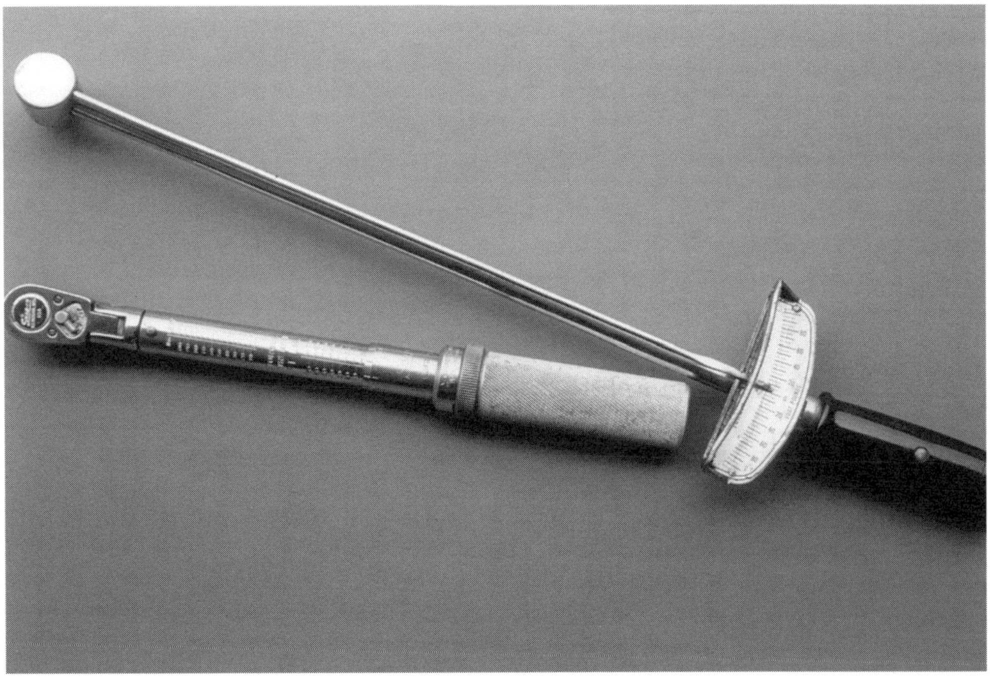

A variety of means can be used to determine the tightness of a particular bolt. Most common is the common torque wrench - available in a number of styles.

How Tight

If you ask a fastener engineer about how tight a particular bolt should be, they describe the tightness as a percentage of the yield (check out Tom Smith's comments on torque in Chapter Two). In other words, they want the bolt to be left with strain, not so much that it fails because the bolt is at the yield point, but approximately seventy or seventy five percent of the yield point.

Though a torque specification might be an imperfect guide, it's all the guide we get in most situations. The key is to keep the threads clean, use the recommended lube (if one is called for) and an accurate torque wrench.

Nylon-collar lock-nuts come in various configurations, including chrome-plated, polished stainless and extra thin for shear applications

What Keeps It Tight

You might think that the lock washer is what keeps the nut on the bolt, or the bolt in the hole. In reality, what keeps the bolt from unscrewing itself is

Torque Approximations for Non-Critical Applications Only

Atlantic Fasteners

SAE GRADE 5

Coarse Thread

SIZE	CLAMP LOAD	PLAIN	PLATED
1/4 - 20 (.250)	2,025	8 ft. lbs.	76 in. lbs.
5/16 - 18 (.3125)	3,338	17 ft. lbs.	13 ft. lbs.
3/8 - 16 (.375)	4,950	31 ft. lbs.	23 ft. lbs.
7/16 - 14 (.4375)	6,788	50 ft. lbs.	37 ft. lbs.
1/2 - 13 (.500)	9,075	76 ft. lbs.	57 ft. lbs.
9/16 - 12 (.5625)	11,625	109 ft. lbs.	82 ft. lbs.
5/8 - 11 (.625)	14,400	150 ft. lbs.	112 ft. lbs.
3/4 - 10 (.750)	21,300	266 ft. lbs.	200 ft. lbs.
7/8 - 9 (.875)	29,475	430 ft. lbs.	322 ft. lbs.
1 - 8 (1.000)	38,625	644 ft. lbs.	483 ft. lbs.
1-1/8 - 7 (1.125)	42,375	794 ft. lbs.	596 ft. lbs.
1-1/4 - 7 (1.250)	53,775	1120 ft. lbs.	840 ft. lbs.
1-3/8 - 6 (1.375)	64,125	1470 ft. lbs.	1102 ft. lbs.
1-1/2 - 6 (1.500)	78,000	1950 ft. lbs.	1462 ft. lbs.

SAE GRADE 5

Fine Thread

SIZE	CLAMP LOAD	PLAIN	PLATED
1/4 - 28 (.250)	2,325	10 ft. lbs.	87 in. lbs.
5/16 - 24 (.3125)	3,675	19 ft. lbs.	14 ft. lbs.
3/8 - 24 (.375)	5,588	35 ft. lbs.	26 ft. lbs.
7/16 - 20 (.4375)	7,575	55 ft. lbs.	41 ft. lbs.
1/2 - 20 (.500)	10,200	85 ft. lbs.	64 ft. lbs.
9/16 - 18 (.5625)	12,975	122 ft. lbs.	91 ft. lbs.
5/8 - 18 (.625)	16,350	170 ft. lbs.	128 ft. lbs.
3/4 - 16 (.750)	23,775	297 ft. lbs.	223 ft. lbs.
7/8 - 14 (.875)	32,475	474 ft. lbs.	355 ft. lbs.
1 - 12 (1.000)	42,300	705 ft. lbs.	529 ft. lbs.
1-14 (1.000)	32,275	721 ft. lbs.	541 ft. lbs.
1-1/8-12 (1.125)	47,475	890 ft. lbs.	668 ft. lbs.
1-1/4-12 (1.250)	59,550	1241 ft. lbs.	930 ft. lbs.
1-3/8-12 (1.375)	72,975	1672 ft. lbs.	1254 ft. lbs.
1-1/2-12 (1.500)	87,750	2194 ft. lbs.	1645 ft. lbs.

SAE GRADE 8

Coarse Thread

SIZE	CLAMP LOAD	PLAIN	PLATED
1/4 - 20 (.250)	2,850	12 ft. lbs.	9 ft. lbs.
5/16 - 18 (.3125)	4,725	25 ft. lbs.	18 ft. lbs.
3/8 - 16 (.375)	6,975	44 ft. lbs.	33 ft. lbs.
7/16 - 14 (.4375)	9,600	70 ft. lbs.	52 ft. lbs.
1/2 - 13 (.500)	12,750	106 ft. lbs.	80 ft. lbs.
9/16 - 12 (.5625)	16,350	153 ft. lbs.	115 ft. lbs.
5/8 - 11 (.625)	20,325	212 ft. lbs.	159 ft. lbs.
3/4 - 10 (.750)	30,075	376 ft. lbs.	282 ft. lbs.
7/8 - 9 (.875)	41,550	606 ft. lbs.	454 ft. lbs.
1 - 8 (1.000)	54,525	909 ft. lbs.	682 ft. lbs.
1-1/8 - 7 (1.125)	68,700	1288 ft. lbs.	966 ft. lbs.
1-1/4 - 7 (1.250)	87,225	1817 ft. lbs.	1363 ft. lbs.
1-3/8 - 6 (1.375)	103,950	2382 ft. lbs.	1787 ft. lbs.
1-1/2 - 6 (1.500)	126,450	3161 ft. lbs.	2371 ft. lbs.

SAE GRADE 8

Fine Thread

SIZE	CLAMP LOAD	PLAIN	PLATED
1/4 - 28 (.250)	3,263	14 ft. lbs.	10 ft. lbs.
5/16 - 24 (.3125)	5,113	27 ft. lbs.	20 ft. lbs.
3/8 - 24 (.375)	7,875	49 ft. lbs.	37 ft. lbs.
7/16 - 20 (.4375)	10,650	78 ft. lbs.	58 ft. lbs.
1/2 - 20 (.500)	14,400	120 ft. lbs.	90 ft. lbs.
9/16 - 18 (.5625)	18,300	172 ft. lbs.	129 ft. lbs.
5/8 - 18 (.625)	23,025	240 ft. lbs.	180 ft. lbs.
3/4 - 16 (.750)	33,600	420 ft. lbs.	315 ft. lbs.
7/8 - 14 (.875)	45,825	668 ft. lbs.	501 ft. lbs.
1 - 12 (1.000)	59,700	995 ft. lbs.	746 ft. lbs.
1-14 (1.000)	61,125	1019 ft. lbs.	764 ft. lbs.
1-1/8-12 (1.125)	77,025	1444 ft. lbs.	1083 ft. lbs.
1-1/4-12 (1.250)	96,600	2012 ft. lbs.	1509 ft. lbs.
1-3/8-12 (1.375)	118,350	2712 ft. lbs.	2034 ft. lbs.
1-1/2-12 (1.500)	142,275	3557 ft. lbs.	2668 ft. lbs.

Based on IFI 5th Edition Technical Data N-12/N-16, using Equation (1) and a torque coefficient, K= 0.20 for nonplated steel fasteners and K = 0.15 for plated fasteners.

These figures represent an estimate of torque (torque being the measurement of friction, not tension) required to induce a given preload (clampload) in a bolt for non-critical applications only. For critical or special applications where greater control is desired this should be experimentally determined. This applies to washer faced or double chamfered hex nuts (or bolts, if bolt is torqued) having a width across flats of approximately 1.5 times the nominal diameter and having threads free of interference.

Because of the many interrelated variables that directly or indirectly affect friction, such as surface texture, type of coating or finish, lubrication, speed of tightening, human error, etc., it is possible to experience as much as ± 25% deviation in preload (clampload) with the use of a torque wrench.

When it comes to either a good nylon-collar lock-nut, or a split-ring lock washer, most experts prefer the lock-nut.

friction between the male and female threads. By tightening the bolt to a point approaching yield, we have in effect stretched the bolt. This stretch, technically called strain, keeps tension on the bolt and the friction intact between the male and female threads. Most locking washers and nuts work not so much by "locking" the nut in position as by working to maintaining this tension between the threads.

Because stronger bolts have a higher yield point, we can tighten the grade 8 bolt *tighter* than the Grade 5 bolt (assuming the female half of this relationship is up to the task) and create more friction and more tension in the bolt.

It takes only a few degrees of rotation to eliminate the stress within a tightened bolt. What this means is that the cotter key that "keeps" the nut on the ball joint, or the safely wire used in competition, is meant primarily to keep the bolt and nut from falling off altogether once they become loose. The cotter key won't keep the bolt tight.

What will help to keep the bolt tight is a ny-

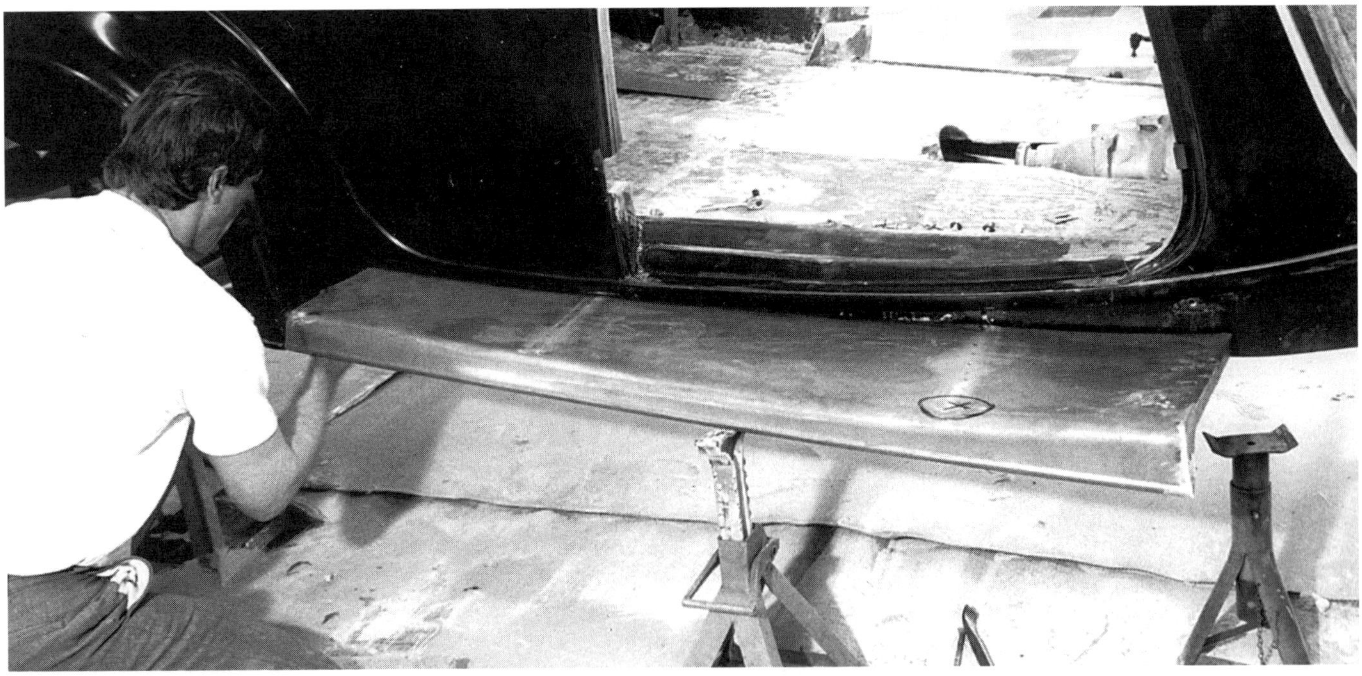

Some jobs, like assembly of fiberglass bodies, require a locking method that doesn't require great tension on the bolt. This is an ideal application for a nylon-collar locknut.

lock type lock nut, an all-metal lock nut, a good split ring lock washer, one nut "jammed" up against the other or a drop of Loctite properly applied. Loctite comes in an a confusing array of grades, some meant for light duty work while others are meant for parts that will never be unscrewed again.

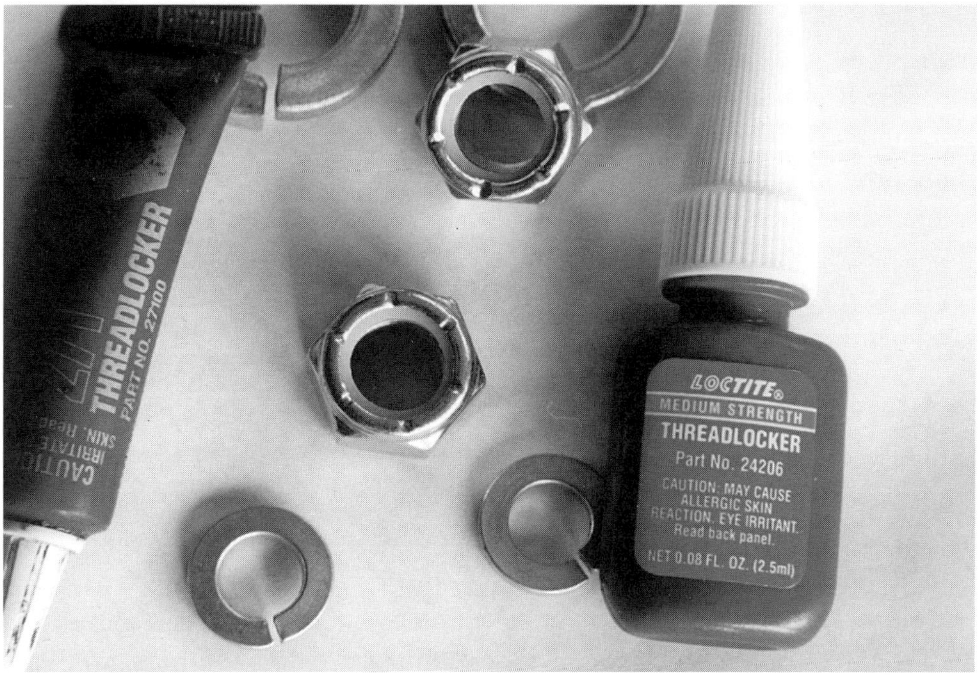

Loctite comes in a wide range of strengths. Most common in automotive shops are the "blue" Loctites (242 and 243) and the red numer 271.

LOCTITE: RED OR BLUE?

Loctite makes a variety of products often used to prevent the loosening of nearly any nut or bolt. Many of us grew up in a two-Loctite world. There was blue and red (never mind the numbers or labels on the little bottles). Blue was used for most of the common situations encountered in an automotive shop, red was the stuff you used to absolutely guarantee that nothing was going to shake apart the bolt.

It turns out there are at least seven different threadlockers from Loctite. What we call blue Loctite is technically a number 242 or 243. Either one is considered by the company to be, "a medium strength threadlocker for fasteners up to 3/4 inch." Number 243 has a slight advantage in that it's slightly stronger than 242, is quicker to set and is more tolerant of a little oil on the threads. Both products protect against rust and corrosion

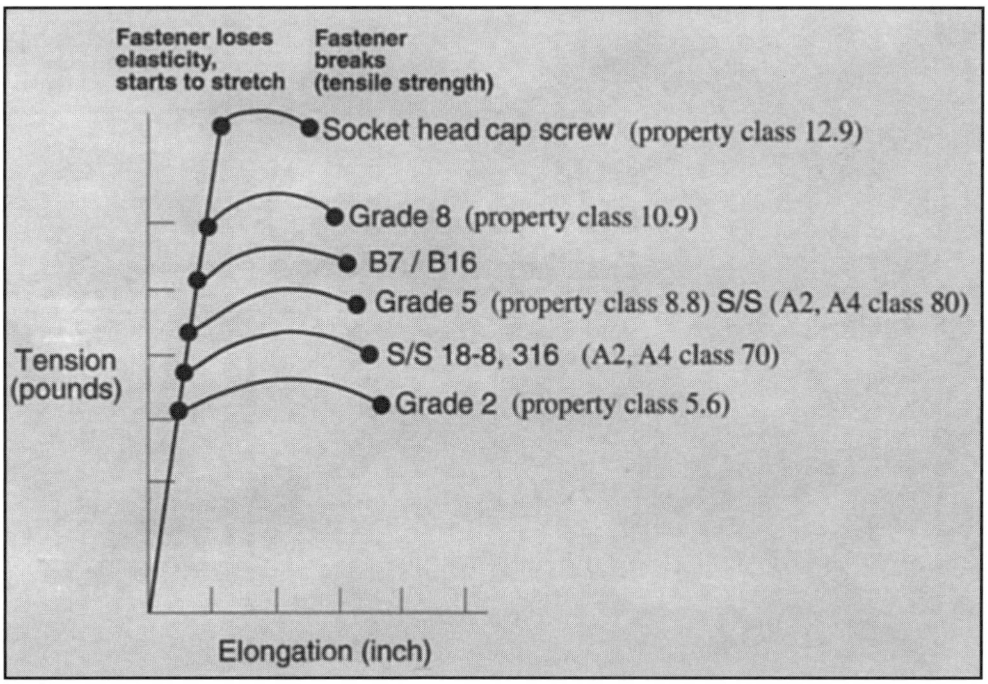

This strength-stretch chart illustrates the fact that weaker bolts also stretch farther before breaking. A Grade 2 bolt hits yield early but then stretches a great deal before rupture. A Grade 8 on the other hand is much "stronger" but won't stretch much after hitting the yield point. Atlantic Fastener

and both allow removal of the bolt or nut with hand tools and no heat.

The Red Loctites include numbers 262, 271, 272 and 277. These are indeed stronger than the blue products, but before reaching for the red material consider that some of these are meant for parts that will not be disassembled (number 270) while the rest of the red-tites "require heat and hand tools for disassembly."

In order to work properly and form a good bond, Loctite requires an oxygen-free atmosphere and active metal ions. In assembling hot rods we often encounter chrome-plated and stainless bolts, which offer the Loctite no free-metal ions to aid the locking process. Which means that when using plated bolts or when screwing a bolt into aluminum it should first be treated with Loctite primer, either the T (which makes for a stronger bond) or the N (which can be used in colder weather).

And despite the fact that the 243 will tolerate oily threads better than some other products, it's always a good idea to clean any dirty threads with Loctite's own Klean-n-Prime, or a product like Brake-Klean, something that leaves no residue behind, before applying the Loctite.

Why Keep It Tight

Tests have shown that bolts tightened to 75% of their yield strength will have a much, much longer fatigue life than the same bolt tightened to 50% or less of the yield strength. While it makes intuitive sense to make sure the bolts are "good and tight" when assembling a car or component, most of us fail to consider the affect this tightness has on the fatigue life of the bolt(s).

When a bolt is properly tightened, it stretches just a bit. And the assembly it's clamping together is compressed very slightly. Without getting in any heavy physics, consider that as the assembly rotates or moves, loading and unloading the joint, the stress on the bolt goes up and down. If the bolt is loose, the bolt will feel the full affect of these cyclic changes. If the bolt is tight however, part of the energy of the rotating assembly will be taken up "uncompressing" the joint rather than adding to the stress in the bolt.

Which means there are at least two good reasons to ensure that we use the right bolts and tighten them to the correct torque (or stretch) value. First, a tight bolt is more likely to stay tight, because the stretch will maintain the friction between the male and female threads. Second, a bolt or capscrew that's correctly tightened will resist fatigue far better than one that's either too tight or too loose.

Ball joints and tie-rod ends often use a cotter key to "lock" the nut in place. Tension between the male and female threads is what actually locks the nut in place, the cotter key just keeps the nut from falling off once it's loose.

Torque Wrenches

We've all seen and most of us own one or more torque wrenches. For the reasons described earlier, a torque wrench is at best a rough indicator of the actual clamping load.

There are three common ways to determine the tightness of a particular bolt. Most of us use a torque wrench to determine the tightness, but stretch gauges are making their way into more and more tool boxes. The other commonly used method might be called the degree, or turn-of-bolt, method. Often used with head bolts, this method specifies that the bolt be tightened first to some nominal torque, like 20 ft. lbs., then turned "one additional turn," or some other specified amount.

When it comes to torque wrenches, mechanics, both amateur and professional, generally encounter four types of torque wrench.

Least expensive of the various torque wrench designs is the deflecting beam. Looking like a breaker bar with a pointer and gauge attached, this tried and true design is simple, effective and inexpensive. Just put the socket on the end and put a nice steady pull on thc handle until the needle lines up with the desired reading on the foot-pound scale. The trouble with this very basic torque wrench is the relatively large size and lack of any pivoting head, meaning it can be hard to get into tight spots. Due to the pointer and graph arrangement you must also be able to see the foot pound scale while putting torque on the nut or bolt.

A more high-tech solution to the problem of precisely tightening those ten capscrews holding the timing cover in place is provided by the "clicker" type of torque wrench. Like a cricket, these wrenches click, but only when you've hit the desired torque. A micrometer style handle allows you to set the torque, typically in one-pound increments.

Clicker-style torque wrenches are very popular and for good reason. First, they include a ratchet head, so in essence the torque wrench becomes a big ratchet. Second, most have a flex-head, meaning it's easier to get them into tight spots. Third, they do not require that you be able to see the scale while turning the bolt. Additionally, they are generally smaller than a deflecting-beam style of torque wrench.

The "cost" of a clicker includes the higher cost than an ultra-simple deflector-beam style, and the fact that the handle must be set back to zero after

Once of the most accurate types of torque wrench are those with a dial that shows the torque being applied to a particular nut or bolt.

each use. These wrenches are also said to lose their calibration fairly easily and can be hard to correctly re-calibrate.

What might be called the dial-style torque wrench rounds out our selection. These are similar to a deflector-beam but instead of a pointer and scale, the wrench has a round dial that indicates the torque. The more expensive models have a light and tone that indicates you've hit the torque setting so you don't have to look right at the dial as you turn the torque wrench.

Though quite accurate these torque wrenches suffer from many of the same ills that trouble the deflector-beam designs. Namely, they are physically big and have no ratchet head, making them hard to use especially in confined spaces.

We live in the computer age and it was only a matter of time before someone would replace the round indicator dial with a digital read out connected to a computer or chip inside the wrench. In industrial situations these can be connected to a printer used to document the torque settings. Advantages include the ease with which the wrench can be converted from inch to foot pounds, or even Newton meters and the fact that common torque settings can be "saved" inside the magic box.

Achieving the Right Torque

It might seem too simple to discuss, but there is a right and a wrong way to use that torque wrench. You've gone to the trouble of buying the torque wrench and looking up the recommended torque, you might as well ensure you're using the tool correctly.

First, it takes more force to start the bolt moving than to keep it moving, so take the final reading while moving the wrench smoothly through an arc. This is especially important for bolts that are tightened in two or three steps. Tightening the bolt in two or three steps makes a lot of sense. The assembly is clamped evenly and gradually. Each time you tighten one bolt part way and then move to the next bolt, the one you just tightened has a chance to relax just a little, to "settle." The shear forces disappear and tension forces remain.

When you tighten the head bolt to 90 ft. lbs in three stages, make sure your second stage is low enough that you don't have to exceed 90 ft. lbs to get the wrench moving on the last stage of the tightening sequence.

For the same reason, when checking, or re-torquing bolts, they must be loosened then tight-

Not a torque wrench at all, this stretch gauge will actually measure how much the bolt "grows" under tension, a much more accurate way to measure stress and clamping load.

Torque Wrenches

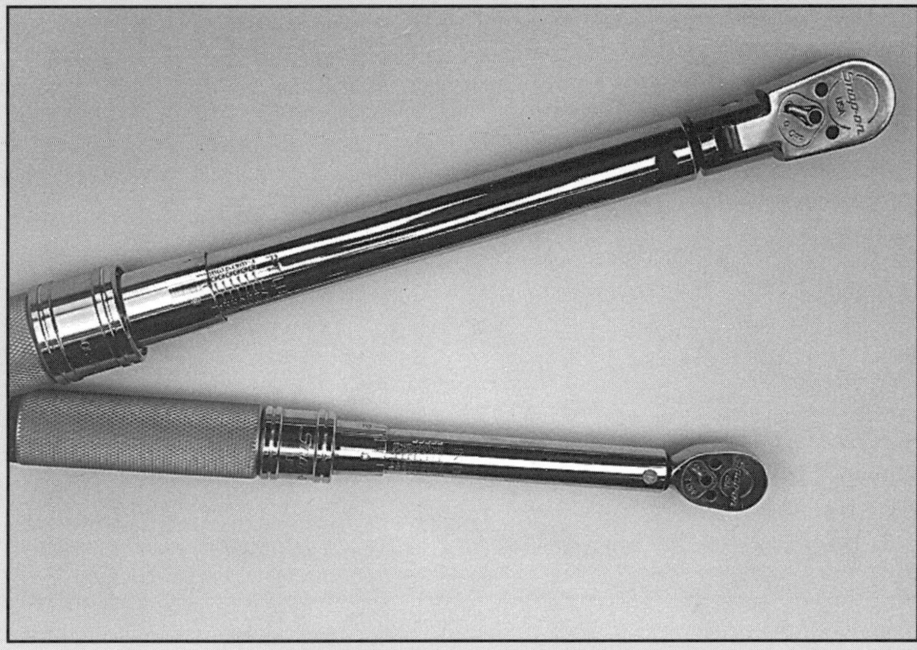

The most common torque wrenches currently in use are the "clicker" style like the two Snap-on models shown here. The upper wrench has a flex-head which makes it much easier to get on those hard-to-reach bolt heads.

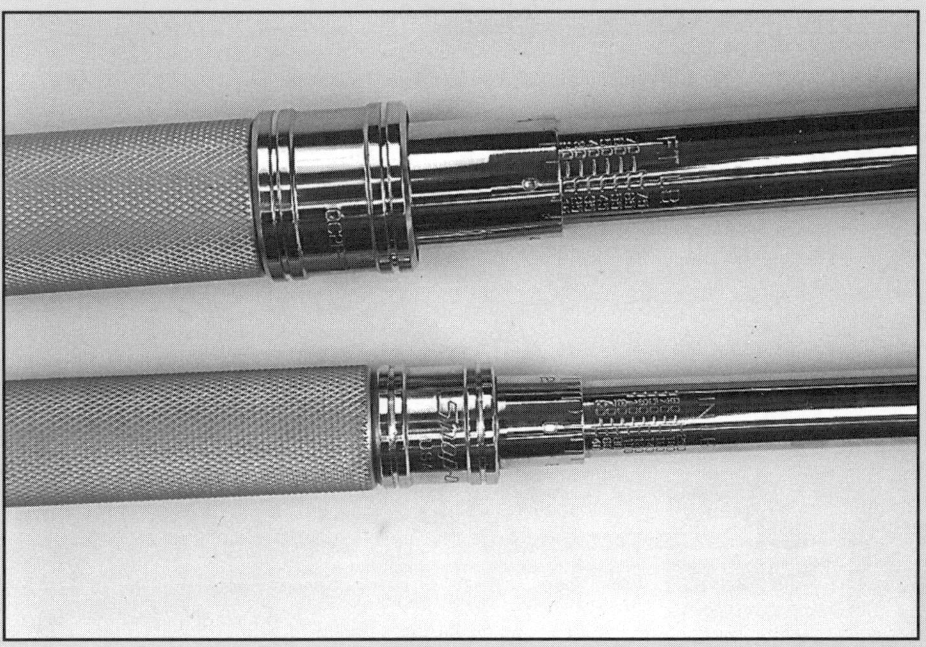

Known as micrometer style, the wrenches are adjusted to a particular torque value then simply turned until they click. These Snap-on wrenches come with a certificate of accuracy. Like all torque wrenches, the final "reading" must be taken with the wrench in motion.

ened again in the method described above. For obvious reasons, crow-foot type extensions that change the overall length of the wrench also change the desired torque readings. Likewise, socket extensions, especially long ones, tend to absorb some of the indicated torque and should be avoided. With the exception of the flex-head found on some clicker-type wrenches, it's important to keep the wrench at ninety degrees to the axis of the bolt.

As noted, friction plays a big part in torque. In a worst case scenario half or less of the torque you see registered on the dial of the wrench is actually applied to achieving the desired clamping force. Minimize the effects of friction by eliminating rusty, dirty bolts. If it's a special bolt that can't easily be replaced, and the threads are dirty (not damaged) clean them with a die before reassembly.

Neal Letourneau adds the following suggestions: Zero the clicker-style wrench after each use. Don't drop the wrench or throw it on the bench. Don't use a pipe on the handle. If you do drop the torque wrench or it's getting on in years have it recalibrated. Most tool suppliers, including Snap-on, Mac and Matco, can recalibrate your torque wrench.

Chapter Six

Plumbing

Moving Fluids

A Short Introduction

Some chapters get a little out of hand, and this is one of those. The problem is two-fold: the subject covers a lot of ground, and the resulting chapter covers a lot of paper. In addition to the standard concise information on plumbing choices and hardware there are three additions to the chapter. On pages 92 and 93 there's a short brake line how-to sequence. Following that are two separate side-bars, one built around an interview with a repre-

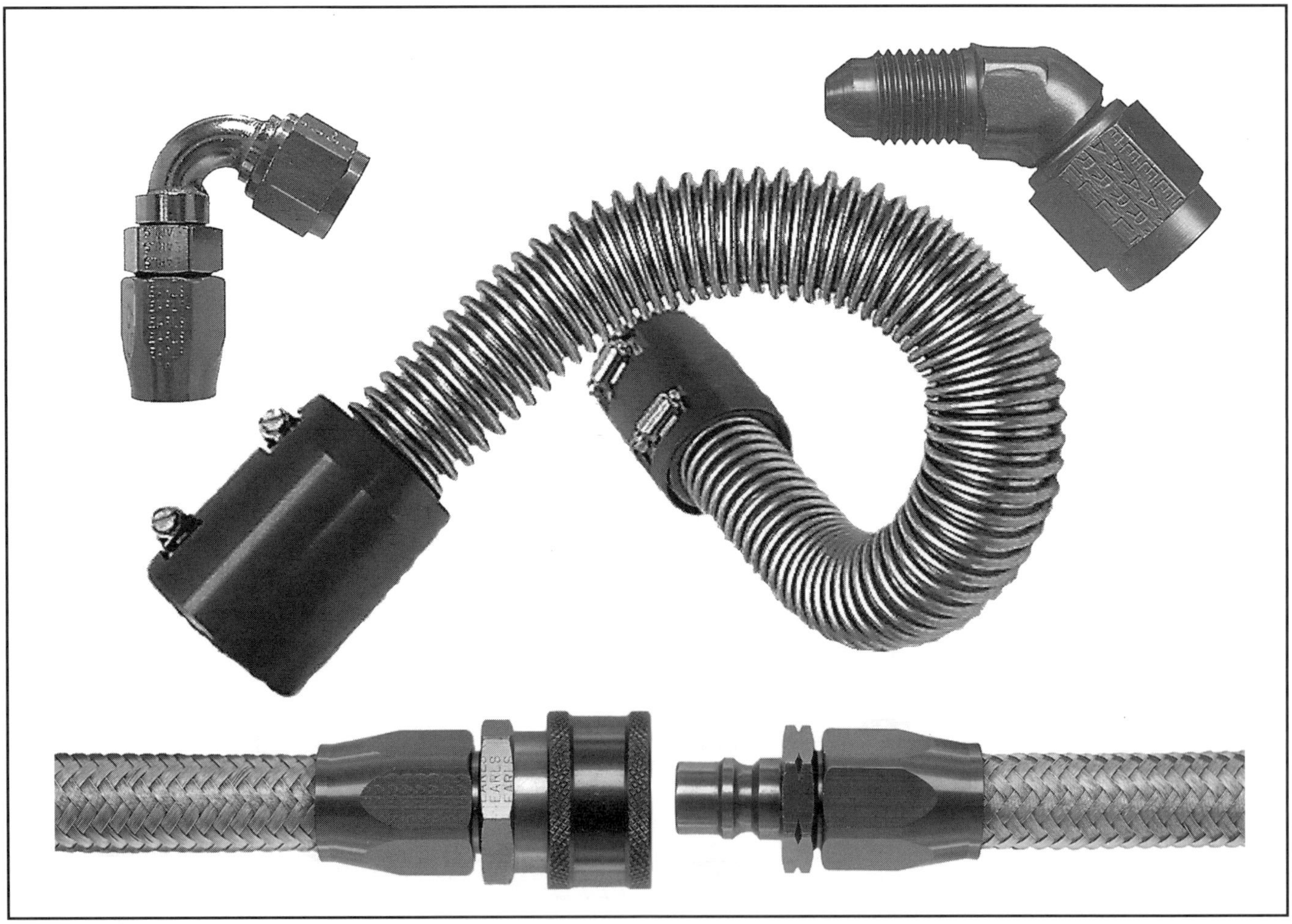

The current automotive aftermarket offers everything from fancy radiator hoses to aircraft grade hoses and fittings. If you can't find what you're looking for you aren't looking hard enough. Earl's

sentative from Aeroquip, and one based on an interview with a representative from Earl's.

On With the Show

When it comes to moving the common liquids around under the hood the aftermarket now provides a vast number of choices. Yes, you can still use the good old OEM stuff or the materials available at the local Pep Boys store. There's nothing wrong with that as long as you use quality materials and install them with care.

When it comes to finding radiator hoses, most parts stores have a huge selection hanging on the wall. Bring along a template to make the search as painless as possible.

In the case of water hoses there's nothing wrong with using standard automotive molded hoses. If you know the size of the inlet and outlet and the approximate shape (you can even bend up a template with a piece of wire or coat hanger) most counter workers at the local auto parts store will help you find the right molded hose from among their substantial stock. The key is to use brand name hoses and avoid the tendency to force the hose into something other than the pre-formed shape, as most hoses will collapse at that point. Be sure too that the hose you use on the suction side of the water pump is reinforced with wire so the hose can't collapse and shut off the flow of water.

When it comes to moving water long distances, it's often easier to use hard tubing with a flexible rubber hose at either end. Many radiator shops cam make up tubing like this with a bead at the end so the hose can't slip off.

The stainless outer braid most of us are so

enamored of is available raw, as are the colored hose "ends" (which are actually covers for the stainless hose clamps) that go along with the braided stainless look. This way you can buy molded hoses and then cover them with braided stainless. The braid does more than provide that nice race-car look. The stainless covering also gives protection from abrasion.

What you want to avoid are the corrugated radiator hoses for aesthetic reasons if no other. If you have to run the water a long distance straight water pipe can be used with rubber "connectors" at either end. It's important that any hard line like this have beaded ends so the clamped ends can't slip off. Any good radiator shop can make up a straight section of tubing and also do a nice job of beading the ends.

Like the water hoses, flexible gas lines can be made up of the black neoprene-type hose available at the local auto parts store. Because current fuels have so many new additives it's important to use only current, brand-name fuel lines. In most cases fuel line like this will slip over a simple barbed fitting where it's secured with a hose clamp. Upgrades in fuel lines include a variety of reinforced and braided hoses available from the aftermarket, most of which use brand-specific anodized ends.

Fuel manifolds are available pre-assembled from a variety of sources. These manifolds are available for most Holley carburetors or a standard three-deuces setup. Because fuel injection systems run at much higher pressures that do carbureted systems, the hose and fittings must be rated for these higher-pressure applications.

An Upgrade in Hoses and Fittings

When it comes to plumbing more and more builders of hot rods are looking for an upgrade. Driven by a desire for quality and certain aesthetic considerations, many builders want braided hose with anodized aluminum ends. Companies like Earl's, Aeroquip and others provide high quality hoses with or without the braided stainless covers, with matching ends. Both the hose and the hose ends are available as extremely high quality components suitable for competition, or in three or four less stringent grades more suitable for street use. (For more on the Earls or Aeroquip product line see the two interviews in this chapter.)

First we have to back up and explain that much of this high-end hose market started as surplus from the military, and thus uses what is commonly called the AN (Air Corps/Navy) measuring system. Fittings are all 37 degree instead of the more common 45 degree used

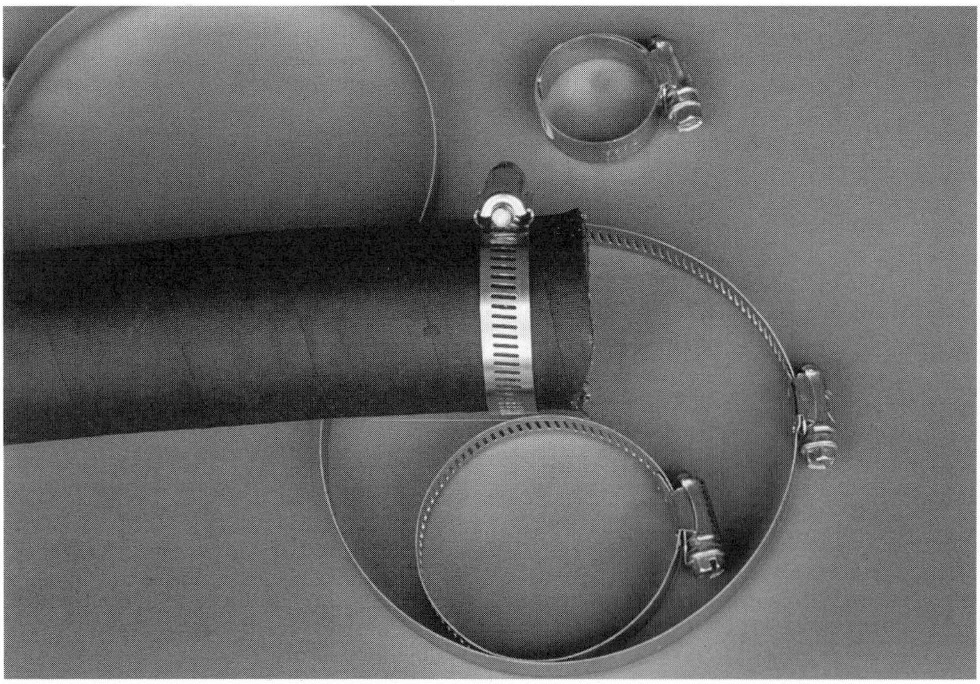

Be sure to use brand name clamps on your water hoses - positioned at least one "clamp width" back from the edge so there's no chance the hose can slide out from under the clamp.

in most American OEM situations. In this system, hose sizes are often indicated by one or two digits, all of which is part of the AN system described earlier.

What's called a "dash three" is generally written –03, or simply, -3. The three is the numerator of a fraction with 16 as the denominator. So the dash three equals 3/16 inch. It gets a little confusing because the 3/16 doesn't indicate the exact I.D. or even the O.D. At the time of implementation each size was designed to replace an existing hard-metal line with a flexible line of about the same I.D. Thus a dash three has about the same I.D. as a standard 3/16 inch brake line. A dash four (-04) has the same internal diameter as a 4/16, or 1/4 inch steel line.

Your choice of hoses depends on the fluid being moved as well as the pressure and temperature of the liquid itself. Yet, many of the high quality hoses offered for sale from companies like Earl's and Aeroquip will handle a number of different fluids and tasks commonly found under the hood of a typical hot rod.

Earl's Perform-O-Flex stainless braided hose, for example, comes in every size from –4 to –24 and can be used for fuel, vacuum and oil lines in the smaller sizes; and heater and radiator hoses in the larger sizes.

Likewise the AQP braided hose from Aeroquip is suitable for use with both standard and synthetic lubricants, as well as fuel, water and anti-freeze. This premium hose comes in sizes as small as –4 and as large as –32.

An overview of the premium hose market would include at least three different hoses from

The plumbing on your engine can be as simple or elaborate as you want. In the case shown here the aesthetic appeal of the multi-carb set up is enhanced by the careful use of high-end plumbing with anodized ends. Earl's

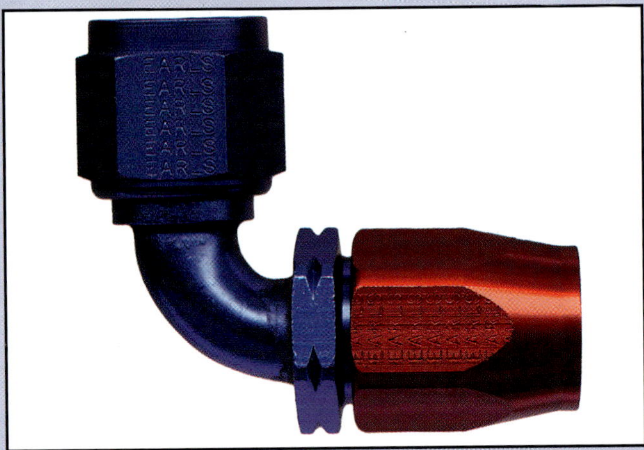

Often used in fuel applications in the smaller sizes, these Auto-Fit ends are a single nipple design (non-cutter) available in sizes 4 through 20. Earl's

For passing through a firewall you may need a single bulkhead fitting like this with AN fittings on either end. Earl's

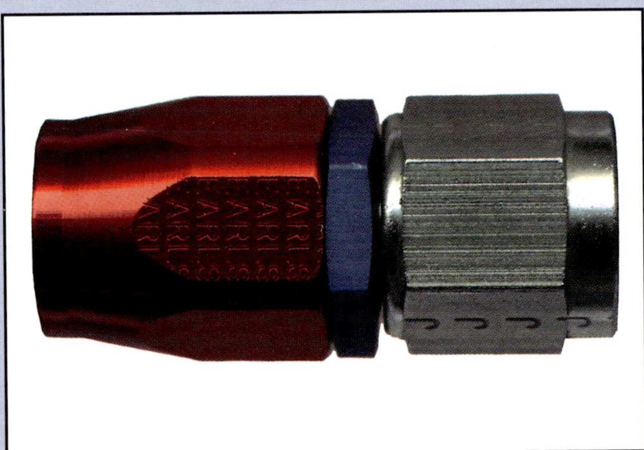

Part of the Swivel-Seal line, (cutter-style) this straight fitting is often combined with the braided Perform-O-Flex hose to plumb fuel, water or oil lines. Earl's

For the budget conscious there are fittings like this that provide a NPT on one end and a straight hose end on the other. Earl's

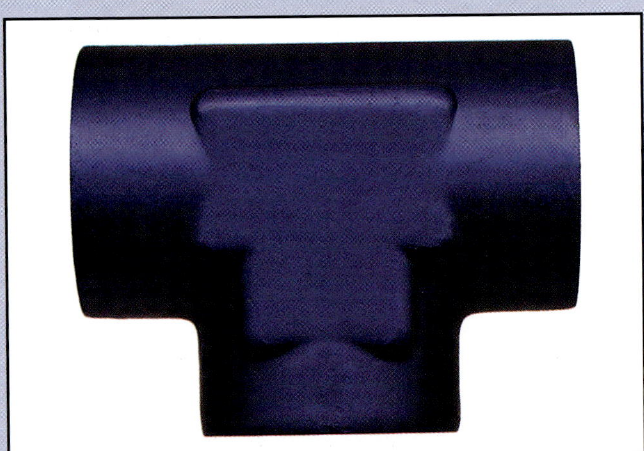

This triple pipe-fitting T comes in 1/8, 1/4 and 3/8 inch NPT sizes and is just one of about a million adapters and fittings available from the aftermarket. Earl's

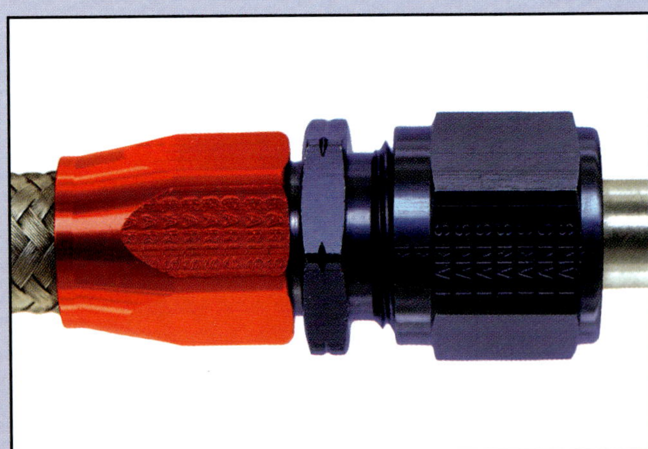

Hard line can be mated to a stainless hose with a fitting like this, available in a wide range of sizes. Earl's

both Earl's and Aeroquip. Before deciding which hose best suits your situation, consider a few of the following criteria. First, do you need and want a hose with a braided stainless covering? Second, how much pressure and temperature must the hose withstand? Third, do you have to follow the rules laid down by a particular racing organization?

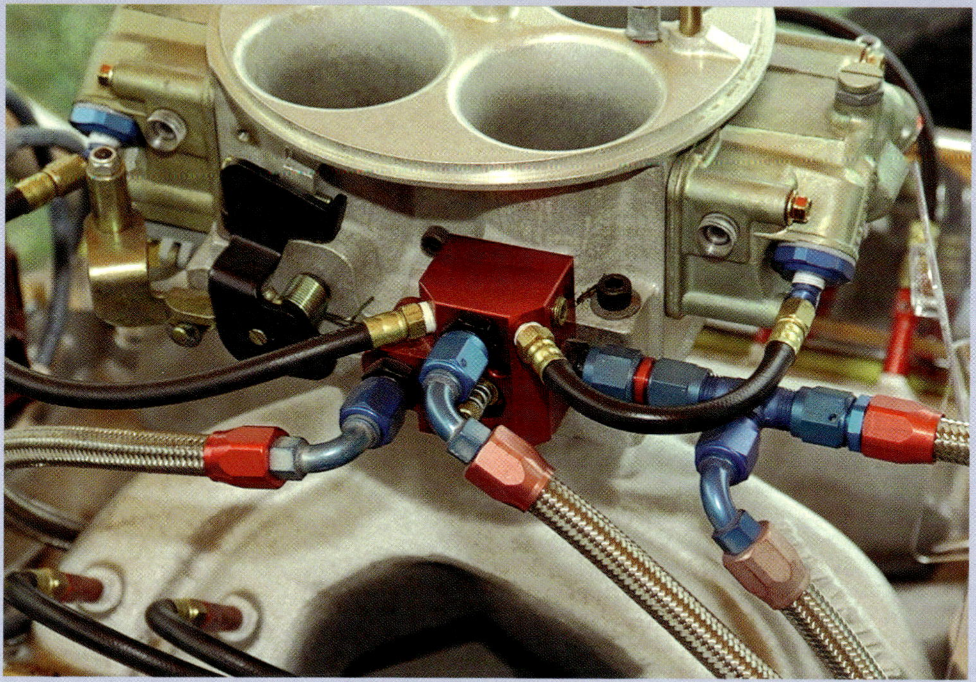

Anodized fittings and stainless braided hose make an installation like this look very sanitary and professional.

Stainless braiding gives the hose an outer armor so that no other hoses, cables or sharp edges are likely to cut through the hose. If the braid is actually bonded to the outermost layer of synthetic rubber, the braid also acts to give the hose a high pressure rating. The proverbial downside is the way the braided outer coating can act as a saw when it comes up against a painted inner fender, or another, unbraided hose. The stainless outer covering also means the hose will conduct electricity. Consider what happens when a braided hose that's connected to the car's ground side comes in contact with a positive terminal at the battery or the back of the alternator. This is why many racing organizations don't allow braided hose to be used under the dash.

In terms of style, a nostalgia car like this doesn't need dozens of red or blue aluminum fittings. Just a neat engine compartment with a molded radiator hose and gas lines with stainless wrap and clamps at either end.

If you have to have stainless braid, there are a number of ways around these apparent problems.

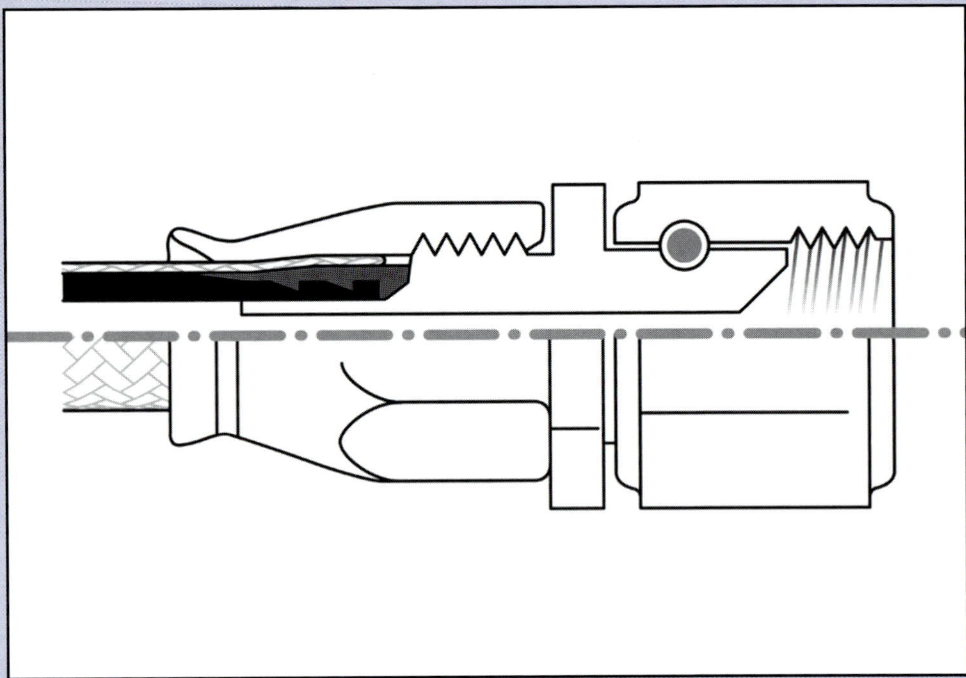

This cutaway shows a Speed-Flex fitting and how it clamps the braided Teflon brake and hydraulic lines. Earl's

Clear, plastic shrink wrap tubing is available and can be shrunk onto the outside of most common sizes of stainless hose. Though the tubing will discolor in time when exposed to UV light, it will eliminate the saw-like effect of a standard braided hose. A better option might be "stainless" hoses with another, non-braided outer coating, like the ruff-stuff hose from Earl's.

Consider too that there are a number of alternatives to a premium hose with a stainless outer braid. For many of us, "stainless" hoses mean quality, and the outer-braid gives them a very business-like appearance. Before deciding that you absolutely have to have stainless hose, consider the non-braided alternatives.

All the major manufacturers offer synthetic rubber hoses with pressure ratings of 200 and more psi. In most cases these hoses can be used for fuel, lubricants, water and anti-freeze. Aeroquip sells their StartLite while Earl's promotes their own Pro-Lite hose. In the case of the Aeroquip product, the hose is made up of a special synthetic inner hose, wrapped in a Nomex flame-retardant cover. The StartLite product uses Earl's own HTE synthetic rubber inner liner and an outer braid of woven

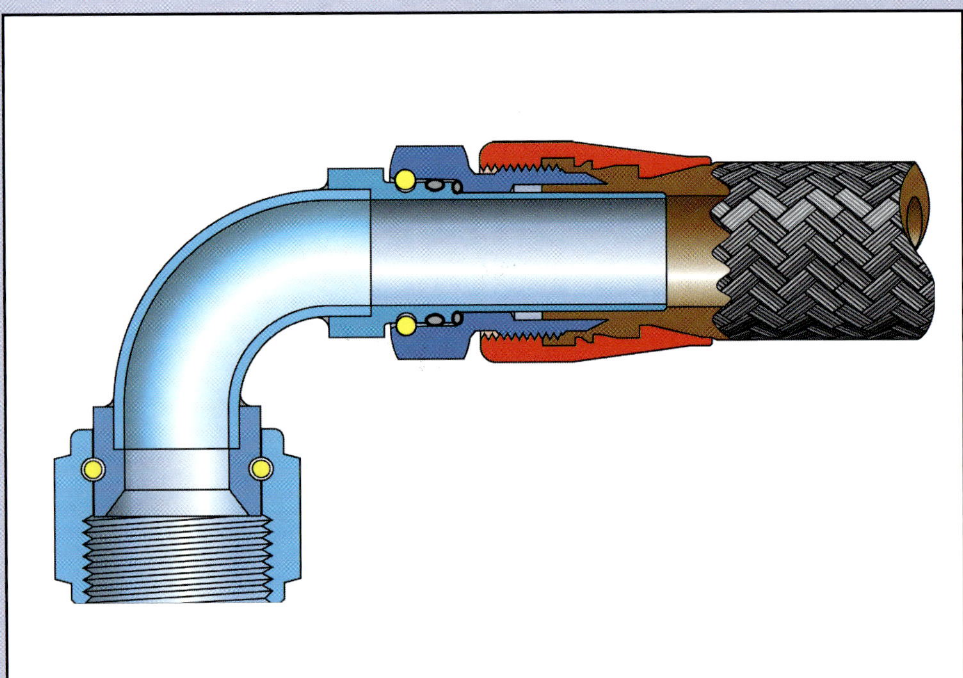

Another cutaway, this one illustrating how the Swivel-Seal cutter-style fitting clamps and seals the hose while allowing the fitting end to turn after assembly. Earl's

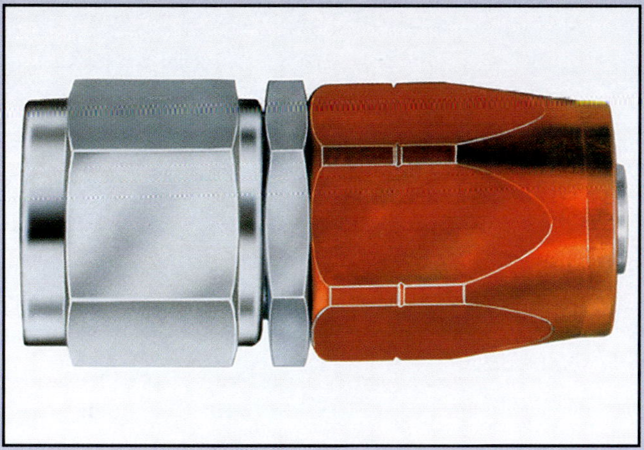

This re-usable single nipple (compression-style) fitting is available anodized or with nickel plating. Can be mated with AQP stainless hose or Startlite hose. Aeroquip

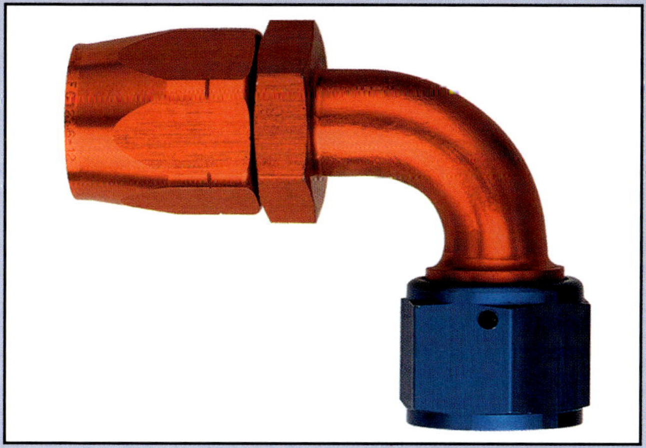

Another single nipple design, this 90 degree aluminum fitting is re-usable, and comes in sizes 6 though 20. Aeroquip

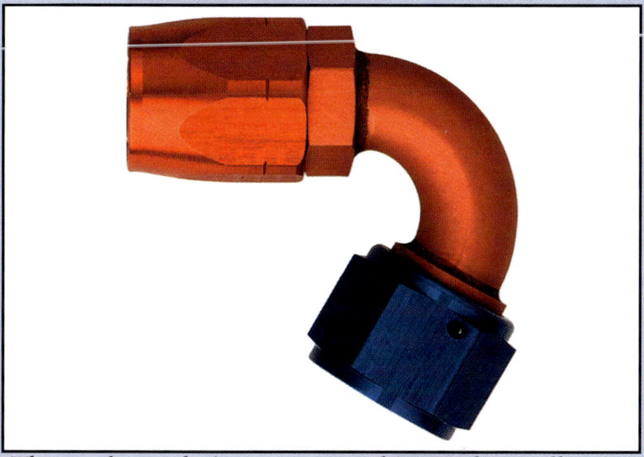

This single nipple (compression-style) 120 degree elbow is the non-swivel model and can be mated to stainless or non-stainless hoses capable of handling gas, water and oil. Aeroquip

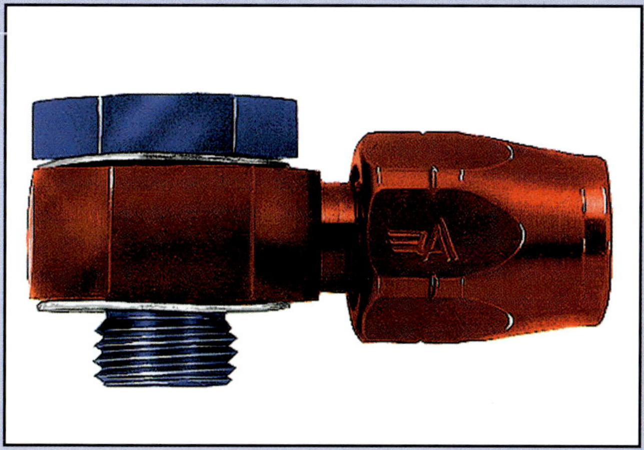

Banjo fittings can be mated to stainless or non stainless hose with fittings like this. Aeroquip

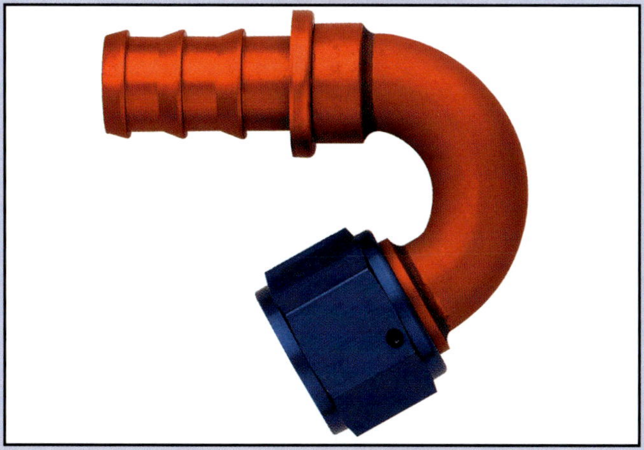

Socketless aluminum fittings are available in sizes 4 through 12, can handle fuel, oil and water, and mate up to Socketless hoses without even the need for a clamp. Aeroquip

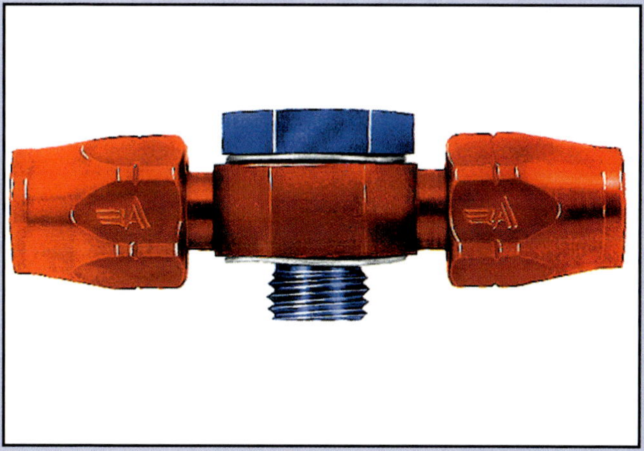

To neatly plumb a multi-carb set up requires two-line banjo fittings like these designed for –6 hose. Aeroquip

Nylon. Most of these hoses are designed to work at a wide temperature range.

Whether the hose you use is wrapped in stainless or nylon, the ends you use on either end will contribute to both the appearance and the performance of that particular hose. What you might call the upper end of the hose-end market is made up of the swivel and non-swivel hose ends. These come in at least three styles and are often anodized to boot.

The best of the hose ends can be broken down in to two or three basic styles depending on how the fitting assembly seals against the hose. Familiar to most of us is the concept of a compression fitting. With this style of fitting, the outer nut is slipped over the hose, the hose is slipped over the inner nipple and the nut is screwed onto the nipple. The action of screwing the outer nut onto the fitting's nipple compresses the hose between the inside of the nut and the outside of the nipple. These fittings may have threads on the nipple (so the fitting is actually screwed into the hose before the nut is threaded into place) or barbs, and may also have barbs on the inside of the outer nut to help hold the hose in place on the nipple (see the illustration).

A second type of hose end might be called the "cutter style" fitting.

With these hose ends the nipple includes a "cutter" that splits the hose as it is forced into place. Manufacturers of this style of fitting feel that by "cutting" the hose they achieve a better seal and a more trouble free hose end.

When trying to decide which type of hose end to use, it might be simpler to just buy the

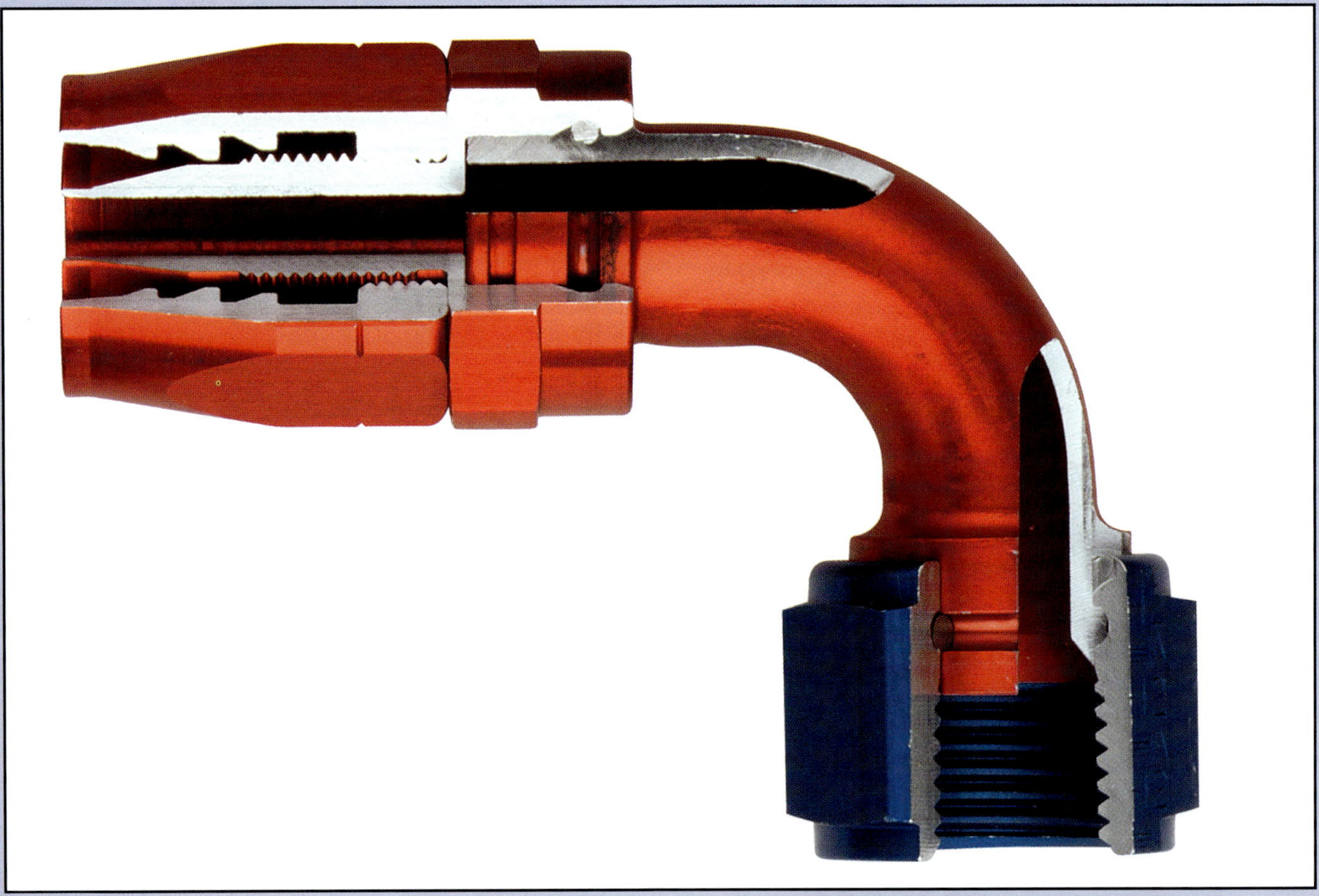

This cutaway shows a swiveling, compression style (non-cutter) fitting made from 2024 aluminum alloy. Aeroquip

hose and ends from the same supplier and thus ensure compatibility. Though both types of hose ends do a good job, the compression style are easier to re-use.

What might be called the "true fittings" (as opposed to a hose clamp and cover on a barbed fitting) can be further subdivided depending on whether or not the fitting can swivel after the hose is in place. Providing the swivel makes for a much more complex fitting, though it's much easier to use as well, particularly if the hose end includes a 45 or 90 degree angle.

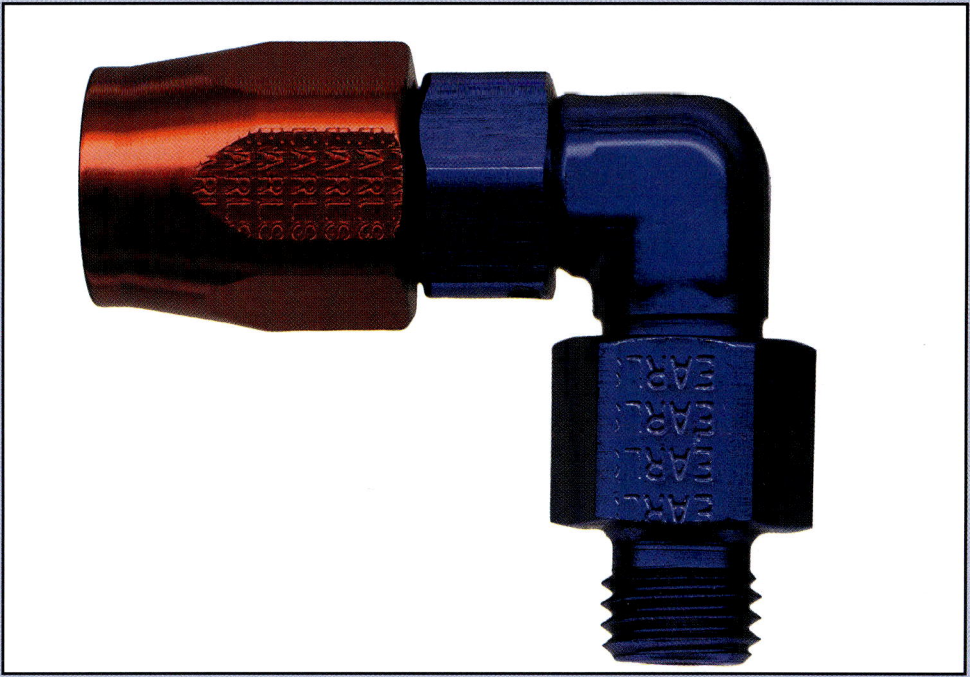

This special line of fittings is designed to mate a braided or non braided hose and Swivel-Seal end with a male "fitting" that swivels so the male end can be screwed into the female counterpart while the hose is attached. Aeroquip

As mentioned earlier, the simple barbed fitting and hose clamp combination we're all familiar with is also available in a deluxe version. A number of the aftermarket companies manufacture the barbed fittings anodized in blue or red, with a matching aluminum cover that slides over the hose clamp. These deluxe clamps and covers can be combined with stainless braid that you purchase raw and slide over the hose of your choice. The combination of anodized fittings and braided hose makes for a very nice looking hose assembly done on a budget.

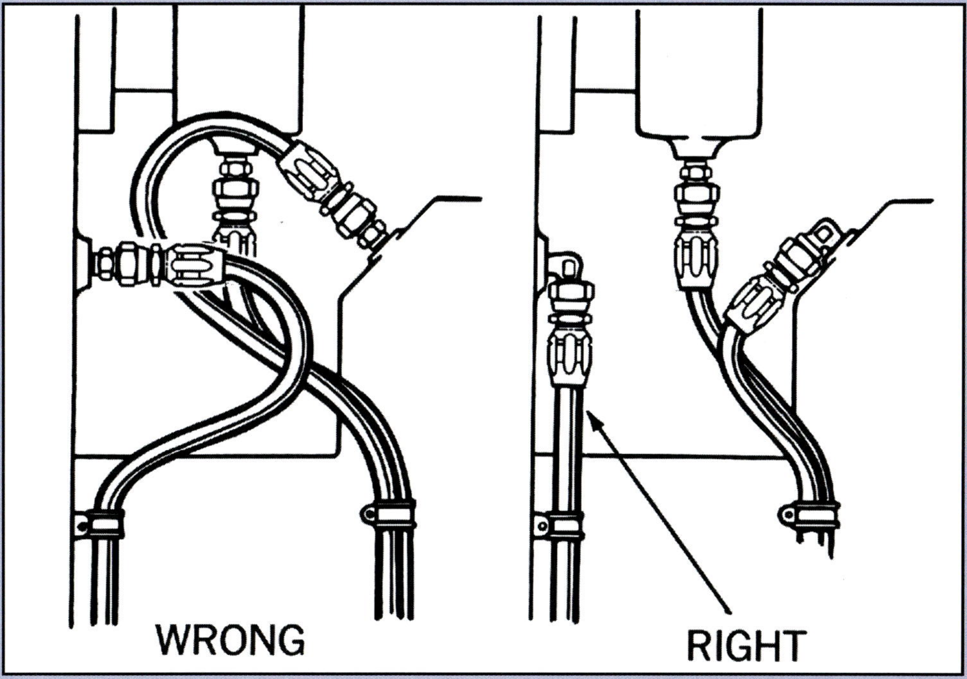

With the incredible range of fittings currently available, there's no reason not to do a very neat hose installation as shown. Aeroquip

Brake Hoses

If you assemble a radiator hose from aftermarket parts and it blows later while cruising down the highway, you've created a mess and an inconvenience. In the worst case, you could damage the engine if the temperature is allowed to go too high before you shut it down. If the same thing happens with a brake hose you've created more than an inconvenience.

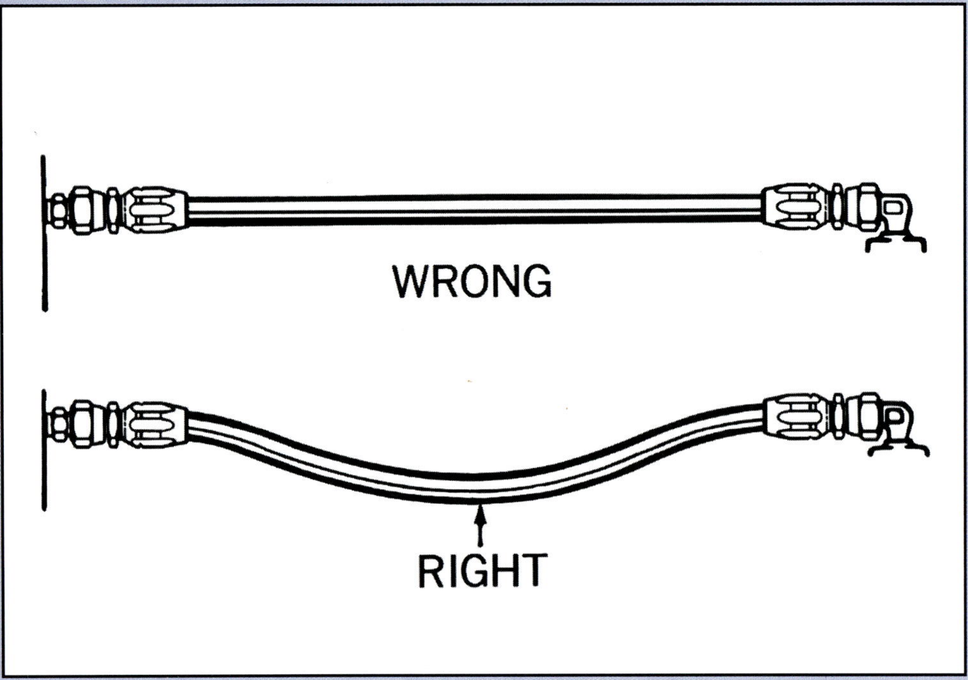

Hoses expand and contract as the fluids inside get hot and cold. For these reasons there needs to be a bit of slack in your hose installation. Aeroquip

The only truly approved hard-line for brakes is the OEM-style steel hose with double-flare 45 degree fittings. Hot rodders lean toward the stainless steel hose with 37 degree single-flare AN fittings. Though aesthetics drives many of these decisions, there's also the "I want this car to have the best of everything" mentality at work here, along with the related refrain, "I want this car to last forever." Yes, a stainless line will last "forever," but in reality a standard steel line will last nearly that long.

When it comes to the flexible brake hoses a similar dilemma arises. The DOT approved hoses are the big, ugly black ones. The hoses that many people want to use are the braided stainless hoses. These braided hoses are made up of a Teflon liner inside a stainless braided

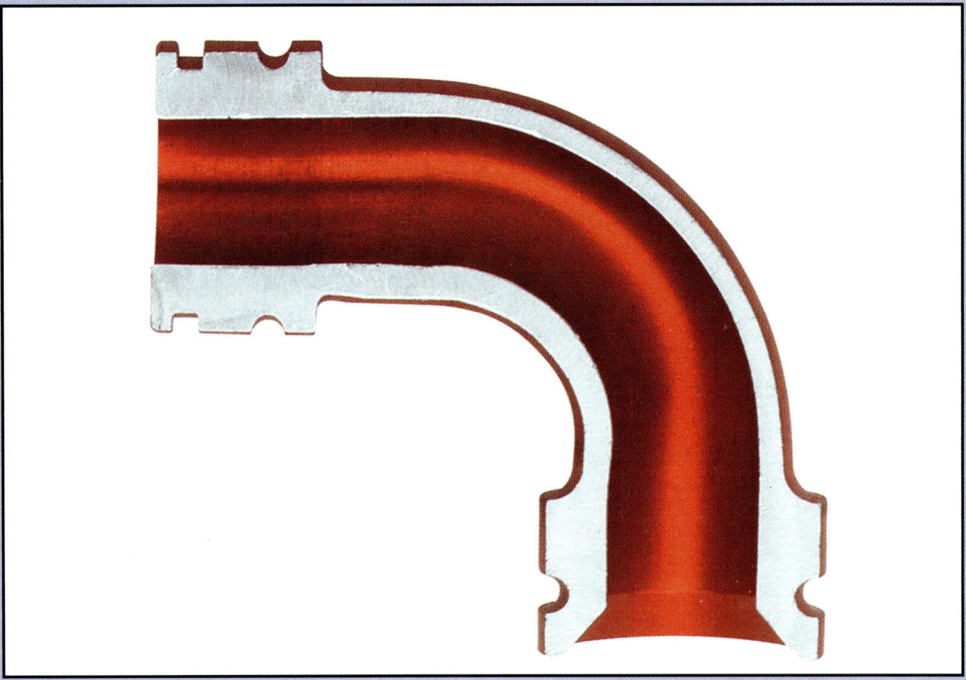

Not all aluminum fitting are created equal. The best are one piece designs intended to offer the greatest possible I.D. for a given fitting size, and to eliminate any constriction inside the fitting. Aeroquip

TECH TIPS-AEROQUIP

TECH TIPS-AEROQUIP

VACUUM

One of the most severe applications of a hose is in vacuum service. Modern dry sump oil systems are pulling more vacuum than ever. It is extremely important to match the hose you are using with the vacuum rating of your application. Aeroquip offers racing hose with a vacuum rating of up to 28in./HG(check hose specifications for vacuum rating). Great care should be taken in the handling and routing of hose used in vacuum service. If a hose is installed beyond the minimum bend radius, the vacuum rating will be reduced. Also, if a kinked or damaged hose is put into vacuum service, the kinked or damaged area will be a weak spot, and the vacuum rating of the hose will be reduced. For severe vacuum applications, an internal support coil may be needed. Contact Aeroquip Technical Support for additional information.

RUBBING YOU THE WRONG WAY

Abrasion is the number one cause of hose failure. Make sure hose assemblies are routed properly to reduce the chance of abrasion. Use a support clamp about every 14 inches to 18 inches to secure the hose. For chafe protection, be sure to install a grommet at any point a hose passes through a panel or bulkhead. However, remember that under pressure, a hose may change lengths. Leave a little sack to allow for any shortening or elongation in the hose.

AN (ARMY-NAVY)

The AN(Army-Navy) standard was established many years ago by the U.S. military to set a common measurement for hose and fittings. It designates the outside diameter (O.D.) of the ridged metal tube that is compatible with each size of fitting. Still today, this AN dash standard is the benchmark measurement for military, industrial and the performance hose applications. These dash sizes are expressed as the numerator of the fraction, with the denominator always being 16. For example, a -04 port is 4/16 or 1/4 inch.

TOO TIGHT AND LEAKING

One of the most common ways the seat or cone on aluminum fittings and adapters can be easily damaged is by overtightening. If a fitting has been overtightened, it may be damaged and prone to leaks. Dirt and debris on the sealing surface are also common sources of leaks. Always use Aeroquip dust caps when disconnecting a hose or fitting to help keep contaminants out of hose and adapters.

SEALING ADAPTERS

Teflon tape or sealant of any type should not be used on AN threads of 37 degree fittings and adapters. These fittings and adapters seal on the seat and cone, and any material on these surfaces could cause a leak. Only tapered pipe threads require a thread sealant. This seal takes place by a wedging action of the mating threads, and a pipe sealant is required to produce a leak-free joint. It also helps to lubricate the thread surfaces to help prevent galling.

cover. The hose can be purchased raw from companies like Earl's and Aeroquip, or pre-assembled hoses can be purchased with a variety of ends factory installed. Most of these are rated at a minimum of 2000 psi operating pressure and a burst pressure of more than 10,000 psi.

When it comes to clamping the brake lines to the frame a number of small clamps are available. The two on the right are stamped from stainless while the two part clamp is cut from aluminum.

Before running out to buy the trick braided brake hoses remember that most of these are not DOT approved. All of this might be no big deal except that more and more states are requiring some kind of safely inspection, an inspection you could fail if the hoses don't meet DOT specifications.

If you do run a braided hose, a dash-three hose is the right size for most brake applications. Clutch hydraulic systems generally require a dash-four because they are moving a larger volume of brake fluid. Call me conservative, but I recommend buying the hoses factory assembled with the ends already installed. They can be ordered in nearly any length, if you can't get exactly the right fitting on the end, a whole raft of adapters are available to convert the pipe fitting thread in the caliper to the AN fitting on the brake line (for example).

When working on brake lines and fittings, pay attention to the flare. Don't try to mate a

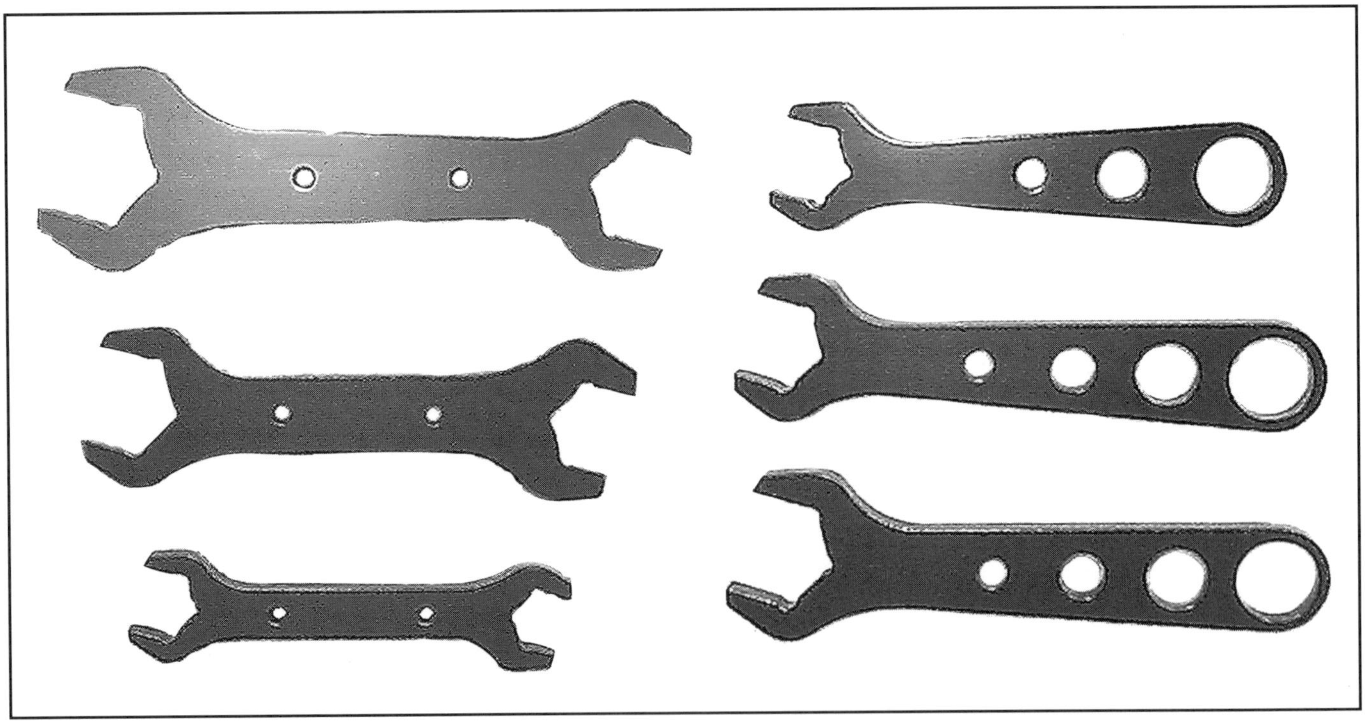

These wrenches, available in single and double end, are designed for fittings and hose ends. Short handles work in cramped spaces and prevent over-tightening. Earl's

37 degree hose with a 45 degree fitting on the caliper or chassis. Yes, the materials are soft and will probably "give" enough to mate the two, but seepage and failure are likely results. If you have to mate the typical American 45 degree system with the AN 37 degree system, conversion fittings are available to do just that.

Be sure all the hoses you mount, especially the flexible ones, can't come in contact with a suspension member or the edge of the tire as the suspension goes from full extension to full compression, or as the tires go from lock to lock. If you run the lines inside the frame, don't put any connectors where you can't see them and be sure to test for leaks, an essential part of the installation process. When everything is finished and the system is bled, get someone to stand on the brake pedal while you carefully crawl around underneath with a light inspecting each and every fitting for any signs of leakage.

Whether you run the lines inside the frame or outside, they must be clamped in place. A variety of aluminum and stainless clamps are available from the aftermarket to make your installation as neat as possible.

We should mention that for individuals who don't want to spend their days measuring, cutting and flaring stainless brake lines, companies like Pure Choice Motorsports will custom cut and flare all the lines and ship them to you ready to install on the car of your choice.

A final word of caution is warranted here. To quote Jim Petrykowski: "The brake lines are one of the last things that is installed in the car, people get into a hurry and use the wrong hose and ends just to get the car on the road right now. You can't use any plastic or rubber-type hoses in place of brake lines. The only thing to use for hard line is the 45 degree steel lines or the stainless lines with the correct 37 degree fittings. For flexible hoses, only use the DOT approved hoses or the Teflon variety with stainless coverings, *the hoses that are meant for brake applications.*"

"All the lines must be routed safely, away from any source of heat or abrasion. Run the suspension through the full range of motion to check for interference with a tire or suspension member. Secure and support the lines to avoid vibration. Your life depends on this. The consequences of a screw up or mistake are just too high, you and your family are riding on this deal. You wouldn't drive the car with only three quarts of oil in the engine….."

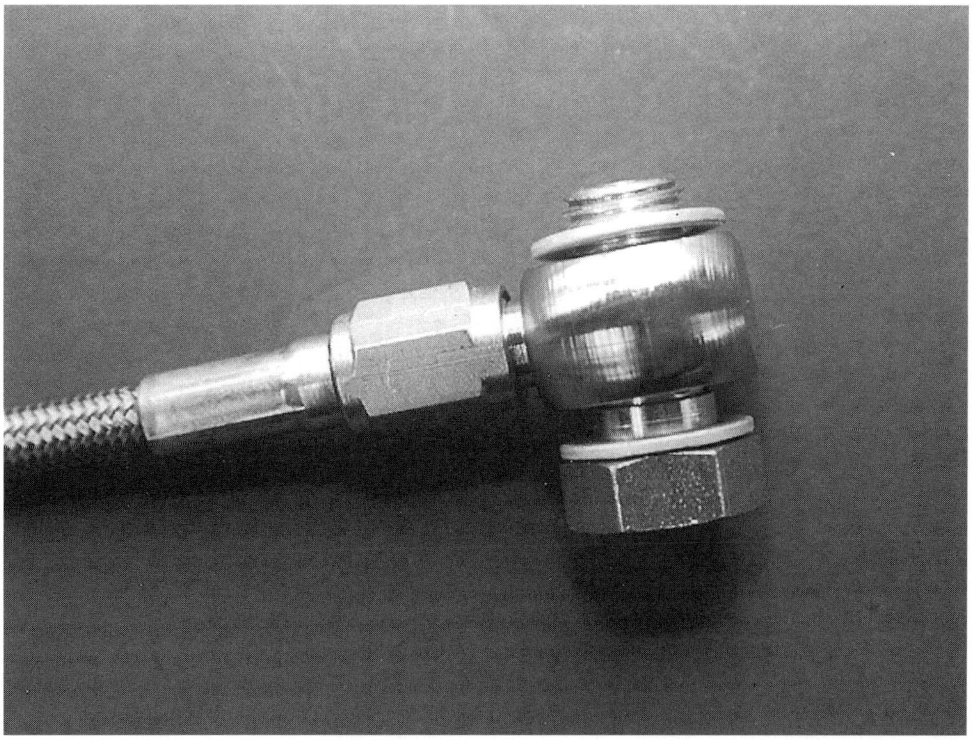

Some brake lines come with a standard AN fitting on the end, which can then be screwed to the correct fitting, a banjo-style fitting in this case.

Neal starts the project by cutting the raw line to the correct length. Note he uses a cut-off wheel, not a tubing cutting, because the cutter tends to crush the end of the tube.

A small sander is used to clean up the end of the tube and make sure the end is cut off 90 degrees to the tube's axis.

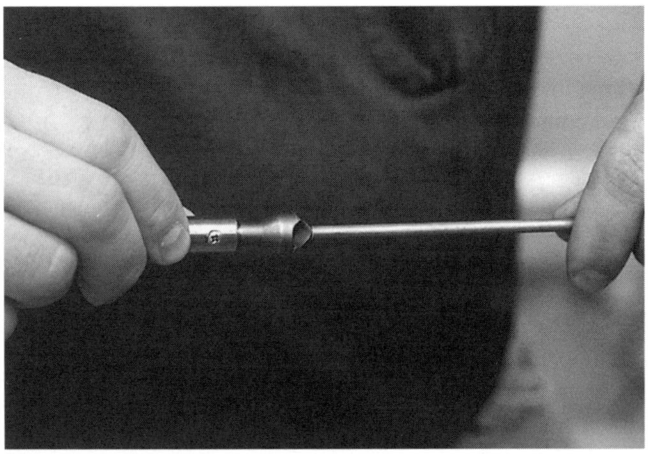

The next step is to de—burr the end: first with the special tool shown here, and then with a small file (not shown) on the outside of the tubing.

Brake line how-to

Presented here is a short brake line how-to sequence performed by Neal Letourneau of Shoreview, Minnesota. This sequence covers the use of stainless line and 37 degree AN fittings (though there's nothing wrong with the use of standard steel brake lines).

Materials and Tools

The hard line used here is 3/16 inch stainless. "These lines have a .028 inch wall thickness," explains Neal, "the material is seamless 304L stainless. The lines must be seamless or they will crack when you bend or flare them. The fittings are AN 37 degree single flare, the type that use a small tube sleeve between the line nut and the flare (see photo to eliminate confusion). These can be obtained from Earl's or Aeroquip, or one of their dealers.

Cutting, Flaring and Bending

Neal suggests that if you're new to this notion of cutting, bending and installing brake lines you might want to mock up the whole thing in standard 3/16 inch steel line, or welding rod before starting in on the stainless. The actual cutting is done with a cut-off wheel on a zinger. After cutting the tube Neal carefully dresses both the outside and the inside of the tube and goes on to explain that, "A standard tubing cutter tends to squash the tubing." Now it's time to flare the tubing, which must be done with a quality flaring tool designed for a 37 degree single flare, not the 45 degree double flare seen on most American OEM applications.

Neal warns that, "The end of the tube needs to be really clean without any nicks or burrs. You can use some taping fluid or lubricant of some kind between the cone and the tube so it won't gall against the tubing. The cone of the flaring tool needs to be nice and clean, without any nicks.

The tubing is positioned so the end is flush with the top surface of the tool. Neal says you have to exert pressure, by turning the cone down against the tubing, until "you can't go any further." The tubing will be damaged if you continue to exert pressure after the tubing has been fully flared out against the clamp.

Plumbing the frame with stainless is pretty much a nuts and bolts kind of deal. Like most parts of a hot-rod building project, a neat job requires good materials, patience and attention to detail.

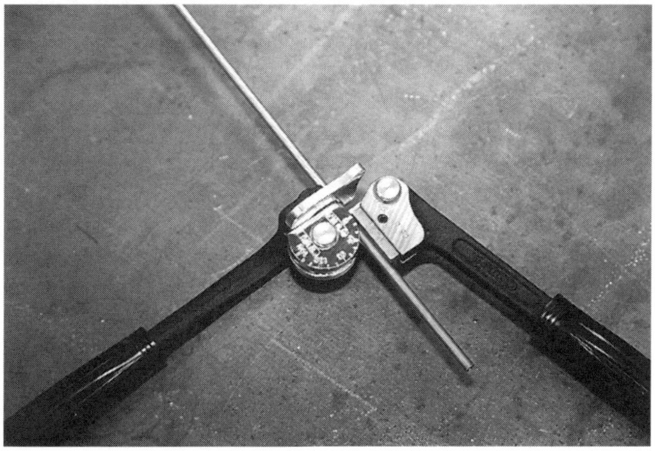

With a quality bending tool like that shown, made by Ridgid, you can make neat bends with a small radius without damaging the tubing.

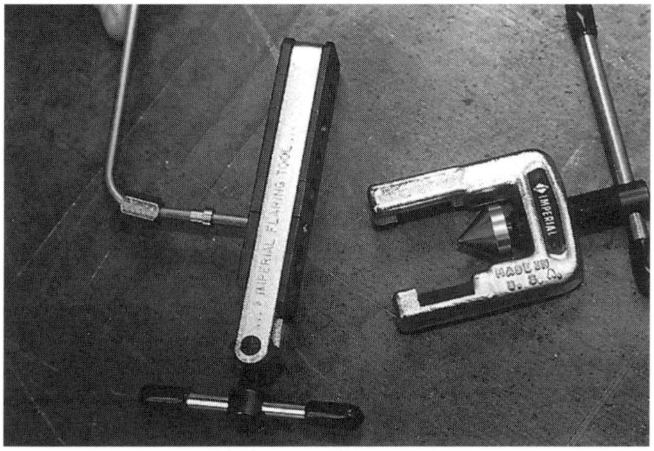

After bending the tubing Neal places the AN nut and the correct sleeve on the tube and positions it in the flaring tool just far enough to be flush with the edge of the tool.

A little lube placed on the flaring tool means it's less likely to gall against the stainless. Stainless doesn't flare and bend easily, and thus requires quality tools and attention to detail if it is to be used effectively.

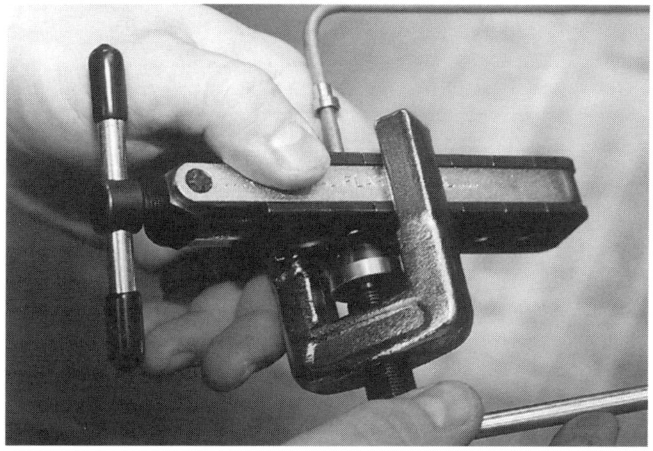

As Neal puts it: "The flaring tool is tightened down against the end of the tubing until you feel the metal stop moving."

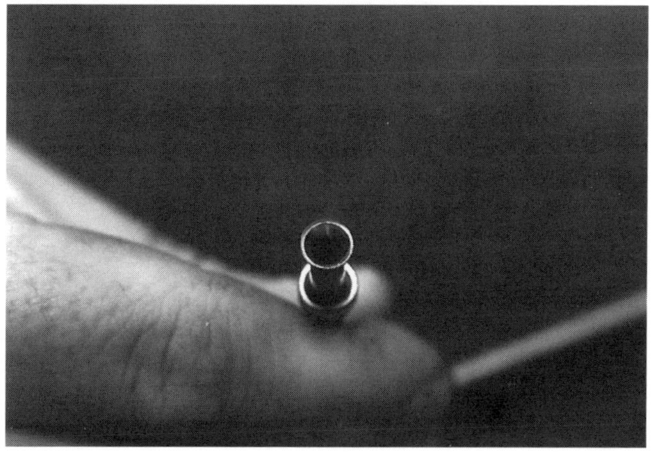

A properly executed flare should have no cracks. Close inspection will show a nice smooth, almost burnished, surface.

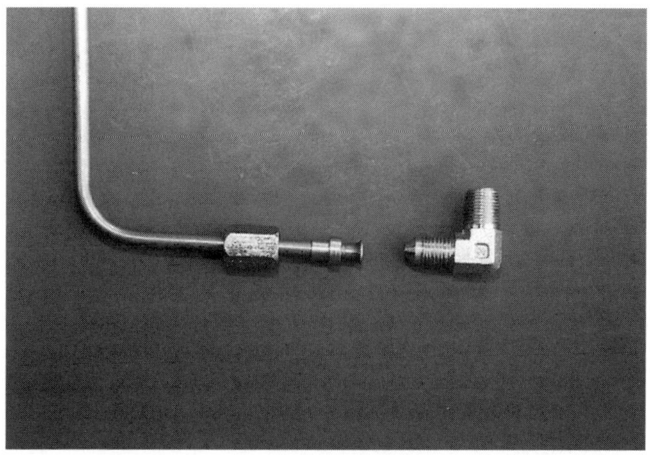

The finished tube, with a nice 90 degree bend, the AN nut, the sleeve, and the right adapter to go from AN to pipe threads.

Aeroquip

A Short Q & A With Fred Grossmann From Aeroquip

Fred, how did Aeroquip get started?

The company got its start at the beginning of WWII, supplying fittings and hoses to the military.

Most of your hoses are rated for more than one kind of fluid. How does the first-time user pick the right hose from among the various choices in your catalog?

In our product line we have braided stainless steel covered hose, Nomex covered hose and rubber covered hose. Which one you choose depends on the performance requirements of your application. Weight, operating pressure, temperature, vacuum and cost all figure into your hose selection.

How do I decide whether or not I need a stainless steel hose?

Our stainless steel hose uses a smooth-bore inner tube made of AQP elastomer. It is compatible with just about any fluid used in an automotive type application. Of course the stainless covering gives it good abrasion resistance, it can rub against something without being affected. The stainless steel hose is extremely durable and has a high operating pressure rating (up to 1000 psi). It also has a good vacuum rating so you can use it on an application like a dry sump oil system.

Do I have to use an Aeroquip fitting on an Aeroquip hose?

Yes, we recommend you use Aeroquip fittings on Aeroquip hoses. Each one of our hoses has a fitting that is designed specifically for that hose. For stainless steel braided hoses we have the reusable compression fittings.

The StartLite hose uses aluminum crimp fittings and our SOCKETLESS hose uses a push on fitting. We are the only leading performance plumbing supplier that engineers and manufactures both the hose and the fittings. We manufacture both so we can guarantee that they work together.

You use a compression style fitting while other firms use a cutter-style fitting, what are the advantages of the compression-style

Aeroquip hoses and fittings are used on many competition cars, including this Pro/Max quarter mile machine.

Aeroquip

fitting?

The compression-type fitting is more user friendly, easier to assemble and disassemble. The nipple is piloted so it is less likely to damage the hose. The cutter style fitting is not as easy to reuse. Aeroquip reusable fittings come in both swivel and non swivel styles. When you swivel one of ours, the nipple does not turn inside the hose, with all cutter style fittings it does, And most of our fittings, 80%, are a one-piece tube design,

AN hoses and fittings, already made up, are available to fit most popular carburetors. Aeroquip

AQP® Racing Hose (with Reusable Fittings)

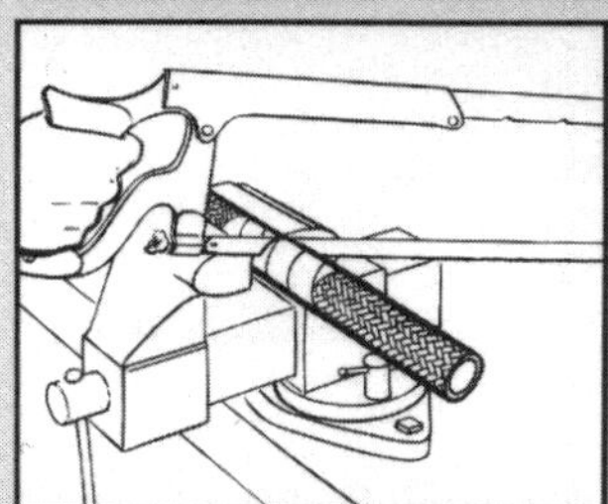

Step 1. Cut hose square to length with fine-tooth hack saw or cut-off wheel. To minimize wire braid flare out, wrap hose with masking tape and cut through tape. Remove tape before next step.

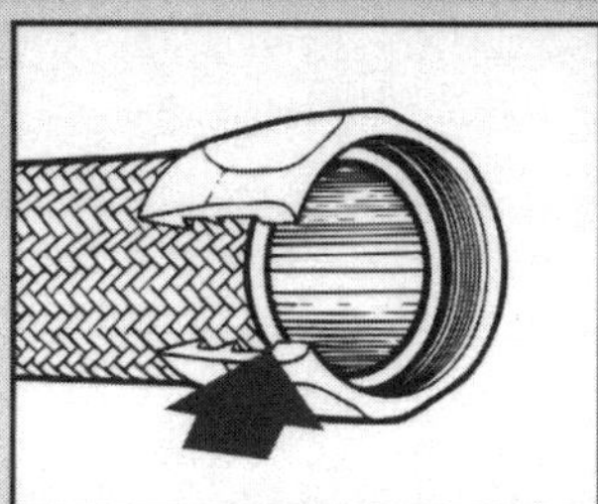

Step 2. Insert hose in socket with twisting, pushing motion until hose is in line with back of socket threads.

Step 3. Important—Mark position around hose at rear of socket with a grease pencil, paint or tape.

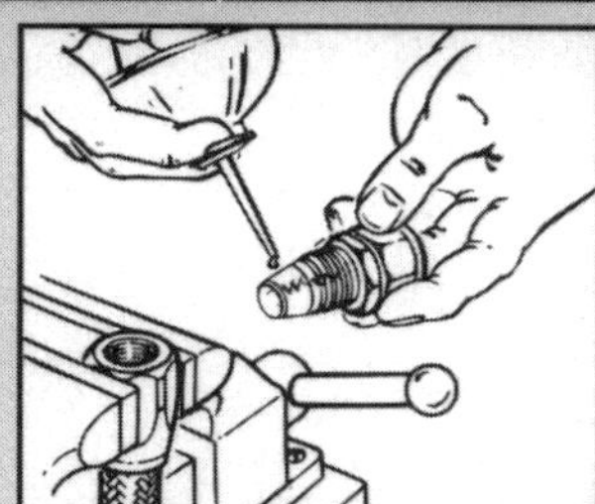

Step 4. Lubricate inside of hose and nipple threads liberally using S.A.E. 30 lubricating oil or Aeroquip FBM3553 Hose Assembly Lube.

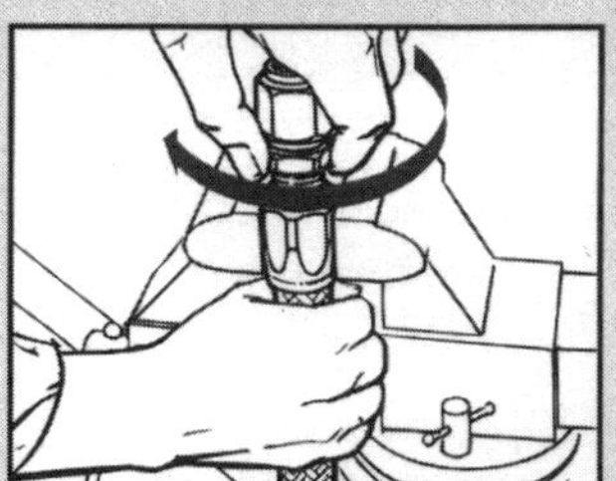

Step 5. Carefully insert nipple and engage nipple and socket threads while holding hose in position with other hand. Make sure hose does not push out of socket by observing mark made in Step 3.

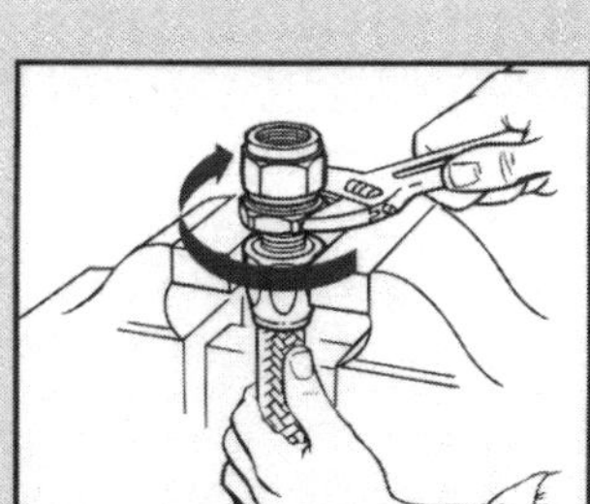

Step 6. Complete assembly using wrench while continuing to hold hose in position. Maximum allowable gap is .031 inches. Your thumbnail is a convenient measuring device.

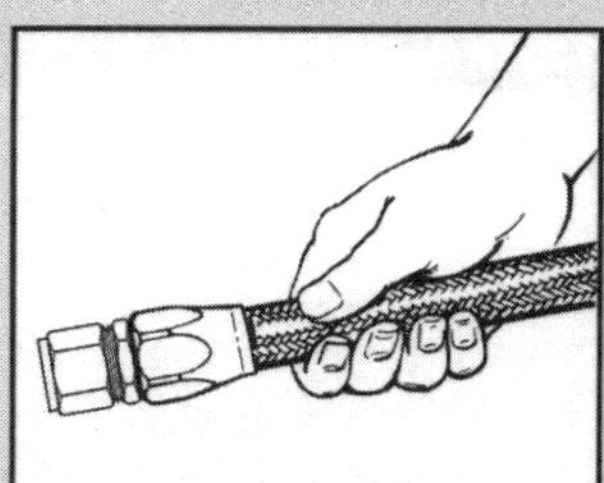

Step 7. Important—Check hose for pushout by observing hose position mark. Pushout should not be evident. CLEAN, PROOF TEST TO TWICE OPERATING PRESSURE AND INSPECT ALL ASSEMBLIES. Disassemble in reverse order.

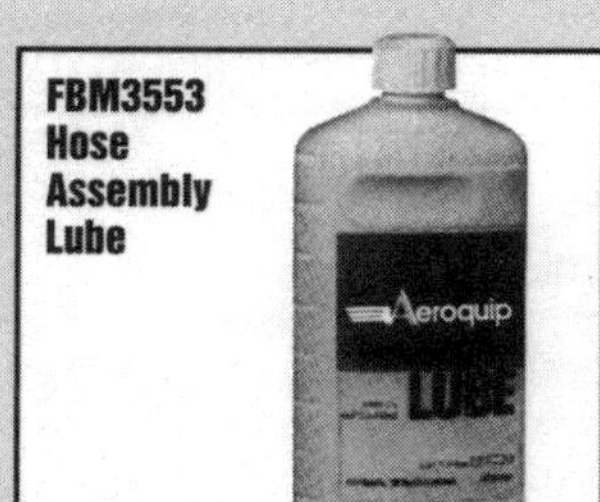

Aeroquip Hose Assembly Lube is a specially compounded lubricant superior to any other lubricant used in hose assembly work. Available in pint containers.

Use for either hand or machine assembly.

there is no brazed joints like there are in the industry standard design. We're able to do this because of our new manufacturing process. With the one-piece tube design the fitting is stronger, it provides for better flow and is Cosmetically superior.

What about crimped fittings, are these designed primarily for big shops?

Yes, the crimp is more for professional race teams where they have the crimping machine. Or someone can have their Aeroquip dealer make up the hoses. The crimp fittings offer some significant advantages including lightweight, savings in assembly time and the ease of assembly.

How about brake hoses, how good are the braided-stainless steel brake hoses?

Ours are extremely durable; the stainless braid gives them a very good resistance to abrasion. The Teflon inner liner is good to 3000 psi maximum operating pressure. And the Teflon doesn't expand at all when you apply pressure like the OEM rubber hoses do, so you get better pedal feel with the Teflon hoses. You can order these in almost any length with ends installed, or you can buy the raw hose and install the

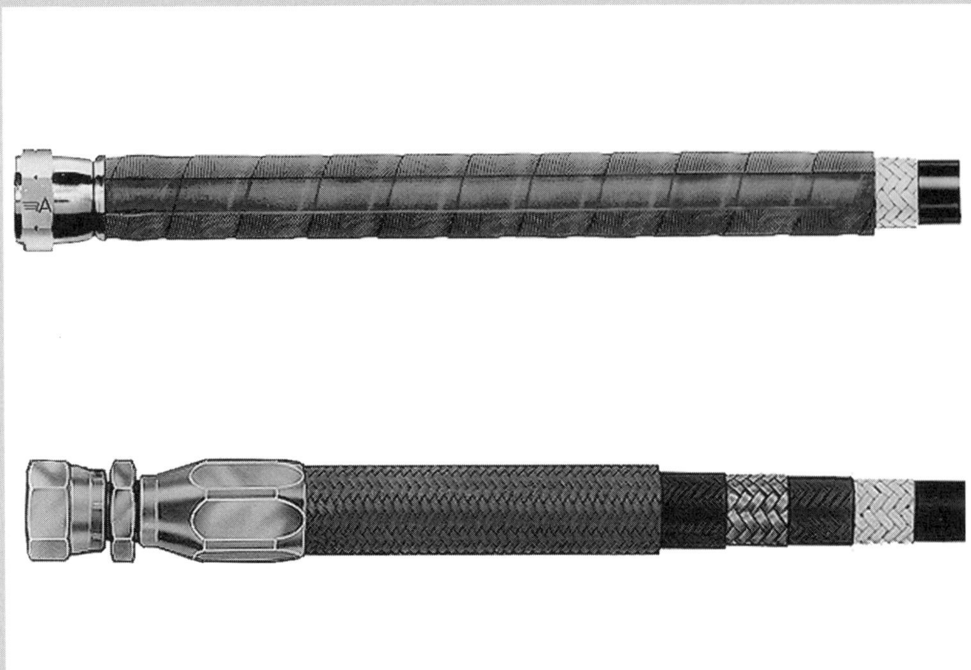

Most high quality hoses are made up of multiple layers. The inner liner determines the hose's compatibility with various fluids and temperatures while the number and type of outer braids determine the hose's pressure rating and how easily it can be bent. Aeroquip

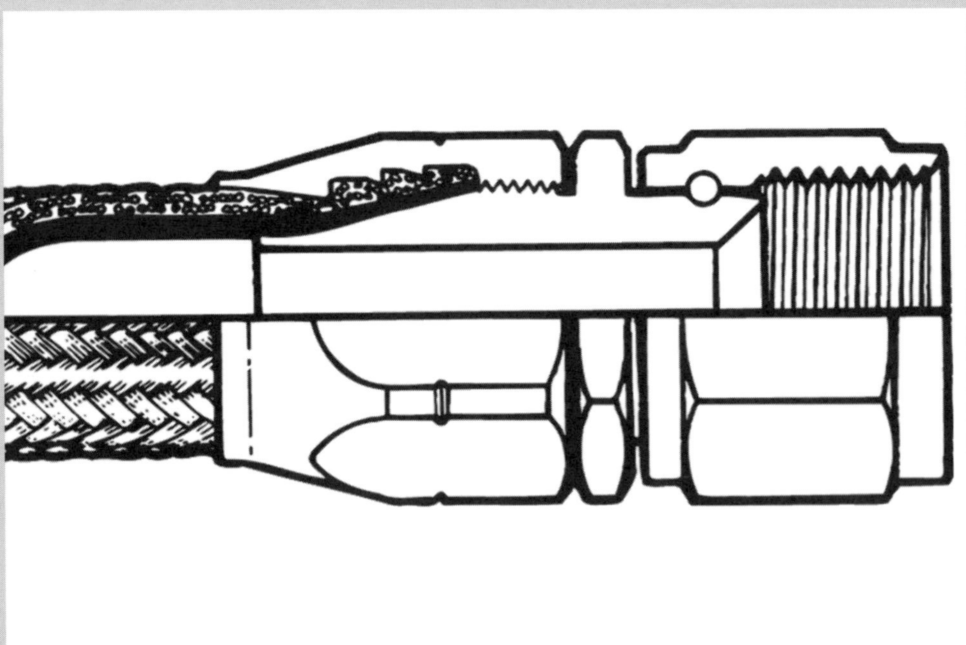

The diagram shows a compression fitting (non-cutter style) and the way the outer sleeve, often called a socket, screws onto the fitting and holds the hose in place. Aeroquip

Aeroquip

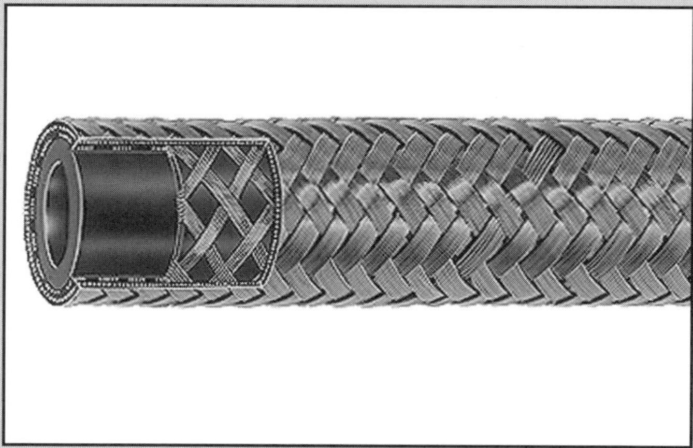

The AQP racing hose utilizes a smooth elastomer inner liner and an outer braid of stainless steel. Aeroquip

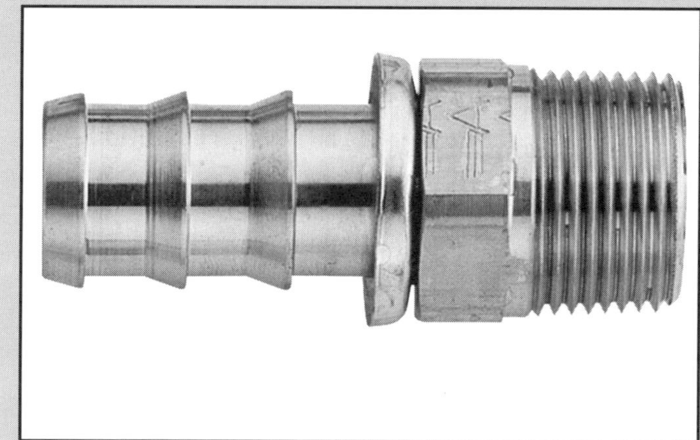

Designed for use with Socketless hose, this fitting screws into a NPT female sized from 1/8 inch to 3/4 inch. Aeroquip

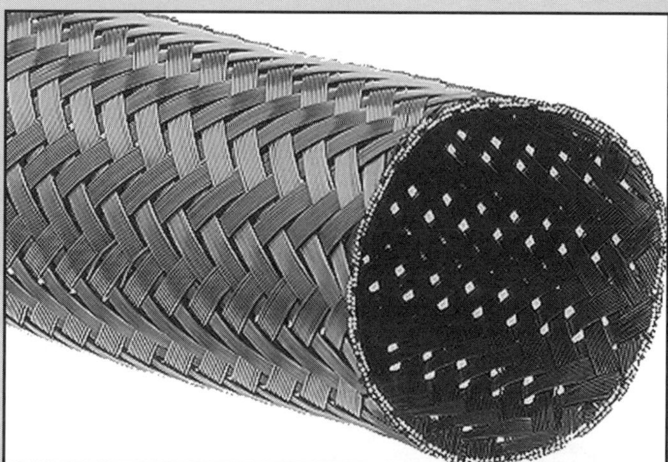

The outer stainless braid can be purchased separately if you need to add it to a standard water or gas line for abrasion resistance or aesthetics. Aeroquip

ends yourself. If you're not experienced though you probably want to let us make up the hose. These hoses are not DOT certified however so they are labeled as being for off road and competition use only.

What are the mistakes that people make, either in choosing, assembling or installing hose?

The biggest problem is abrasion. The hose rubs on something like a frame rail and that creates a problem. You have to be sure to route it correctly. If the hose goes through a bulkhead or the firewall, a grommet should be used. When you secure the hose, be sure to leave a little slack so it can move a bit because a hose will grow slightly when in use.

People sometimes have a problem when they install a reusable fitting. When people install a fitting on a hose they need to follow the instructions. As those instructions show, when you put the socket on the hose you need to mark the hose with paint or grease pencil. That way you know the hose is fully seated even after the fitting is completely installed (see copy of instructions). The other thing people have to understand is the fact that all the fittings we have are AN with a seal of 37 degrees, not a standard automotive fitting with a 45 degree fitting. What looks like it may fit, may not. We have a wide range of adapters to help the end-user meet just about any plumbing need.

People often install these hoses and ends for their aesthetic appeal. Are there any colors besides the anodized red and blue that most of us are familiar with?

Yes, we have a new series of fittings, both the reusable and the SOCKETLESS with electroless nickel-plating. These fittings have a really nice bright shine that looks good under the hood of a lot of street cars. It goes well with the stainless steel hose and our new black SOCKETLESS hose.

Earl's

A Q & A with Alvin Rocha, marketing manager for Earl's Performance.

Alvin, can you start by giving us some background on Earl's

Earl's was started by Earl Fouts. Earl was in the surplus business. He would buy components, fasteners, hose and hose ends from the military and re-sell them. Earl did business with George Bignotti of Indy-car fame and pretty soon George's car was plumbed with aircraft hose and fittings that he bought from Earl. The other racers followed George's example and pretty soon Early was selling a lot of hose and fittings to race car owners. Then the surplus market dried up. At that time Aeroquip had a patent on the cutter-style hose end. So Earl tried to buy hose and ends from Aeroquip but they wouldn't sell to him.

Earl and his son Bob decided to design their own fittings. They used an O-ring to seal in the fitting which also meant the hose could be turned after the fitting was installed on the end of the hose. This was the Swivel Seal hose end, the start of Earl's own product line.

The problem was obtaining the right hose. They had to make a commitment to a hose manufacturer to buy enough hose that the manufacturer would produce it to their specifications. That hose is our Perform-O-Flex braided hose, the standard in the industry. From there, once they had the ends and the hose it was a matter of working with racers and trying to get better and better distribution. Race cars always take special adapters. Earl's would respond to almost any request for special adapters, so you could plumb almost anything with their stuff. And they've always worked to have the best products.

The first-time buyer who opens your catalog might be confused by all the different hoses, many of which overlap in the types of fluids they will handle. How does the buyer choose the right hose?

In general there are two kinds of stainless braided hose, the Auto-Flex and the Perform-O-Flex. The other side of the business is the Teflon lined hoses - a wrap of stainless braid over the top of the Teflon liner to hold the pressure. The advantage of the Teflon line is it's impervious to anything and has high structural strength. But it's harder to bend and assemble. Brake and hydraulics are the two applications where people use the Teflon hose.

Our Pro-Lite hose is a nylon braided synthetic rubber hoses, this is good for race car applications where light weight is important. The working pressure is 200 psi for most sizes.

The Perform-O-Flex and Auto-Flex and Pro-Lite all have

AN T-fittings are available zinc plated and in sizes from 3 to 16. Earl's

Earl's

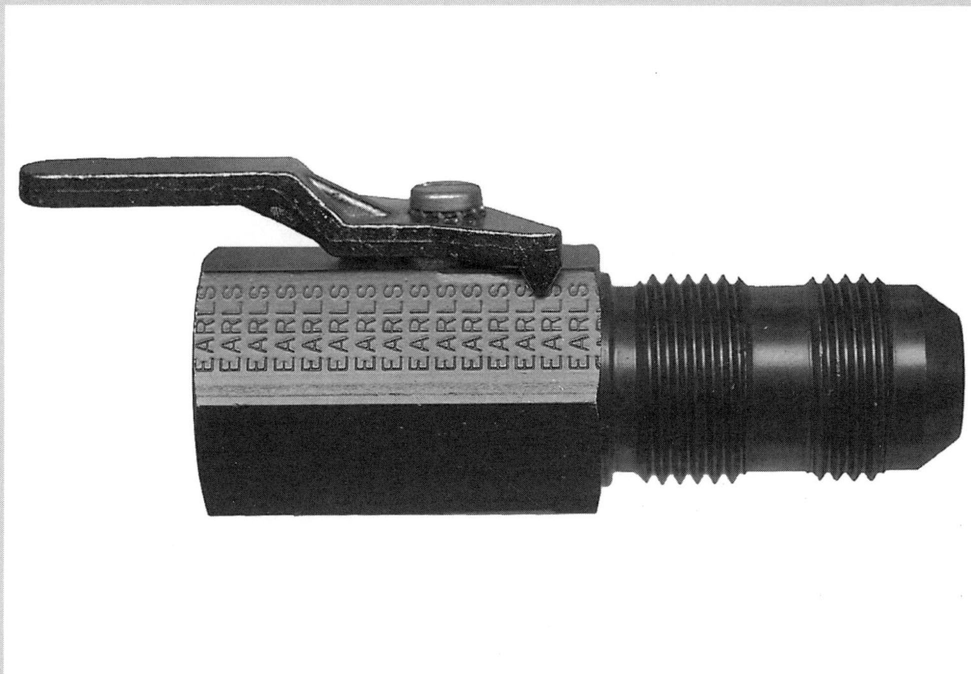

These fuel shut off valves come in various NPT sizes on the female side, and assorted AN and AN-bulkhead fittings on the male side. Good for emergency shut off or as an anti-theft device. Earl's

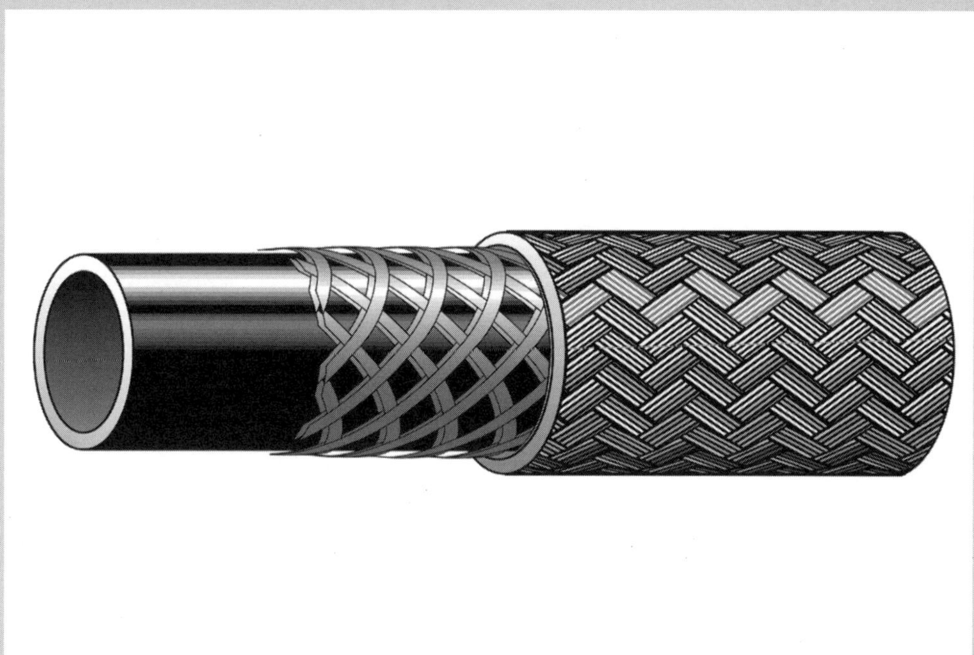

Designed to a answer the need for a stainless hose at an attractive price, the Auto-Flex hose is made up of an HTE synthetic liner with bonded fabric textile braid, all encased in a stainless braid. Good from -40 to 300 degrees F with a clamped max pressure rating of 250 psi in most sizes. Earl's

the same inner liner of HTE synthetic rubber. The difference is in the way the hose is constructed. Pro-Lite is nylon braided, the other two have a stainless braid. The Perform-O-Flex has an outer and an inner wrap of stainless and as a result has the highest rating:1500 psi from size -4 to size -8. The application is high pressure.

The Auto-Flex hose has the same outer weave of stainless but the inner wrap is a textile. This gives it a somewhat lower pressure rating and also means that it bends more easily. Our Perform-O-Flex has a marker wire in the outer braid, one band that's copper so the hose can be easily identified.

In general the stainless outer braid hose is good for high working pressure and situations where there's any chance of abrasion. Some racing organizations dictate that the lines be either hard line or stainless.

Do you recommend the use of Earl's fittings and ends on Earl's hoses?

We do recommend that our hoses be used with our ends. There are comparable hoses on the market that will work with our ends though. Some hoses, however, have a slightly different cross section, the wall thickness is different that ours, so our compression fittings don't work.

You have both cutter and compression-style fittings in the catalog, can you talk about the advantages of each?

The cutter-style fitting is the premiere fitting in the industry. Our Swivel seal fittings are a cutter style, The Auto-fit is a compression style fitting and those do not swivel after assembly.

The Swivel-seal fittings have a slightly larger I.D. in a given size than the Auto-Fit do, but if you're not a hard-core racer the Auto-Fit is probably just fine.

The compression-style fittings are probably easier to re-use. The cutter style fittings can get pieces of rubber stuck up between the sleeve and the cutter when the hose and fitting are disassembled. Then the new hose won't seat completely and may leak.

You have a pretty extensive line of Teflon-lined brake hoses, can you describe the programs?

There are three different ways to get a brake hose from Earl's. Originally, you would buy the Speed-Flex hose, then buy ends like you buy ends for anything else. That way you can build the hose to any length and with any fittings you want.

We also have the hoses available with the ends installed. We stock standard lengths, they can be ordered in different configurations, female AN on one end with a banjo fitting on the other for example. The range of available lengths and fittings should take care of nearly any vehicle.

The third way to buy stainless-wrapped Teflon brake hoses is to buy them already assembled and built to fulfill specifications developed by the Department of Transportation. This is our Higher Stop program. Each hoses has a code stating that it meets DOT specifications and also gives the application.

These three brake hose programs all use the same hose. Sometimes the ends are a little different, some are slightly different to make it easier to

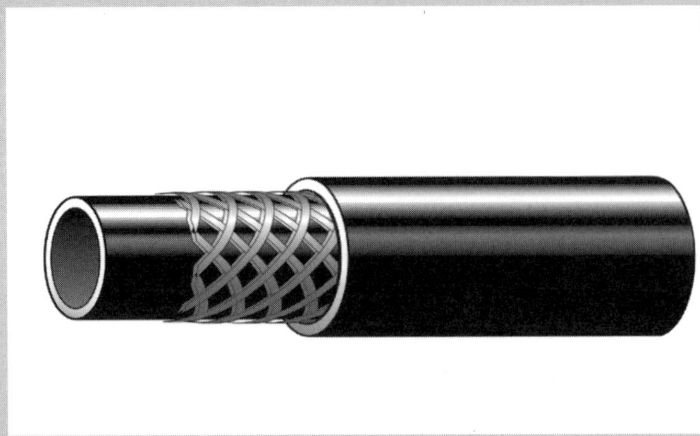

Suitable for gas, oil or water, Super Stock hose uses an internal textile wrap to provide safe use up to 250 psi. Available in sizes 4 though 12 in red, blue or black. Earl's

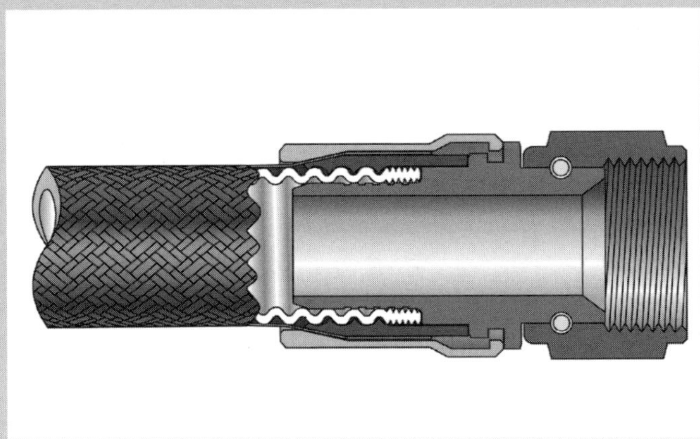

Some hoses use a factory crimped collar to provide the seal between hose and fitting. Earl's

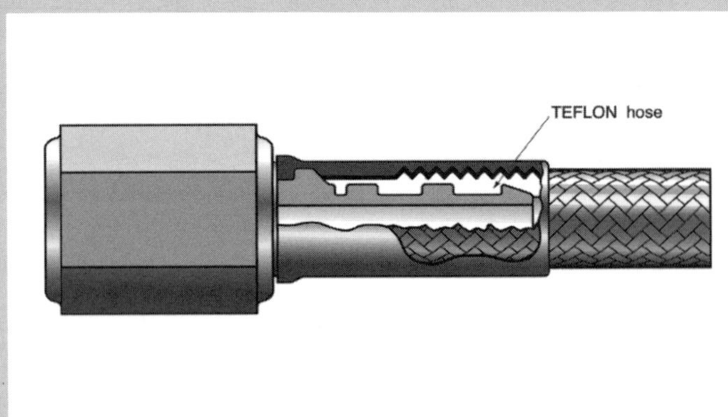

Assembled at the factory, these Speed-Flex hoses use a crimped or swaged fitting. Available with various ends, AN, Metric and assorted banjo fittings. Earl's

Earl's

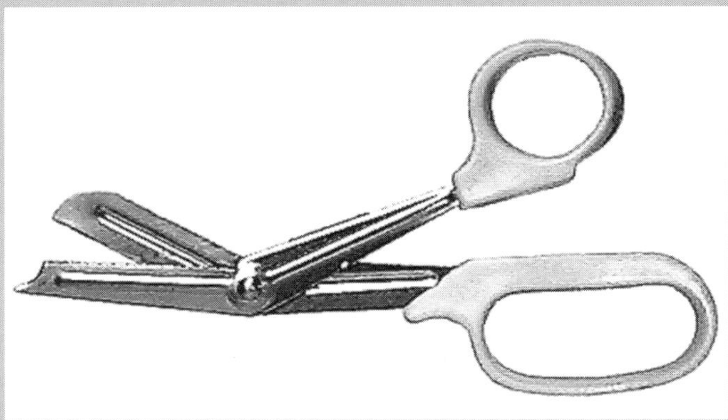

Not just any old scissors, this one is designed to cut through the toughest hose, even the stainless wrapped variety. Earl's

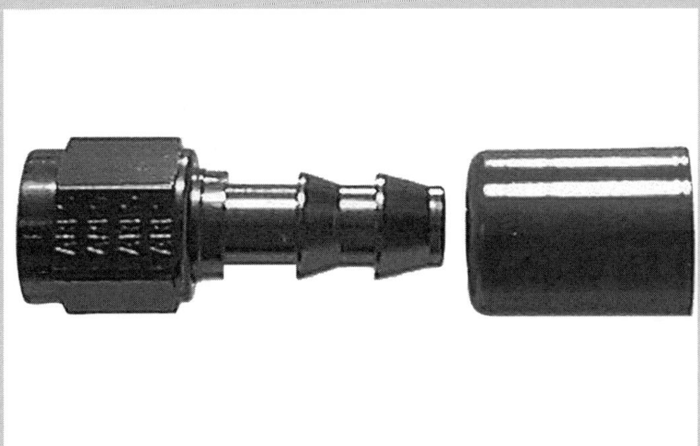

Super Stock hose ends are intended for matching hose, the collar can be crimped for extra insurance, though it isn't necessary. Earl's

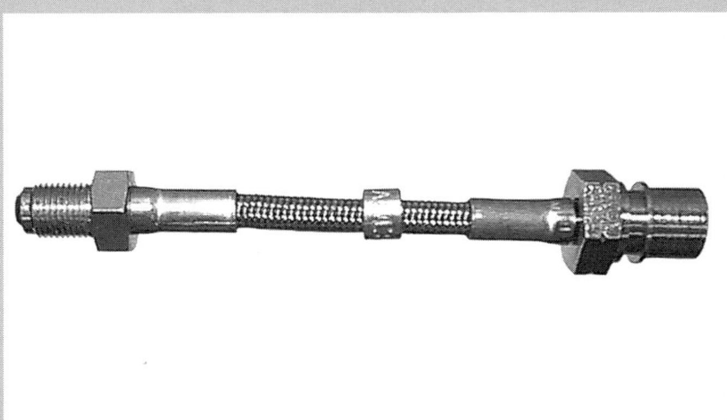

Already assembled hoses like this utilize the Speed-Seal Teflon lined, stainless wrapped, hose with factory installed ends. Earl's

comply with the testing that's done to meet the specifications developed by the D.O.T. We try to recommend that first-time buyers purchase pre-assembled hose. We pressure test all the hoses before they leave our factory, you simply can't test the hose at home.

What kind of mistakes do people make, either in choosing or installing hose and fittings?

There's a lot of stuff. In brake lines they run all braided hose with no hard lines. But the Teflon still expands more than a hard line so you get a really bad pedal. You need to run as much hard line as possible and only use the Teflon-lined hose at the wheels. And where they run stainless tubing straight through the firewall, a grommet isn't good enough. The firewall eventually cuts the grommet and then the hose, they should use a bulkhead fitting instead. Sometimes they stack up 2 or 3 adapters. If they did their research they would find there are a tremendous number of adapters. You can find the right adapter if you look.

What separates Earl's and the Earl's product line from similar companies?

Earl's biggest thing is, in hose, we have a wide range of hoses that other companies might not. We have Super-Stock for example and Pro-Lite and all the rest. We have a tremendous number of adapters and hose ends. In hose ends we do straight and various bends in low profile. In the other lines we have 90, 120, and 150 degree bends.

Our adapter section is a major strong point. We have all the standard adapters plus lots of unusual adapters and some that aren't even in the catalog. We also stock the tools, the AN wrenches and a braid separator for Teflon hose, along with the clamps to keep the hoses out of the way. The other thing is our complete line of coolers and heat exchangers.

Chapter Seven

Chassis Hardware

Beyond Nuts & Bolts

What follows is a discussion of some specialized hardware often used on a hot rod chassis. Though we all like to use high quality parts throughout the chassis, there are also times when a simple bushing works better than a sophisticated rod end.

SPHERICAL ROD ENDS

Like Allen bolts, the term Heim joints is a misnomer. "Heim" is a trade name. More accurately, these specialized supports and pivots are spherical rod ends and like most hardware they

The typical steering shaft uses one or more U-joints and some kind of vibration reducer. With the combination shown here (in polished stainless) you can buy one component that combines the U-joint with the vibration reducer. Borgeson

come in a bewildering array of sizes, styles and quality levels.

The least expensive spherical rod ends, known as economy grade, are usually a two-piece design. The body of the rod end, often aluminum or low-grade steel, is formed around the inner ball. The ball itself may be made from sintered iron instead of true steel. Some use a grease zerk as a means of providing lubrication, though the hole drilled for the zerk weakens the outer assembly. Lubrication may also be provided by an inner ball made from a "permanently lubricated" oil-lite type material.

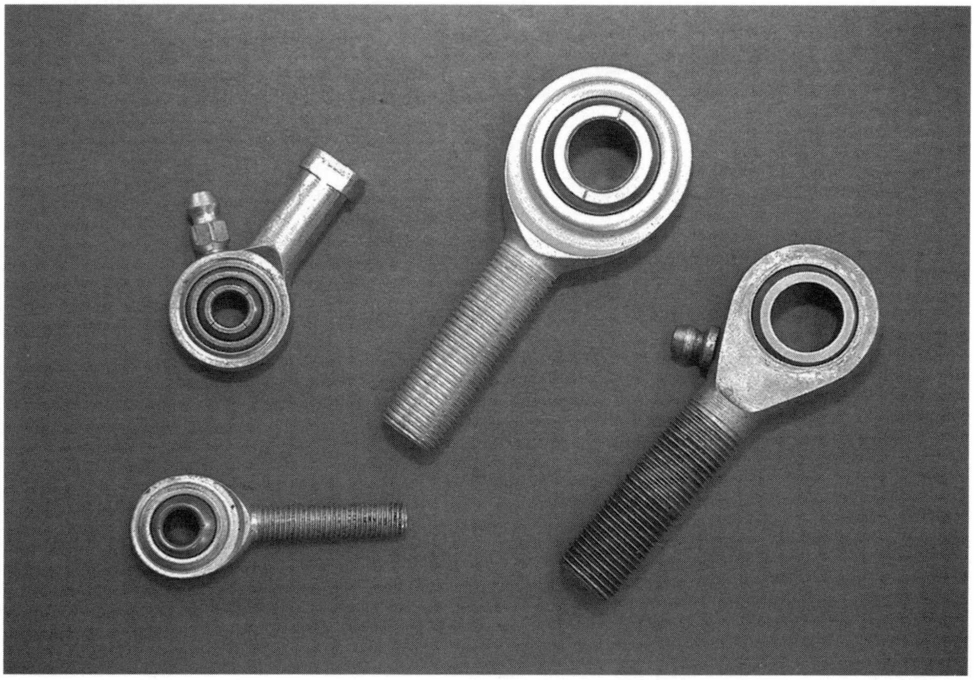

Spherical rod ends come in a vast variety of sizes, with male or female threads, with or without an external means of lubrication.

As the quality level of the rod end increases, two things happen. One, the design changes to a three or possibly four-piece design. (check the illustration here). Second, the quality of the outer housing or lollypop increases. Not only is it a one-piece design, the material is upgraded to a material like 4130 chrome-moly or high-strength stainless steel. At this quality level the threads are rolled with great care, often after heat-treat like a high-quality fastener to increase their fatigue strength. Third, both the race and the ball are manufactured from high-quality heat-treated alloy, never sintered iron.

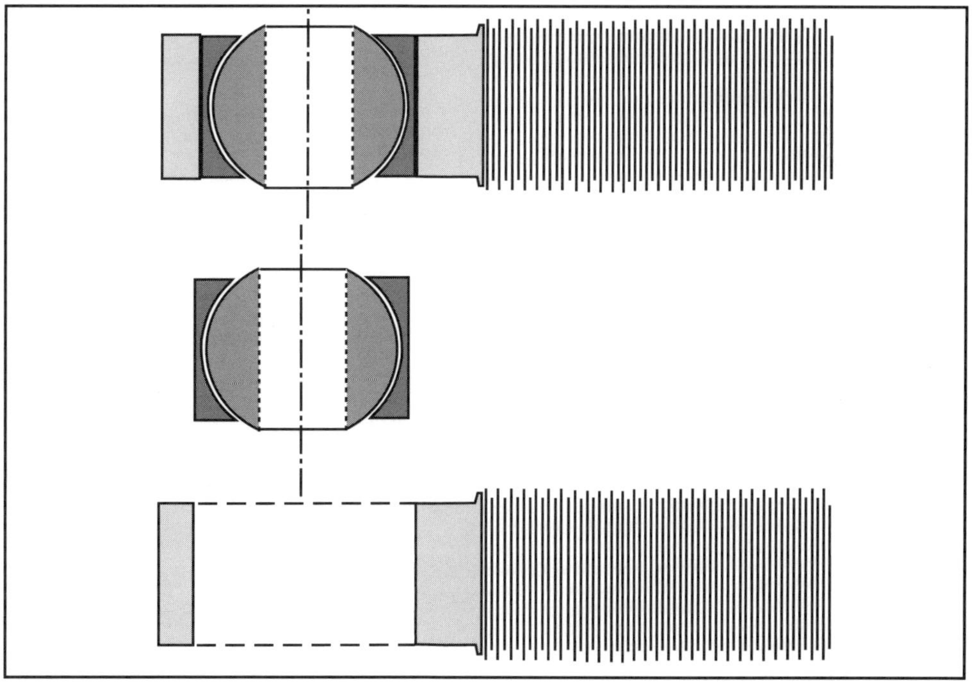

In a three piece rod end the ball is contained in a separate race and the two are then pressed into the outer body or lollipop.

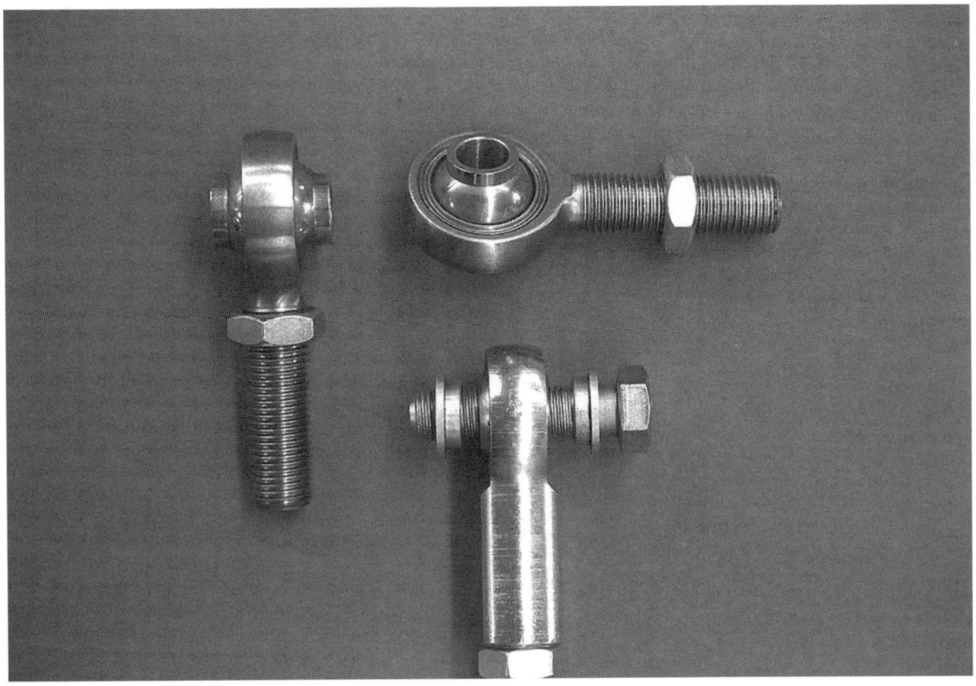

On the top you see two high-misalignment rod ends while below is a rod end with the special spacers or washers that accomplish the same thing.

Lubrication may be provided by a Teflon liner or with a layer of PTFE-impregnated fabric bonded to the inner race. These very high quality rod ends are generally known as "precision" rod ends. Nearly all rod ends are available with male or female threads.

Up to this point rod ends come in standard or nominal sizes. That is, a rod end with a 1/2 inch shank will also have a 1/2 inch hole in the ball. To upgrade further in quality is to move into what the manufacturers call their heavy duty series. The advantage in using a

These are the special "U-joints" that more closely resemble the CV joint in the axle of your front-wheel drive car. Sometimes used by an OEM in the shift linkage, these joints do not have to be kept in phase like conventional U-joints.

heavy duty series spherical rod end is in the sizing. Because of their strength you can use a rod end with a smaller bolt. This means you might run a 3/4 inch shank but only a 1/2 inch fastener through the ball, which leaves everything a bit more petite looking.

The very best spherical rod ends are manufactured to MS specifications. The housings are made from forged alloy with Teflon liners to create a self-lubricating rod end, some of which have "wipers" at the edge of the race to the clean the ball during rotation and prevent dirt from getting inside.

Generally seen on either end of a four-bar linkage, these urethane bushings assemblies can be purchased separately so you can build your own suspension components.

In order to increase the range of motion or degree of misalignment that a rod end can endure, many of the manufacturers make special rod-end spacers. These precise "washers" move the ball farther away from its attachment point thus increasing the clearance between the housing and that attachment point. These are available from Aurora, Baker and others

Most bearing and rod-end manufacturers also make what they call a high-misalignment rod end. These are made with shoulders or washers "built in" on the inner ball, which increases the amount of misalignment the rod end can tolerate before the outer end con-

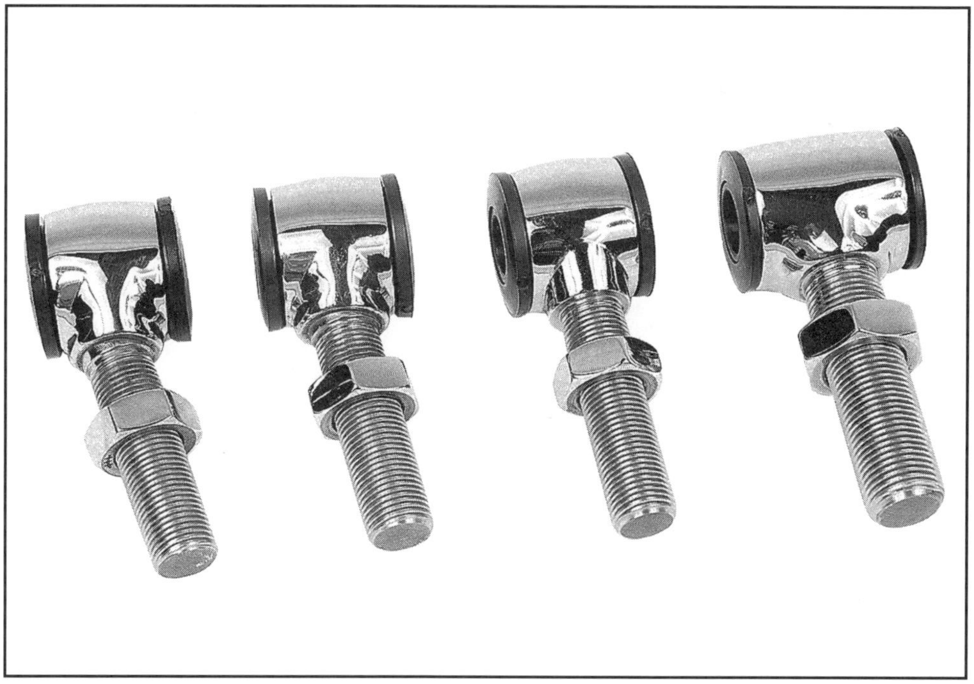

These adjustable rod ends come in stainless steel with urethane bushings. Available in straight with left or right-hand thread, or in 7 or 11 degree angles. Deuce Factory

tacts the mounting bracket. Most rod ends, no matter what the grade, are available with a stud already pressed in place in the inner ball.

When I asked Jim Petrykowski from Metal Fab about spherical rod ends, he warned me about one style of rod end that looks most appealing, yet has no place on a street-driven car. "A number of companies make spherical rod ends from forged aluminum. They're anodized and look great, but these are throw-away parts, meant for race cars. They have no life. They're inexpensive and seem at first to be a really good deal, but they are not meant for the street."

These polished U-bolts are made from 304 stainless and come with nylon-collar type of lock nuts (be sure to use anti seize on the threads). Deuce Factory

Rod ends typically wear out because of dirt that gets between the ball and the outer cage or race that it runs in. The dirt of course acts as an abrasive. Spherical rod ends, especially those used outside the car, should be the high quality ends with Teflon liners fit tight enough that dirt simply can't enter. The greaseable rod ends, though they would seem to be the answer, are in fact weaker and of a lower overall quality, than industrial or heavy duty rod ends with no grease zerk.

Designed to match the U-bolts, spring pads are available in polished stainless, and come in standard height and a raised version. Deuce Factory

What breaks rod ends? A load that's too much for the rod causing the ball to tear out of the housing or an installation with misalignment that exceeds the design parameters of that particular rod end.

"Heim joints" have a wide range of uses, from shift to throttle linkage. The one place they don't belong is on the ends of the four-bar links that hold the solid front axle in place. Though they seem at first a much more precise way to locate the four bars to the axle, there is a problem. The problem is a fact that you only want the axle to move in one plane, up and down. The rod ends, especially when used at both ends of the axle, allow a certain amount of radial movement that you don't want. So skip the overkill and stick with the bushings that came with the four-bar kit.

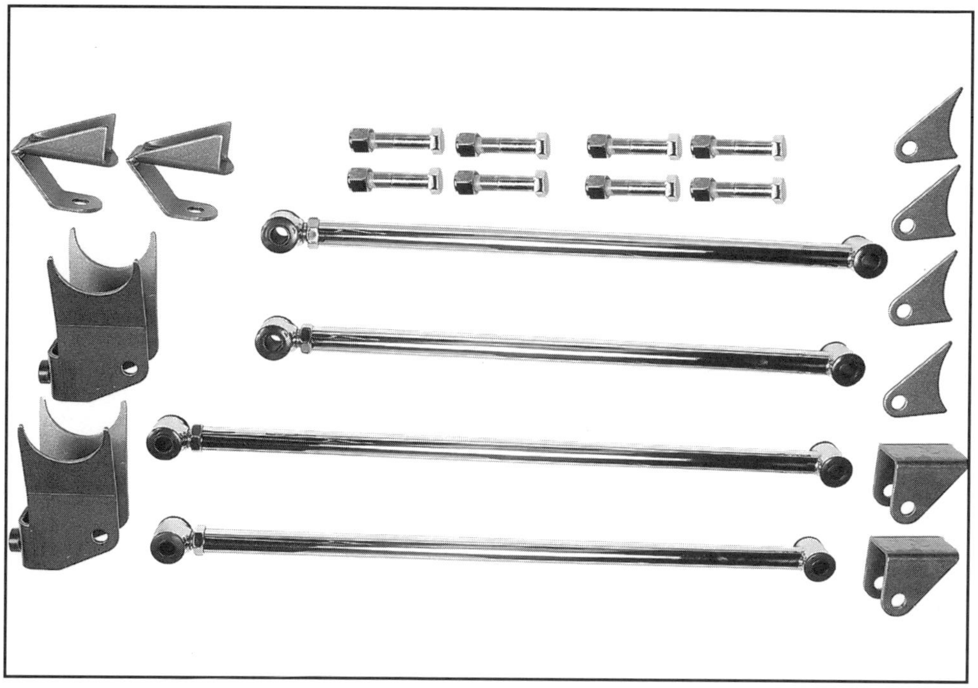

When it comes to four-bar suspension set ups simple rod ends with urethane bushings works better than the more sophisticated spherical rod ends. Deuce Factory

Urethane Bushings

What should be used on the ends of the four bar links are good old urethane bushings. These offer a number of advantages over the seemingly more precise spherical rod ends.

First, the urethane material is impervious to UV rays and grease, and is available in both soft and hard "compounds." This material won't crack and won't dry out. When properly used the life span of a urethane bushing is very long indeed. The

Yes, you can make all your own brackets for that new chassis but why not take the easy way out and use ready-made brackets like these for attaching suspension members and all the rest.

material is so well liked in automotive circles that the aftermarket now offers urethane bushings for more than four bar ends or A-frame bushings. Both body mounting bushings and transmission mounts are now available molded from urethane instead of the more typical rubber or neoprene material.

As already mentioned, at least one street rod supplier warns that urethane bushings and rod ends can't always be swapped.

Seen in the Metal Fab shop, this chassis shows just some of the ways spherical rod ends are employed in a suspension.

By using two spherical rod ends, one male the other female, you can create an adjustable link like this on the sway bar.

Chassis Engineering warns their customers that four-bar installations should use urethane bushings (like the ones that come with most four-bar kits) and not spherical rod ends.

U-Joints

The U-joints in a steering shaft, used to connect the steering column with the steering box, must be of high enough quality to do the job for years and years.

Though the U-joints offered for sale by well-known companies like Borgeson are of a quality level that's easily good enough for automotive use, there are joints on the market meant for industrial and not automotive use. Sometimes these do find their way under the hood of our hot rods.

If you look in a catalog of U-joints the least expensive models are the simple block and pin designs. These open, flexible joints have no needle bearings and are meant for fractional horsepower connections. Little better than a U-joint from your socket set, these u-joints have no longevity, no corrosion resistance and are defi-

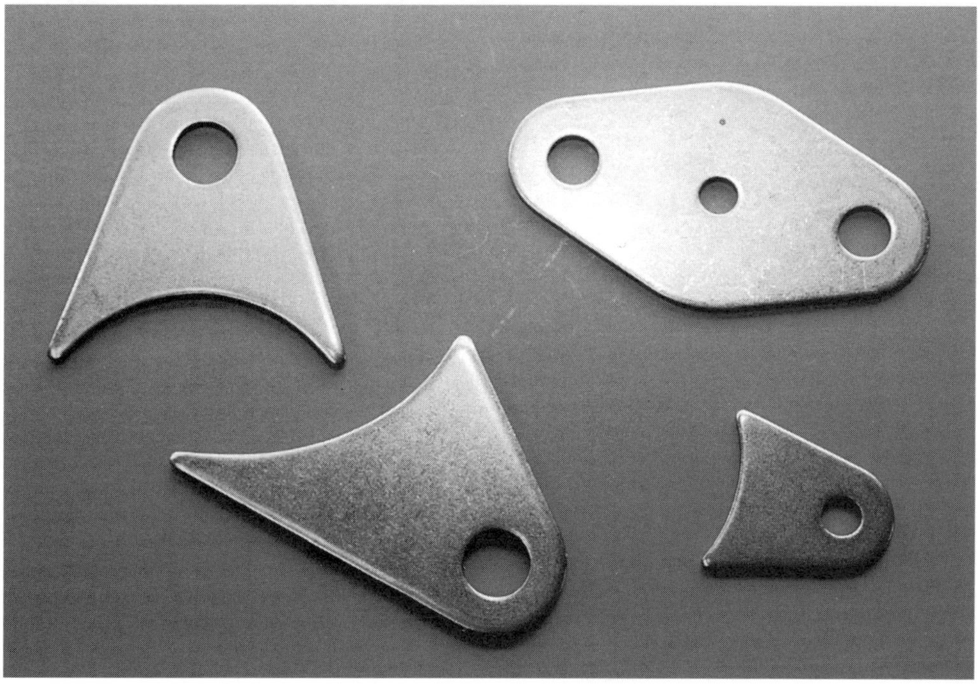

Ready-made tabs like these come in handy as mounts for suspension members or to create a flange that can be unbolted for maintenance.

nitely not strong enough for automotive use.

Next up in quality are the universal-joints made either as a screw machine product or a forged assembly. The better ones have needles and cups like those used in the driveshaft of your hot rod. These latter needle bearing joints are definitely good enough for automotive use. These joints, available from hot-rod suppliers like Borgeson and Flaming River, or industrial companies like Sweet's, are available in

The upper shock mount you use on that street rod doesn't have to be an ugly utilitarian bracket. These upper mounts from SO-CAL Speed shop are a perfect blend of form and function.

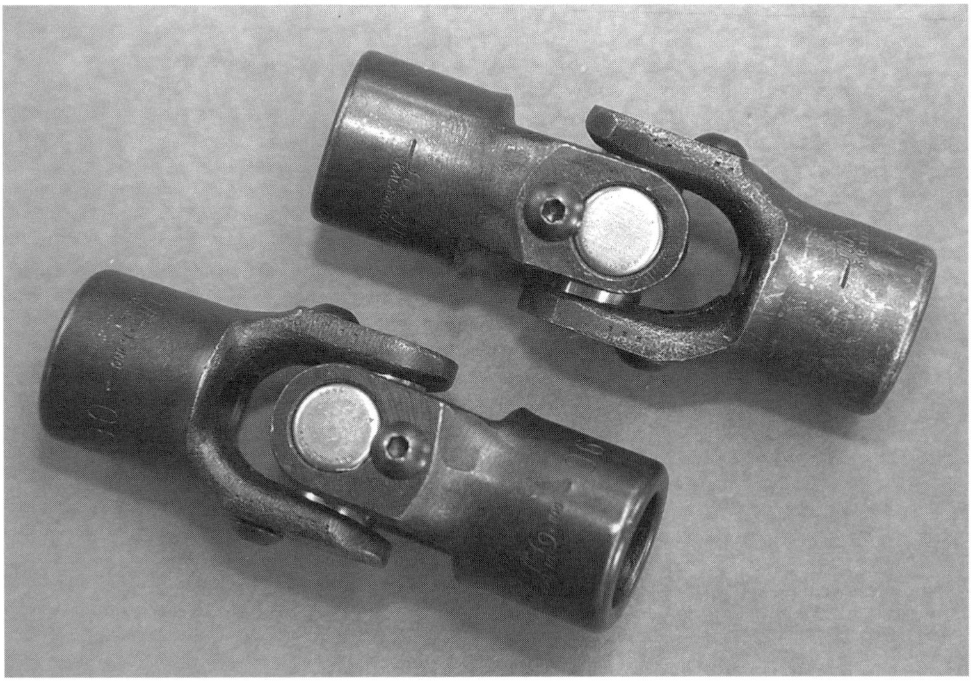

These high-quality U-joints from Sweet's use needle bearing cross shafts and forged yokes.

standard sizes with or without splined yokes.

Though seldom seen on hot rods there are some very precise universal joints available that are good enough for automotive use. These small units are more like a mini CV joint than a typical U-joint. In addition to their small size they offer one additional advantage, they don't need to be phased like a standard U-joint.

Before installing the steering shaft remember that the U joints must be kept in phase (see the illustration). Borgeson recommends that their single joints not be used at an angle of more then 35 degrees. Column support is critical as well. "You need good support on both ends of the steering column," suggests Jim Petrykowski. "And where the steering shaft connects to the rack there can't be any slop or side play."

Like all good U-joints, this 16 series item uses needle bearings. Unlike most U-joints, this one is made from stainless steel, polished to a bright shine. Borgeson

Too often, hot rod builders install the engine and exhaust, and leave installation of the steering column, shaft and gear for last. As mentioned by Alan Zordan from Borgeson, the best installations are the simple ones. Yes, you can use six U-joints, but does that make a better system?

Take time to mock up the engine in the frame. Install the body if possible, and then consider where the driver is going to sit and where that puts the column. In the case of a worm-style gear, the exhaust headers or manifold are often pretty close to the gear, whether it's power steering or not. You probably want to clamp or tack-weld the mounting plate for the steering gear to the frame, in what seems like the most logical location. Then install the engine and check the clearance between the shaft and gear, and the engine, mount and exhaust.

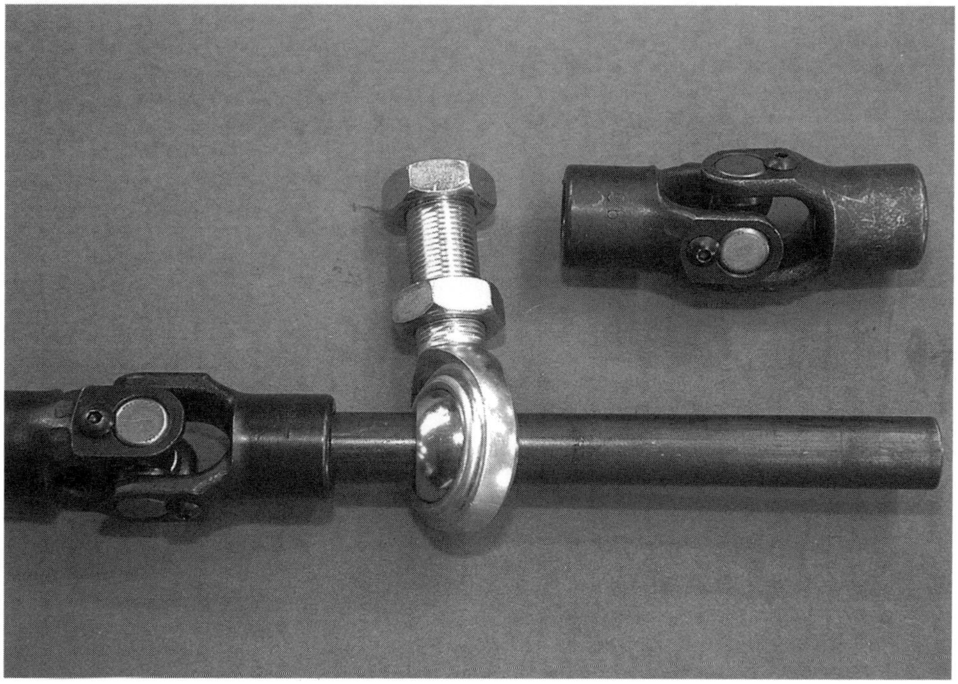

The use of a steering shaft with more than two U-joints requires a support bearing (see the interview in this chapter), a good use for a spherical rod end.

Unless the car is a bucket T, mount the column high enough where it goes through the firewall that it doesn't get in the way when the driver moves his or her feet from the gas to the brake pedal. Make sure the column and steering wheel are in a logical and comfortable spot for the driver.

Remember that it's often easier to find a different type of header or manifold than it is to build a steering shaft with multiple U-joints. Care in the planning and mock up of the chassis are the keys to designing and installing a safe, simple steering column and shaft.

Interview: Alan Zordan from Borgeson

When it comes to hot rods and steering shaft components, the best known name is Borgeson. Not only

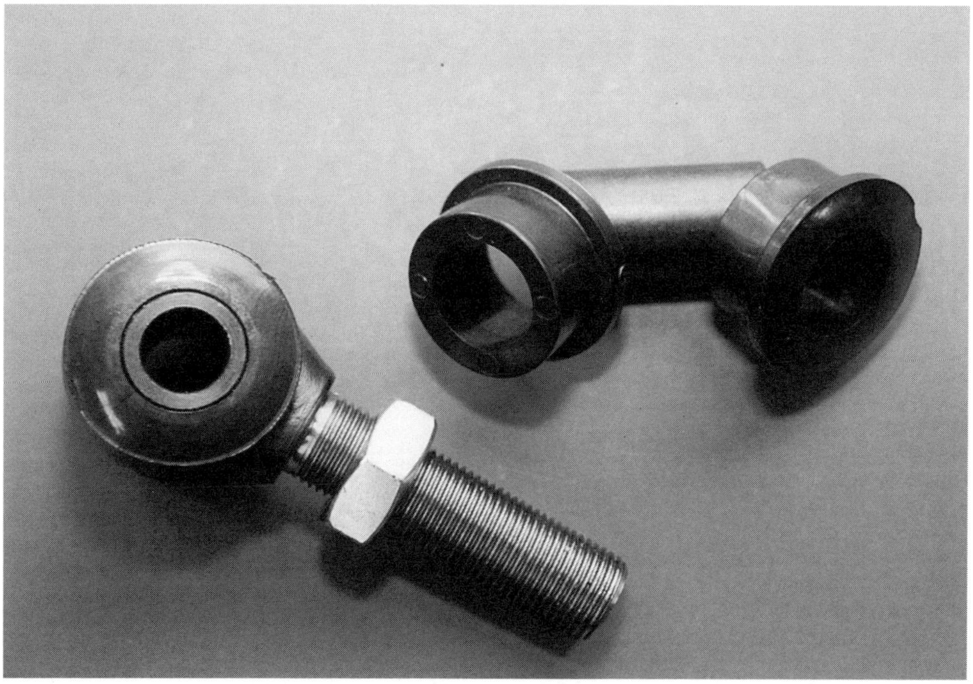

The urethane bushings commonly used on the ends of a four-bar link are available in different sizes and can often be used to manufacture other components - like heavy duty motormounts.

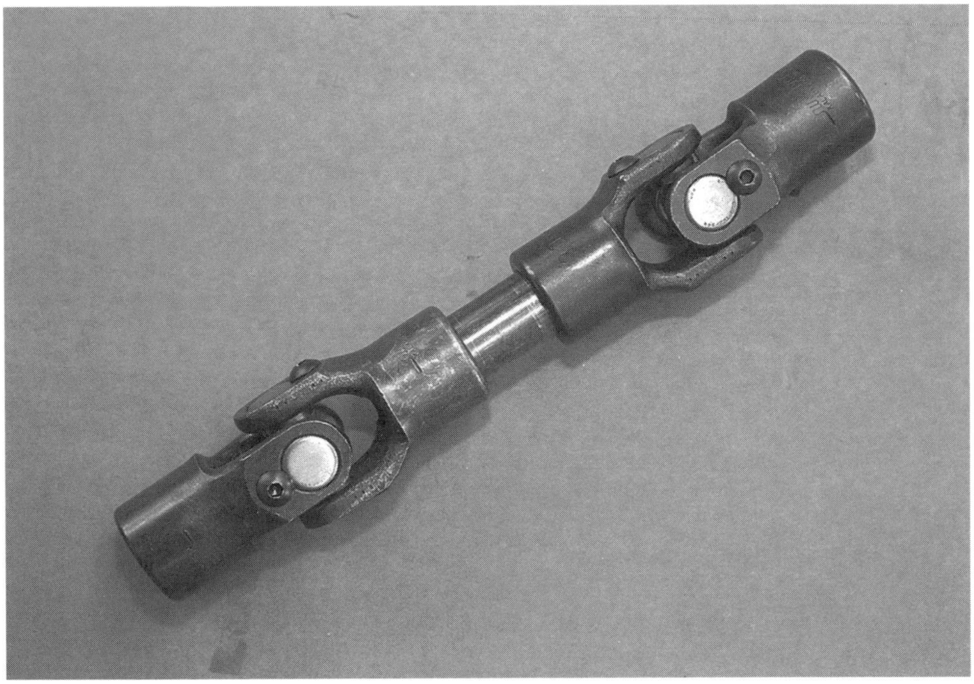

When two or more U-joints share a common shaft they must be kept in phase - check out the joints on the driveshaft some time.

do they make the majority of U-joints seen in hot rods and street rod steering systems, they attend booths at most of the major shows. This provides them an opportunity to listen to their customers, and examine some of the installation work being done by your average hot rodder.

For a little insight into the inner workings at Borgeson, and the right and wrong way to install a steering shaft, we spoke with Alan Zordan. Alan is a fifteen year employee of Borgeson and currently serves as vice president.

Alan: Can you give us a little background on Borgeson?

We've been manufacturing U-joints for automotive applications since 1914. We've manufactured U-joints in some early Ford concept cars, military vehicles, even electric vehicles. If it has to do with steering we've done it.

What makes a good U-joint from a steering standpoint?

There are two things that need to be examined. The first is strength, if it's not strong enough you shouldn't put it into your car. The second thing is the type of U-joint. You need a needle-bearing U-joint. There are other types, which for street applications are not a good choice, like some of the U-joints made for race cars,

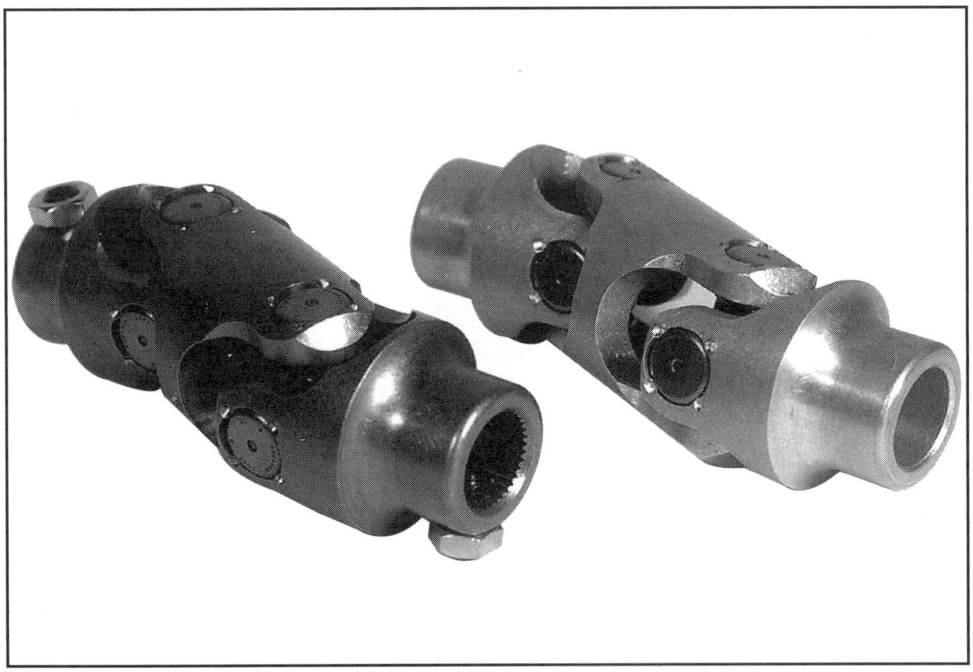

These double U-joints allow the shaft to turn a much steeper angle than a single joint, as much as 70 degrees. They are, however, two U-joints meaning a support bearing must be used if a double joint is combined with a single joint on the same shaft.

What about aluminum and stainless steel U-joints?

We've been manufacturing stainless steel U-joints for 60 years, mainly for cosmetic purposes. If the car owner has stainless accessories in the engine compartment we can match it with stainless joints and shafts.

The aluminum U-joints are a product we've made for 12 years, primarily for the competition market. We've recently redesigned these aluminum joints so they are stronger and now we can sell them for the street. We've done it so the owner can use them to match the billet parts under the hood. Our aluminum joints are made from aircraft grade material and tested at over 150% of the OEM standard.

When do you like to see people use collapsible shafts?

If you have a two-joint system, the two joints will act as a collapsible system in an accident. Where the shaft only uses a single joint or if it's a straight shaft, then, you should use a collapsible shaft. If you're using a column from a late model car, many of those are collapsible, so you can take care of the problem that way.

This 8000 series U-joint uses needle bearings and steel yokes to ensure long life and smooth operation at angles up to 35 degrees. Borgeson

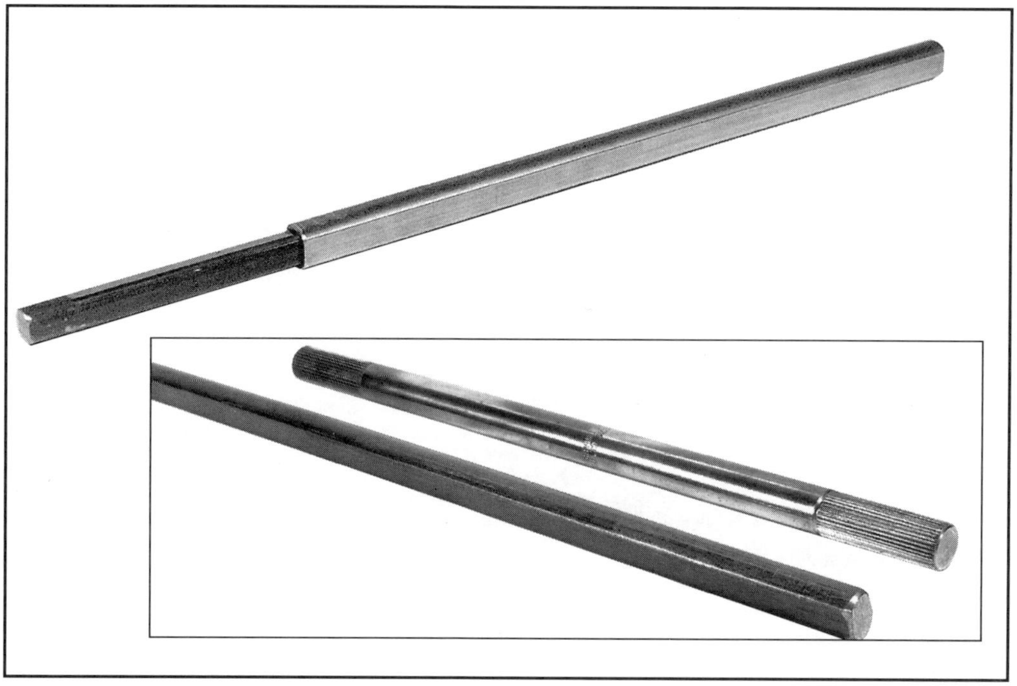

Ready-made steering shafts come in a number of different styles, including telescoping for safely, and ends. Borgeson

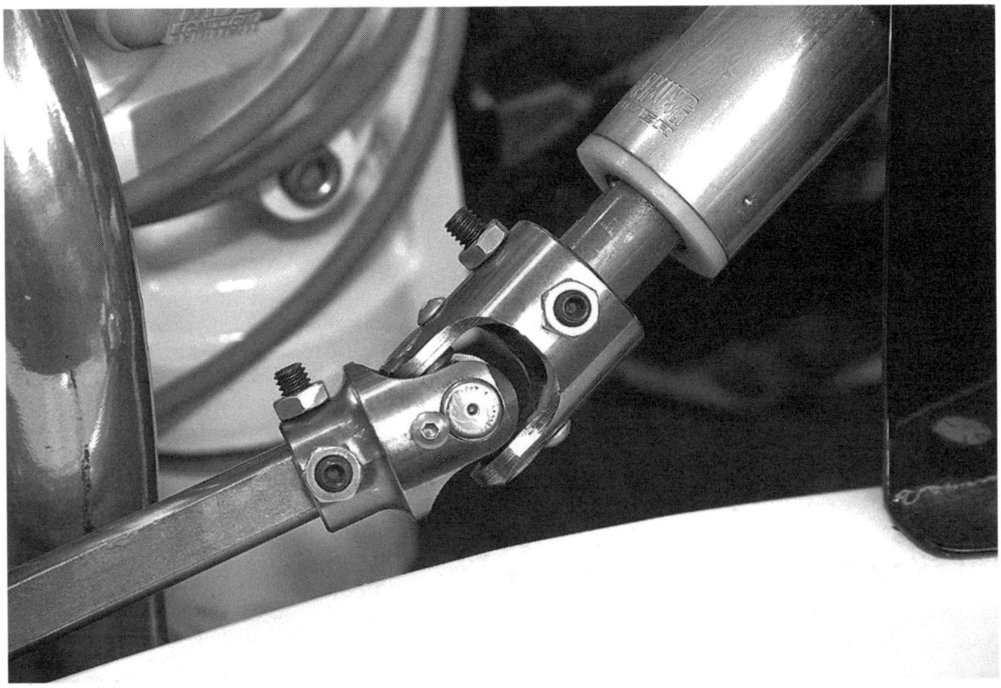

The ideal is to design a steering shaft that needs a minimum number of joints, each one operating at as shallow an angle as possible.

How about some guiding principles for the layout of the shaft, column and steering gear?

Keep it as simple as possible, you can use as many U-joints as necessary, but for cost and design purposes, you should try to use only two or three. You need careful planning to figure out where they need to go.

When is a support bearing needed and where should they be positioned?

A support bearing is needed for every U-joint over two. A system with three joints needs one support. A system with four joints needs two supports. On a three-joint system the support should be as close to the center joint as possible though it can be on the upper or lower shaft.

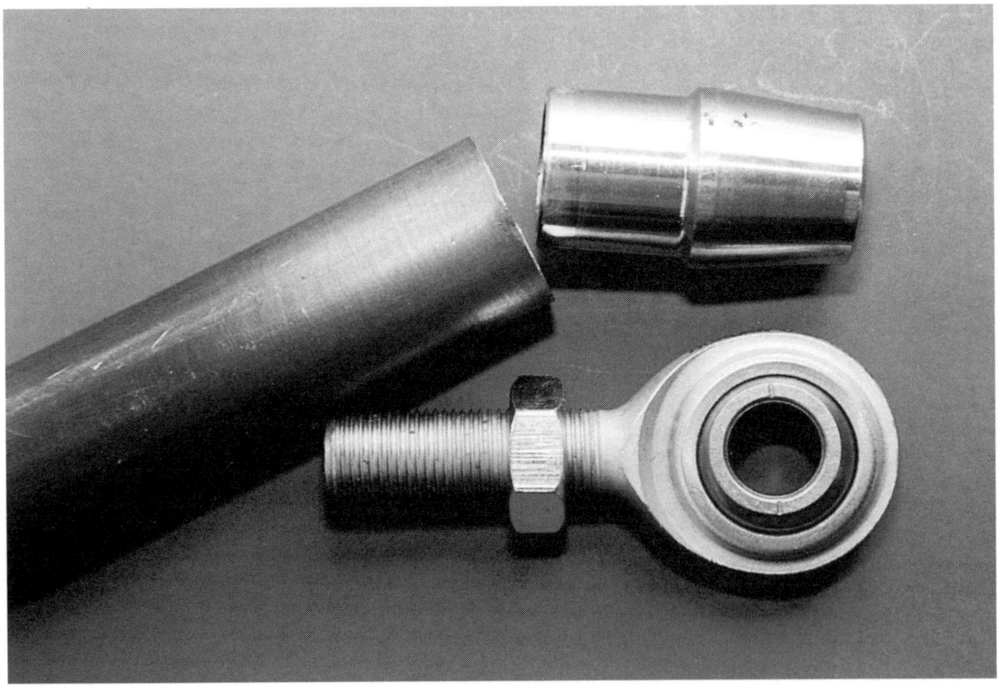

Call them accessories to go along with a spherical rod end. The tubing end seen in the upper right is tapped to accept the male threads on the rod end, and necked down to slide into a common size of steel tubing.

What are the biggest mistakes people make when they design and install the steering shaft?

The two biggest mistakes are: Using an improper U-joint. We've seen everything from a 1/2 inch drive u-joint out of the Craftsman tool kit, to small military joints that were not designed for steering.

The other big mistake is poor welds. Many people still weld the steering together and a lot of those are backyard welders. They don't know what they're doing,

These compact vibration reducers are a good way to isolate the steering wheel from the noise and harshness of the road. Borgeson

difference between a straight u-joint and one with a built in vibration damper.

The dampers themselves are made up of two separate pieces of metal encased in urethane. There's a steel safety pin, so even without the urethane you would still be able to steer the car.

they end up with stress cracks in the steering components and if any of those components break later they're going to have an accident. The other problem with welding is heat, they can cook the joint with too much heat. We tell them to weld small sections at a time, and use a damp rag around the joint to dissipate the heat.

Do you prefer non-welded steering systems?

Yes we do. You avoid the problems that come with heat and poor welds, and the system is easier to disassemble if you need to do any service or make any changes to the steering.

Alan, do you have any final comments or suggestions?

At the shows we get questions about vibration dampers. The OEM manufacturers have used them since the 1970s. They reduce driver fatigue by reducing vibration. This is especially important when you consider that low-profile tires absorb less vibration. The other factor is rack and pinion steering, which is more sensitive and transmits more vibration to the steering wheel. For the minor cost difference, we recommend putting one in. There's only a 30 dollar

Alan Zordan from Borgeson is a man who's seen the good the bad and the ugly of steering systems. His recommendation, use good components and keep the system as simple as possible.

Chapter Eight

Body Hardware

Hinges & Latches

When it comes to door latches, many builders are all too eager to throw the stock latches in the trash can and start over with something "better" from the aftermarket. In reality, many of the original latches, even some of the older ones, are just as good as the new ones from the aftermarket.

At least one big California shop, SO-CAL, reports that they almost always use the original latches. To quote Shane Weckerly from the SO-

Body hardware includes much of what you can and can't see on the car, and how it all goes together. These very important parts include the trunk, hood and door hinges (visible or not) and all the latches.

What we call a bear claw is a rotary design door latch with two positions. The good ones meet DOT specifications.

want to avoid is the cheap latches meant for tool boxes or trailer doors. The quality aftermarket latches are DOT approved, are spring loaded and use heat treated components. This is another of those instances where you don't want to buy the cheap stuff.

What we call "bear claw" latches come in more than one size. As Don from Don's Hot Rods explains, "there are differences in sizes and

CAL speed shop: "Almost all of our cars use stock OEM factory door latches. There are a couple of exceptions, ... when the original design isn't very good. But all of our '40 Fords and Deuces use Ford latches. The stock '32 latch works good, especially when we tweak them so they're properly adjusted and lubricated. When we first fit up the car, we take the time to make sure the door fits correctly and we stiffen up the pillars, so the door jamb doesn't just bend in when you close the door."

At Metal Fab in Minneapolis, Jim Petrykowski feels the same. "The OEM stuff is usually pretty good. If you want something newer and smaller, steal the latches from a late-model Honda or something. They're very small and very strong. After all, those cars have passed all the Federal crash tests. Because they're so small, some of these OEM designs work well for updating the trunk latch too."

Good latches are rotary designs, the latch rotates as it grabs hold of the pin. Any good latch will have the two-click, or two-step latch mechanism we're all familiar with. What you

One of the keys to a door that closes properly is body support. Here we see a Model A body about to be reinforced with metal tubing, though original-style wood kits are also available.

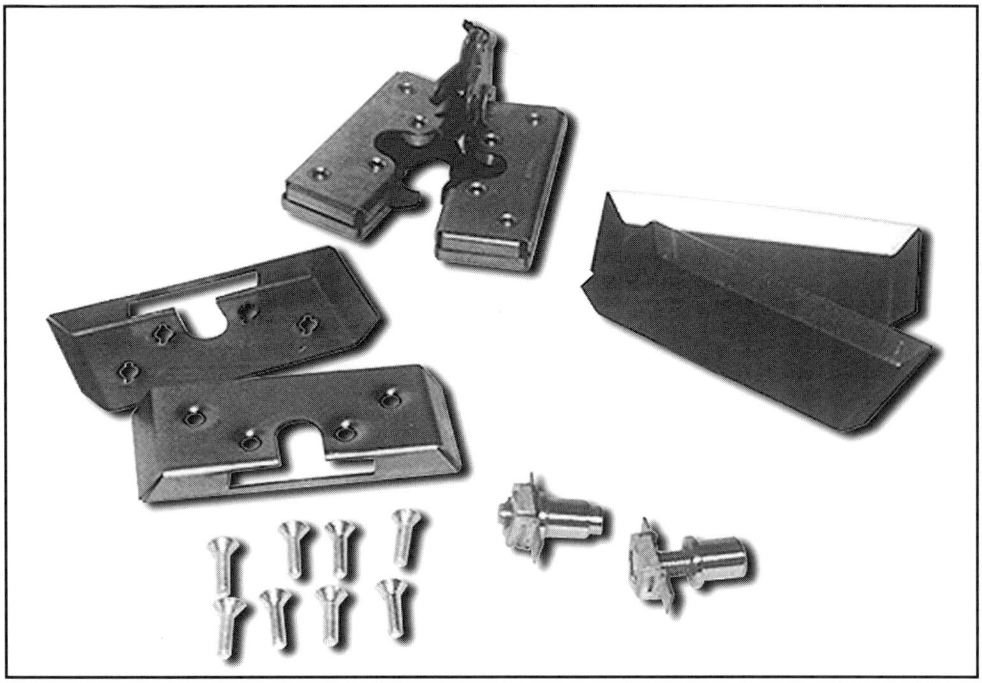

These bear-claw kits feature a true two position latch, with stainless striker pins and latch covers for a neat installation. Don's Hot Rods

configurations. Some are smaller and mount with three bolts while most are larger than that and mount with four bolts. We try to always use the bigger four-bolt bear claw latches though sometimes in Deuce and Model A roadsters you have to use the smaller latches."

Don explains that the trouble people sometimes have with latch installation is really a matter of putting "the cart ahead of the horse." "They get in a hurry and put latches in before they have the door totally aligned. Then later the latches don't line up properly because they've changed the way the door fits and that affects the latch. In our shop, before we do latches, we have the door totally aligned with the floor pans in and the car sitting just the way it will when it's finished."

When it comes to electrifying the door latches you can buy kits from about a hundred different suppliers. The main difference is in the type of solenoid these kits use. While some are true solenoids, like the one that engages the drive on the starter, some are actually screw motors. To quote Don again, "Some of the solenoids are better than others, they resist vibration better. But when we can we like to use the screw motors, we

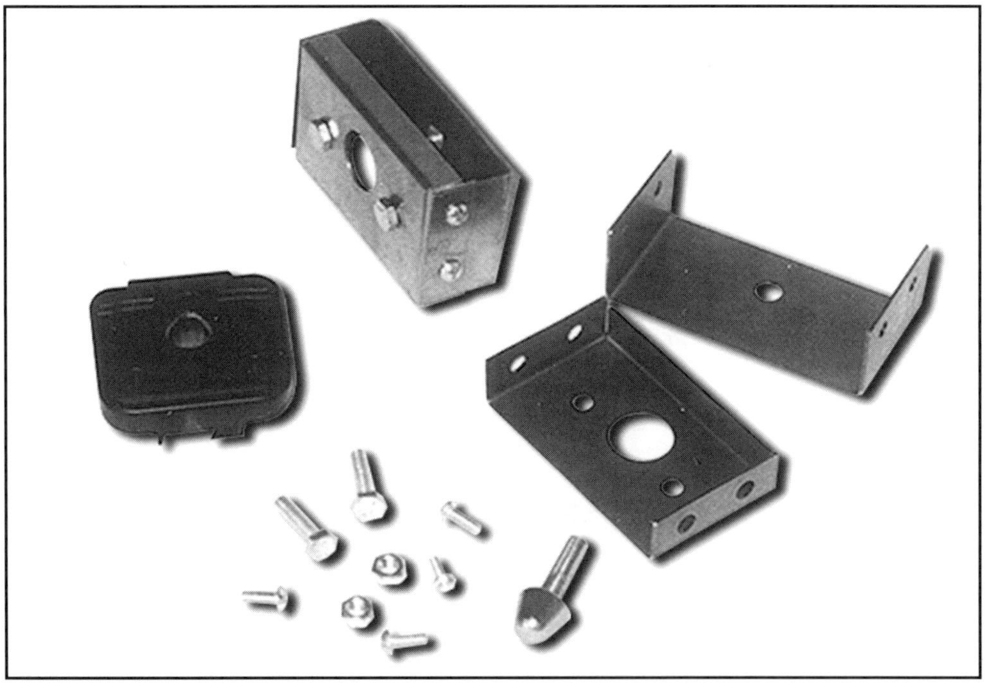

This hood pin and latch comes in kit form for installation into nearly any car. Don's Hot Rods

like those better than the solenoids."

Hood and deck lid latch kits are available as well. Many, like those from Don's Hot Rods, can be ordered with built in solenoids. Some come with a cable for easy installation of the inside release handle.

Hinges

When it comes to hinges, door hinges in particular, there is again nothing wrong with the original hinges that came with the car. Worn hinges can often be swapped for new OEM-style hinges available for many of the popular cars. Or the mechanically inclined can have the worn hinges reamed slightly and a new oversize pin installed. For better visuals, stainless steel pins are available for many hinges from companies like The Deuce Factory.

The trouble with the original hinges is their obviousness. Many of us want our cars smooth and that includes elimination of the door hinges. Some Model As allow the owner to eliminate one of the three hinges while still maintaining a solid two-hinge support system. But to eliminate the hinges altogether requires a move to the proverbial hidden hinge.

Most cars that have been converted to hidden hinges use a hinge assembly borrowed from another

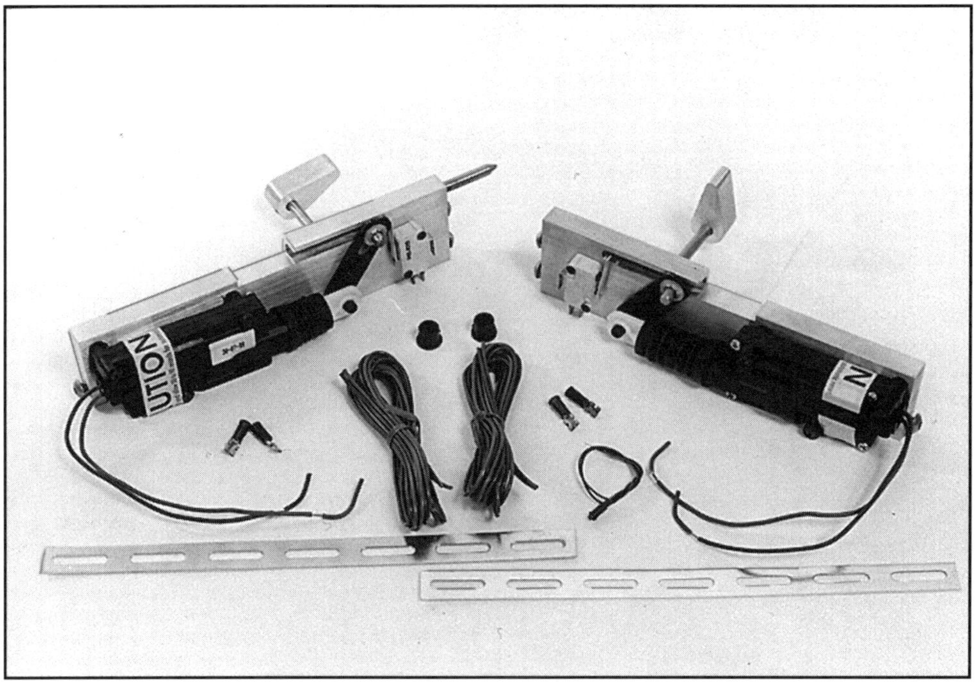

Extra security, especially for suicide doors, is provided by these power door locks. Rock Hinge Company

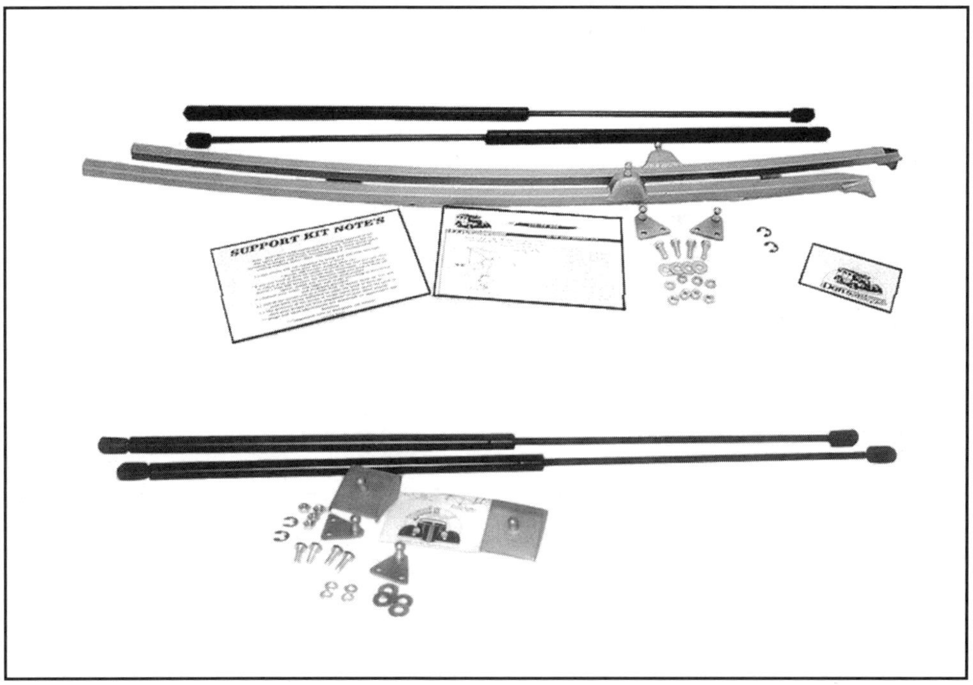

Designed for certain fat Fords, these hood support kits include two gas shocks and the necessary brackets. Similar kits are available for many deck lids. Don's Hot Rods

These hidden hinge kits feature a one-piece swingarm with a 3/8 inch pivot welded to 1 inch square tubing for a design that's simple and strong. Rocky Hinge Co.

application, or perhaps fabricated from scratch by the enterprising builder. The move to hidden hinges is often part of the larger plan to convert the doors to "suicide" operation. As in all other parts of the hot rodding game, a number of firms now offer hidden hinge kits and many of these can also be used to convert to reverse opening.

Rocky Hinge Company manufactures a hidden hinge assembly that can be used to suicide the doors at the same time. "The main thing is to get that hinge out against the outer skin as far as

Seen at the Metal Fab shop, this Model A was converted from a three to a two-hinge door at the same time the top was chopped.

possible," explains Rocky, "so the door will swing out without hitting anything." A number of firms make hinges for specific models, like Lobeck's V-8 Shop with hidden hinges for the '32 and '34 Ford.

Like doors, trunk and deck-lid hinges are fast being converted to hidden and smoother operation with assemblies provided by the aftermarket. While many are built for a specific application, there are just as many designed to fit a variety of vehicles.

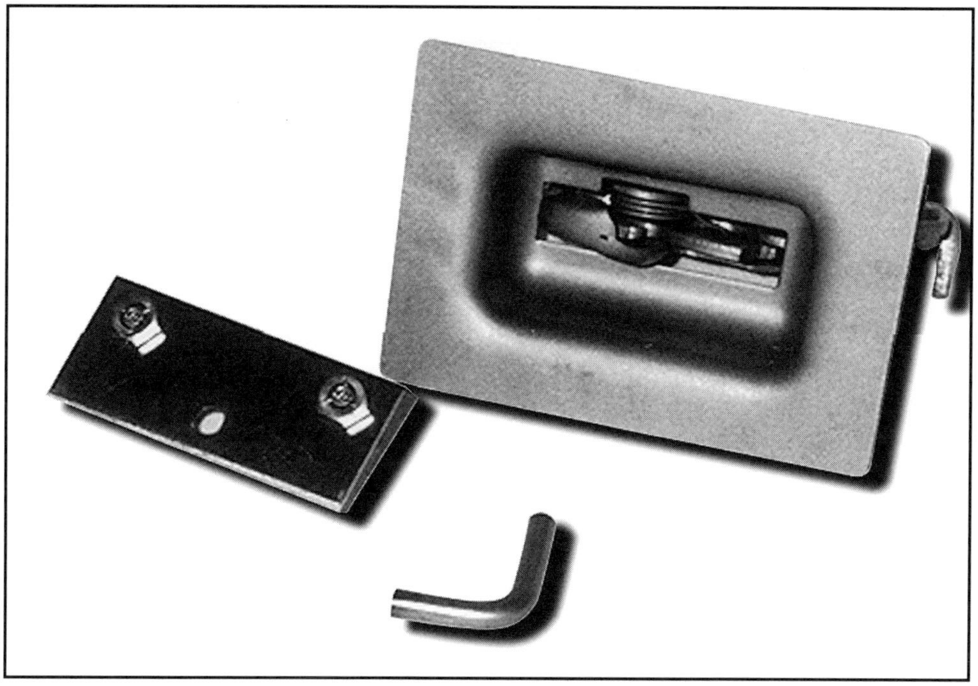

Designed to fit a wide range of cars, this universal latch kit can be used in mechanical or electric modes. Don's Hot Rods

THREE-PIECE HOODS

If there's one piece of hinge and/or body hardware that's not common in the aftermarket it's hinges and latches designed for a three piece hood. Dan Fink Metalworks makes two hood hinge and latch kits for three piece hoods. One allows single opening from one side only while the more deluxe kit allows the owner to open the hood from either side.

They say a picture is worth a thousand words, so we've included part of a hood installation story, using Dan Fink hinges and latches, that ran originally in *Street Rod Builder*. We are grateful to John Dianna and Buckaroo Publications for the use of this material.

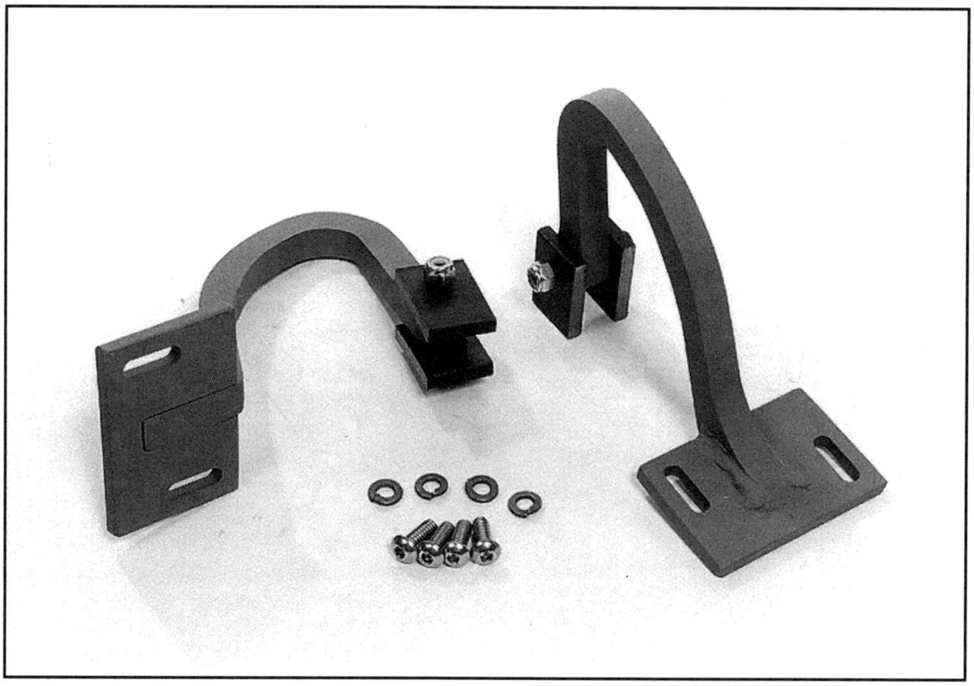

Don't like the trunk hinges that came with the car? Try these steel hinges from Rocky Hinge Company

Install A Three-Piece Hood & Hinge

Reproduced with permission of Buckaroo Communications. Written by Stephen K. Anderson, photography by Scott Kileen

With so many different rodding companies creating various components these days, it seems there is something for every market; all but one, that is! While you can buy a great variety of bodies from several sources, nobody has you covered with a hood. After all, just as each body and grille shell differs, so to do the hoods that span the distance between them.

As the challenge of bridging this gap has been baffling rod builders for many years, we thought we would bring you some insight into how a high-quality hood is created.

To assist us through the twists and turns of this process, we look to the considerable talents of Jack Hagemann. As one of the nations top aluminum fabricators for many years, Hagemann has refined his own method of building hoods, and he'll pass it on to you.

While you might not have all of the tools seen here, know that you can achieve the same results with simple hand tools. All it takes it patience in learning what Hagemann has been perfecting for his entire career. Still, you can do it, if you remember that failure is often part of the learning process, and that in the end, you will succeed in the hood!

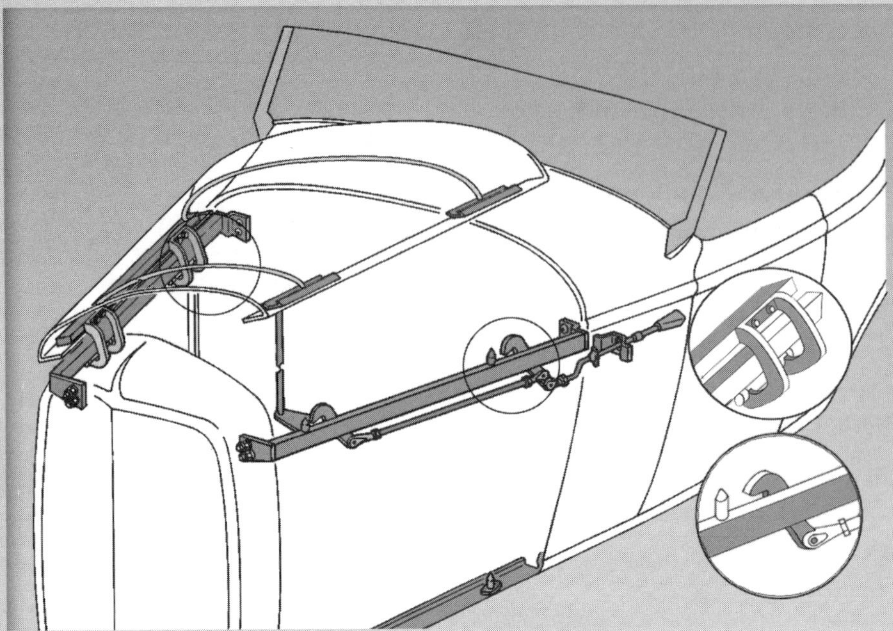

D.F. Metal works manufactures both a single and double-opening hood hinge and latch kit. Shown is a diagram of the single opening kit. D.F. Metalworks

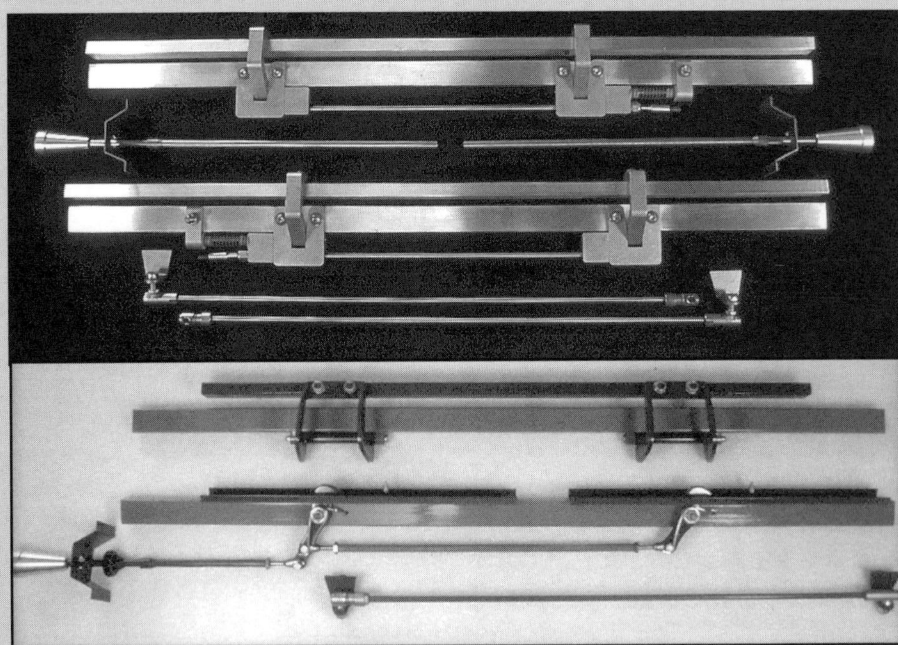

Seen here are the two kits laid out. The single opening kit is the one used in the following photo sequence. D.F. Metalworks

Install A Three-Piece Hood & Hinge

Before you install the hinges you first need a hood. Here Jack Hagemann makes a cardboard pattern of the hood. SRB

Midway through the hood forming operation Jack checks the fit of the new aluminum hood. SRB

At this point a Dan Fink Metalworks hinge kit was used to attach the hood. First the hood is clamped to the upper supports so the mounting locations can be determined. SRB

Everything must be done in sequence. After the basic shape is formed, the reveals must be added, then the flanges that mount the hood hinge and latch are folded in, followed by a little fine adjustment. SRB

Install A Three-Piece Hood & Hinges

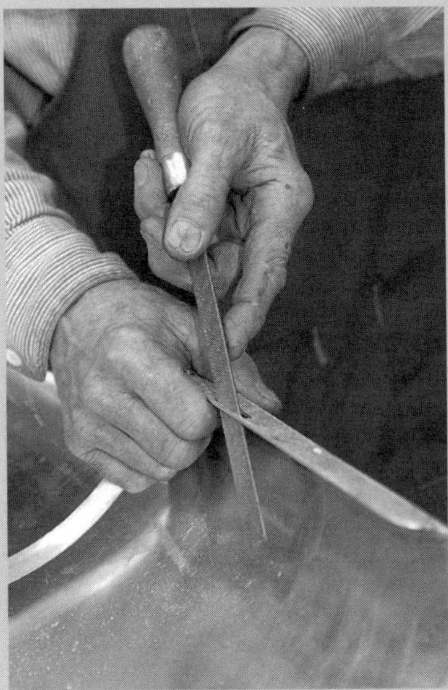

The slots have been cut for the hood latch and then filed for a clean fit. SRB

Once the mounting points have been determined for the hinge assembly, holes can be drilled for the six mounting screws. SRB

You can build your own hood braces like these or purchase similar versions from Dan Fink. Keep in mind that the braces are important for good hinge and latch operation. SRB

Essentially finished, Jack works on the fit of the side panels. Note the hinge assembly on the right side and the latch plate on the hood's left side. SRB

A Few Common Mistakes

When it comes to nuts, bolts and fasteners there are a few things that you should never do. Some of these tips might be common sense and general knowledge. Others, however, are more obscure and certainly not well-enough known. If you're like me, at least some of this information is new despite the fact that you've been hangin' around cars and bikes for more years than you care to admit. Though smaller in number, there are likewise a few issues that surround the use of plumbing equipment and supplies. Though the list is shorter there are a few things here that all of us should know.

Things you should never do to a bolt or hose.

Cut more threads onto the unthreaded part of the shank.

Why? Because you will "undo" the careful way the manufacturer blended the threads as they meet the shank. As mentioned, the manufacturer did it that way to avoid creating stress risers, which is exactly what those new threads are.

Use a fully threaded bolt or capscrew in a shear application.

Why? Because the load should be supported by the shank, the part of the capscrew that has no threads. This shank should have an O.D. large enough that there isn't excessive play between the shank and the load. The fully threaded bolt has too small an O.D. and has a surface that's hardly conducive to the support of the load. There may be situations where you have to order an airframe bolt in order to get exactly the right amount of unthreaded shank relative to the bolt's overall size.

Use a stainless steel or chrome bolt, especially when it's screwed into a nut of the same material, without anti-seize or Loctite.

Why? Because in the case of the stainless, the nut and bolt have an affinity for each other and are sure to gall. In the case of the chrome bolt, the chrome can flake off and make disassembly very difficult.

Install a stud tighter than finger tight.

Why? Because the threads don't run straight and true all the way to the bottom of the tapped hole. When you crank the stud down into the hole you put all the load on one or two bottom threads. Instead put the stud in finger tight. Some mechanics drop a small ball bearing down into the hole and screw the stud in until it contacts the bearing. Use Loctite to keep the stud in place.

Install the nut on the bolt or capscrew in such a way that there is more than two threads, or none at all, showing past the end of the nut.

Why? To get "full engagement" and full strength from a nut and bolt combination you need about one and a half threads showing past the end of the nut (opinions vary slightly here). Less than that and you give up strength, more and you've got a sloppy installation.

Mate an AN 37 degree fitting with a 45 degree American OEM-style fitting.

Why? Well, I wouldn't have included this again accept that people in the field tell me this happens all the time……

Install a hose like a radiator hose on a beaded connection with the clamp up against the very end of the hose.

Why? Because hoses can "cold flow" or slide out from under a clamp. The way to ensure this can't happed to you is by positioning the clamp one-clamp-width back from the end of the hose.

More Great Books From Wolfgang Publications!

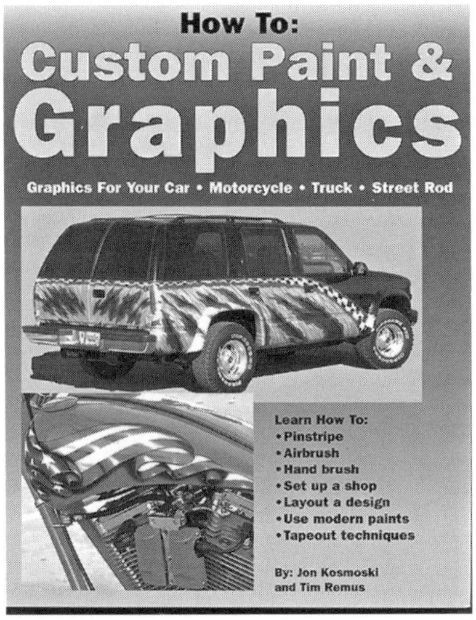

How to: Custom Paint & Graphics

Over 250 photos, 50% in color

7 chapters include:

- Shop tools and equipment
- Paint and materials
- Letter & pinstripe by hand
- Design and tapeouts
- Airbrushing
- Hands-on, Flames and signs
- Hands-on, Graphics

A joint effort of the master of custom painting, Jon Kosmoski and Tim Remus, this is the book for anyone who wants to try their hand at dressing up their street rod, truck or motorcycle with lettering, flames or exotic graphics. A great companion to Kustom Painting Secrets (below).

Seven Chapters 144 Pages $24.95

Kustom Painting Secrets

250 photos with color section

7 chapters include:

- History of House of Kolor
- How to Set up a shop
- Color painting sequences
- Prepare for paint
- Final paint application
- Hands-on, basic paint jobs
- Hands-on, beyond basic paint
- Hands-on, custom painting

More from the master! From the basics to advanced custom painting tricks, Jon Kosmoski shares his 30 years of experience in this book. Photos by publisher Tim Remus bring Jon's text to life. A must for ayone interested in the art of custom painting.

Seven Chapters 128 Pages $19.95

Build the Ultimate American Hot rod

Over 250 photos

11 chapters include:

- Planning
- Which frame to buy & why
- Suspension choices
- Brake components
- Wiring & accessories
- Horsepower: how much?
- Reproduction bodies: glass or steel

Your best first step in building your very own Ultimate American Hot Rod. Publisher Tim Remus goes to the top professional builders for the inside scoop on the best products, concepts and techniques. Get your dream rod off to the right start and enjoy years of high-quality cruising.

Eleven Chapters 144 Pages $19.95

Sources

Eaton Aeroquip
Industrial Division
Performance Products
3000 Strayer Rd
Maumee, OH 43537
419 891 5100
www.aeroquip.com

ARP - Automotive Racing Products
531 Spectrum Circle,
Oxnard, CA 93030
800 826 3045
FAX 805 981 1329

Atlantic Fasteners
49 Heywood Ave
West Springfield MA 01089

Aurora Bearing Co.
970 So Lake St
Aurora, IL 60506
708 859 2030

Baker
310 427 2375

Behling Racing
5170 No 125th St
Butler, WI 53007
800 255 4117

Borgeson Universal Co
187 Commercial Blvd
Torrington CT 06790
860 482 8283

British Tools and Fasteners
Phil Brown
2030, Andre Ave
Los Osos, CA 93402
805 528 0418

Coventry Spares
John Healy
229 Loland st
Holliston MA 01746
508 429 4221

Chassis Engineering
119 No. 2nd.
West Branch, IA 52358
319 643-2645

D.F. Metalworks
17872 Metzler Lane
Huntington Beach CA 92647

Deuce Factory
424 Rowland Ave
Sant Ana CA 92707
714 546 5596

Don't Hot Rods
2643 B Dayton Pike
Germantown, OH 45327
937 855 3605

Earl's Performance Products
189 W Victoria St
Long Beach CA 90805
310 609 1602

Gardner-Wescott
10110 Six Mile Rd
Northville, MI 48167
800 521 9805
www.gardner-wescott.com

Hillco Fastener Warehouse
10462 B Stanford
Garden Grove, CA 92840
714 534 6882

Lake Erie Screw
13001 Athens Ave
Cleveland OH 44107
216 521 1800

Letourneau, Neal
308 Lion Ln
Shoreview, MN 55126

Metal Fab
1453 91st Av NE
Blaine, MN 55434

Pure Choice Motorsports
2155 W Acoma Blvd
Lake Havasu City, AZ 86403
520 505 8355

Rocky Hinge Company
1720 Wilson Ave
Girard, OH 44420
888 539 6295

Sharp Enterprises
Glenn Sharp
1005 Cole St.
Laclede, MO 64651
660 963 2330

Snap-on Tools
Gerald M. Schlagel
421 Laurie Lane
Stillwater, MN 55082

Stage 8 Fasteners
15 Chestnut Ave
San Rafael, CA 91702
800 843 7836
Specialty header bolts nd other fasteners

Wickes Aircraft Supply
410 Pine St
Highland, IL 62249
800 221 9425